## THE AGING OF AQUARIUS

There is no group of individuals more iconic of 1960s counterculture than the hippies – the long-haired, colorfully dressed youth who rebelled against mainstream societal values, preached and practiced love and peace, and generally sought more meaningful and authentic lives. These "flower children" are now over sixty and comprise a significant part of the older population in the United States. While some hippies rejoined mainstream American society as they grew older, others still maintain the hippie ideology and lifestyle. This book is the first to explore the aging experience of older hippies by examining aspects related to identity, generativity, daily activities, spirituality, community, end-of-life care, and wellbeing. Based on forty in-depth interviews with lifelong, returning, and past residents of The Farm, an intentional community in Tennessee that was founded in 1971 and still exists today, insights into the subculture of aging hippies and their keys to wellbeing are shared.

Galit Nimrod is a professor at Ben-Gurion University of the Negev, Israel. Aiming to deepen the understanding of wellbeing in later life, Nimrod has published over 100 articles in leading scientific journals and collective volumes and presented her studies at numerous international conferences. Her significant contributions have been acknowledged, among others, by Academia Europea and the American Academy of Leisure Studies.

# THE AGING OF AQUARIUS

*The Hippies of the 60s in Their 60s and Beyond*

**Galit Nimrod**

Ben-Gurion University of the Negev

CAMBRIDGE
UNIVERSITY PRESS

## CAMBRIDGE
### UNIVERSITY PRESS

Shaftesbury Road, Cambridge CB2 8EA, United Kingdom

One Liberty Plaza, 20th Floor, New York, NY 10006, USA

477 Williamstown Road, Port Melbourne, VIC 3207, Australia

314–321, 3rd Floor, Plot 3, Splendor Forum, Jasola District Centre,
New Delhi – 110025, India

103 Penang Road, #05–06/07, Visioncrest Commercial, Singapore 238467

Cambridge University Press is part of Cambridge University Press & Assessment,
a department of the University of Cambridge.

We share the University's mission to contribute to society through the pursuit of
education, learning and research at the highest international levels of excellence.

www.cambridge.org
Information on this title: www.cambridge.org/9781009304078

DOI: 10.1017/9781009304047

First published 2023

*A catalogue record for this publication is available from the British Library.*

*Library of Congress Cataloging-in-Publication Data*
Names: Nimrod, Galit, author.
Title: The aging of aquarius : the hippies of the 60s in their 60s and
beyond / Galit Nimrod, Ben-Gurion University of the Negev.
Description: Cambridge, United Kingdom ; New York, NY : Cambridge
University Press, 2023. | Includes bibliographical references and index.
Identifiers: LCCN 2022032398 | ISBN 9781009304078 (hardback) | ISBN
9781009304047 (ebook)
Subjects: LCSH: Hippies – United States – History. | Counterculture – United
States – History. | Older people – United States – History. | Aging – United
States – History.
Classification: LCC HQ799.7 .N389 2023 | DDC
305.5/680973–dc23/eng/20221027
LC record available at https://lccn.loc.gov/2022032398

ISBN 978-1-009-30407-8 Hardback
ISBN 978-1-009-30408-5 Paperback

*Dedicated with love to all the people who were interviewed for this book
and to their extraordinary generation that tried to change the world
and, to some extent, did.*

# Contents

# Figures

# LIST OF FIGURES

# Tables

# Acknowledgments

Many family members, friends, and colleagues supported this journey. First and foremost, my partner, Eran Tzur, encouraged me to travel to the United States to conduct the study, read all the drafts, provided detailed feedback, and spent numerous evenings discussing the findings and insights with me without losing one ounce of curiosity along the way. Similarly, my parents, Rachel and Assaf Nimrod, and my children, Mika Tzur and Yuval Tzur, were significant partners with whom I could brainstorm and test my ideas throughout the writing process. I really cannot thank them enough.

Others who supported this project offered helpful advice whenever needed. Their names are listed in alphabetical order without details about their specific contribution. Yet, their handprints are well recognized on every page of this book. These include Hanna Adoni, Ayelet and Meiron Atias, Nir Aviely, Irit Axelrod, Liza Berdychevsky, Patrick Bunier, Avishai and Tamar Chelouche, Susan Doron, Yael Edan, Nelly Elias, Vera Gallistl, Alma Ganey-Har, Yaniv Garty, Michal Hanuka, Tal Hanuka, Noa Ilsar, Amit Kama, Dana Kivel, Douglas Kleiber, Amy Klein, Inbal Klein-Avraham, Michal Kromer-Nevo, Maya Lavie-Ajay, Sara and Michael Leitner, Dafna Lemish, Rinat Lifshitz, Lea Mandelzis, Eyal Milles, Alex and Orit Mogel, Guy Nimrod, Sarit Okun, Patrick Owen, Halleli Pinson, Hagay Ram, Yael Ram, Li-Mor Raviv, Zvi Reich, Ido Rendlich, Yael Ron, Steven Rosen, Dennis Rosenberg, Arie Rotem, Efrat Sar-Shalom, Sharon Shalev, Eyal Solomon, Gabriela Spector-Mersel, Avi Staiman, Judy Tal, John Tower, Gonen Tzur, Mor Yachin, Oded Zafrani, and Amalia Ziv.

Lastly, I would like to express special thanks to Murray Foreman, who told me about The Farm and educated me quite a bit about the 1960s counterculture, to Micaela Ziv, who copyedited the typescript, and to Janka Romero of Cambridge University Press, whose enthusiasm makes one believe that books still matter.

# Abbreviations

ACIM    A Course in Miracles
ACP     advance care planning
BPC     Book Publishing Company
CCRT    Community Conflict Resolution Team
DUP     Dance of Universal Peace
KSNP    Karen's Soy Nutrition Program
KTC     Kids to the Country
LSD     lysergic acid diethylamide
PSOC    psychological sense of community
STD     sexually transmitted disease
U.S.    United States
WELL    Whole Earth Lectronic Link

# CHAPTER 1

# Introduction

I T WAS 2:20 p.m. on a cold, bright winter day when I reached the gate of The Farm. After a five-hour drive from Marion, Illinois, where I spent the night in a small motel near the highway, I was too excited to feel tired. "Finally, I'm here," I thought, but at the same time, I asked myself, "What on earth are you doing here?" I started driving slowly along the main road (Figure 1.1). Having spent the past eight months reading about The Farm and watching many videos available online, I had a good

1.1 The Farm's main road.

**1.2** The peace sign as an ornament.

idea of what the place looked like. Still, it was different from how I had envisaged it: It was far more spacious and peaceful than I had ever imagined.

There was a large meadow to the left of the road, and on the right lay a forest. While driving, I noticed several buildings, a stable with horses grazing next to it, large solar panels, and old grain bins beautifully painted with images of colorful mushrooms, clouds, and what seemed like an indigenous woman holding a torch in her hand. A couple of people were walking next to the road and they smiled and waved at me as I passed them. I thought they must have confused me with someone else, but later I understood that greeting strangers was the norm around there. On the fence of one of the few houses on the main road, I saw a flag with the peace sign in its center next to two gold ornaments of that same sign (Figure 1.2).[1] "I'm probably in the right place," I thought.

Forty minutes later, I was at the community center, waiting for people to gather for a "Dance of Universal Peace" session. Although I had just arrived and had not even taken my bag out of the car, I took my hosts' advice to attend the session in order to start interacting with the community and maybe recruit some interviewees for the study I was hoping to conduct. Several musicians were preparing for the session in the center of the small space, but there were very few attendees. Later, I learned about "Farm time," a term suggesting that punctuality is not a primary value around there.

I sat down on one of the wooden benches next to the wall and observed the people gradually showing up. The majority were older adults, and many of them were pretty slim and wore colorful clothes (including a couple of tie-dye items). Most men had a ponytail or a braid, and most women had not dyed their hair. Still, I could easily imagine how they looked when they first arrived at The Farm, almost fifty years earlier. They all hugged and kissed each other when they met, and some approached me and introduced themselves. One of them, who later became my first interviewee, took me by the hand and introduced me to the others.

At 3:20 p.m., there were enough people to get started (about thirty, not including the musicians). Nicholas – who led the event – taught us the lyrics of each song we were about to dance to. The words combined different languages, including English, Hindi, Hebrew, and Arabic, but the contents were all about love and peace. Next, he taught the melody and only then demonstrated the steps. Occasionally, his spouse stepped in and explained the meaning of a specific word or movement. Putting our palms together and then "pouring" what was in them over our heads, for example, meant "bathing in love."

The dances were simple and involved a lot of mutual touch, such as holding hands or putting a hand on the next dancer's shoulder. The atmosphere was positive and even humorous at times. Often, the participants laughed at their dancing skills, and one even asked if Mother Earth – the theme of one of the songs – could pay his bills. However, most of the time they were pretty focused and intentional, often closing their eyes while dancing and taking a deep breath between the dances. Because my first name means "wave," and I was there to conduct a study on aging, one of the participants asked Nicholas to include a "Grandmother Ocean" dance for me. I was touched. In another dance, participants were split into couples and had to switch partners after each repetition of the song, so eventually, we each danced with all the other participants. The words of the songs were, "I accept you just the way that you are, I accept me just the way that I am…" and while singing these words, we all looked into our current partner's eyes. After several rounds of that dance, I realized I was smiling.

Fifteen months later, during a long walk in the park near my house in Tel Aviv – something that I had started doing daily upon my return from The Farm – I thought about the "daily mix" by Spotify that I was listening to on my mobile phone. It occurred to me that the app's algorithm must have concluded that I am an old hippie, as that mix only included American rock created between 1965 and 1975. Amused by my musical preferences in the past year, I started making a list of how The Farm and its people had affected my life, and the list was long. It included items such as starting to eat organic food and even growing most of it, adopting new leisure activities such as walking and qigong, and going back to reading spiritual texts such as *A Course in Miracles*. However, the most dominant impact may be described as a profound change in my "new-day aspirations": I no longer wake up in the morning thinking about the data I am about to analyze or the article I will write. Instead, I contemplate how I can be a better person and do good in this world.

My interest in aging hippies began in 2013, when my family and I spent the summer in Amsterdam, the Netherlands. One day, while having coffee in an outdoor café next to one of the canals, I noticed an older couple walking by, holding bicycles in their hands and talking to each other. Although I have seen many older couples on the streets of Amsterdam, this one drew my attention: Both had long white hair, were wearing tie-dye clothes, and had beads around their necks with peace signs as a medallion. Suddenly it hit me: *Some hippies have remained hippies to this day!*

The hippies were the most salient countercultural movement that emerged in the United States (U.S.) during the 1960s. Opposing the war in Vietnam and rejecting the mainstream American lifestyle, this movement originated on college campuses but quickly spread throughout the U.S. and many other countries. I am not sure why I assumed that the hippies, at least the original ones, had all adopted a mainstream lifestyle after the heyday of the 1960s counterculture was over. I think it may have had to do with an Israeli song that I liked as a teenager.[2] The song described the hippies most romantically but ended with the following verse:

4

Bill took 30 pills, and John works with his dad,
Jean has a child from Woodstock or Canada,
Norman has a store for natural foods and dairy products,
he took Katy to be his wife
and will pay a mortgage all his life.

Born in 1968 in a rural area in central Israel, I did not witness the hippie movement in real time, but I can clearly remember the first time I saw men with long hair. It happened on a bus ride with my mother to the nearest town. I was only four years old, so I could not understand that there was something different about them. My mother, however, thought that their long hair was hilarious and even sent me to ask them why they did not tie their hair in a ponytail.

Growing up and having learned about the hippies from various media content such as the film *Hair*,[3] I could easily see their effect on me and my generation in Israel. My friends and I were all pacifists, we all attributed great importance to music, and thought that psychedelics promoted spiritual growth and that free love was part of being a free spirit. In addition, many of my friends, myself included, were vegetarians, had a relatively developed awareness of environmental issues, and generally opposed consumerism. Accordingly, we wore clothes bought in flea markets and experimented with walking barefoot until the Israeli sidewalks, burning in the Mediterranean sun, taught us otherwise. As we all ended up living rather normative lives that included having careers and families, I assumed that the hippies had done the same.

Seeing the hippie couple in Amsterdam made me wonder, for the first time, where all the hippies from the 1960s had gone. I was flooded with questions: What did they do for the rest of their lives? Did they become, as I believed, part of the mainstream and abandon all their ideals and dreams? How are they doing now as older adults? Do they still believe in love and peace? Do they meditate and practice yoga all day? What about sex, drugs, and rock-n-roll? Is anything of their somewhat wild and rebellious lifestyle left? Did they come up with a new, creative, and better way to age? What do they think when they look back and reflect on their lives? Do they believe that their generation changed the world? Are they happy with the world in its current state or do they feel they have failed? Do they still consider themselves hippies at all?

Wondering if anyone had ever dealt with these questions, I checked several bibliographic databases to see if anything had been written about aging hippies. However, I could not find any in-depth inquiry into this group. I marked it as a topic for future research, but it took six years before the opportunity to do so presented itself. I was at a conference in Canada when, in a casual conversation, a colleague of mine mentioned The Farm. He described it as an intentional community of hippies located in Tennessee and said it still existed as far as he knew. As soon as I got back home I started learning about The Farm. Eight months later, I was there, at its gate, with a rented car and great curiosity.

## THE STUDY

The purpose of the study described in this book was to explore the aging experience of people I initially described as *hippies who remained hippies*. By using The Farm as a case study and examining issues related to identity, daily activities, and wellbeing, the project sought to discover how such individuals considered later life, whether and how they preserved the hippie ideology and lifestyle in old age, what changed and why, and to what extent their unique characteristics supported their aging process.

The Farm is considered the largest commune out of the thousands of countercultural experiments in communal living during the 1960s and 1970s, and it is one of the couple of hundreds that still exist today. The people who founded The Farm in 1971 were predominantly hippies, or at least were described as hippies in numerous media reports that covered The Farm's story. Accordingly, it offered an excellent springboard for research on aging hippies.

The study's primary source of information was in-depth interviews with forty people who were either among the founding members of The Farm or joined it during its early days (in the early 1970s). During my visit at The Farm, I interviewed founding members currently living there, either continuously since the 1970s or those who had left for some time and then returned. After realizing that many of the early members who left The Farm were still in touch with the community, visited it, donated money to its various actions, and so forth, I decided to expand the study to include such former residents and explore if and how the years they spent at The Farm connected with their present identity, daily activities, and wellbeing. Eventually, therefore, the study included three groups of founding members:

1. Lifelong residents – thirteen individuals (seven men, six women) who have lived at The Farm for most of their adult lives, such as Cindy, who has dedicated her life to preserving nature and educating about it, and Nicholas, who guides Dance of Universal Peace sessions in and outside The Farm.
2. Returning residents – nine individuals (five men, four women) who joined The Farm in its early days, left it for an extended period (more than twenty years), and then moved back, such as Shirley, a lawyer and a Zen master, and Sam, who serves on the community's Board of Directors and plays guitar in a rock-n-roll band that performs covers of the Grateful Dead.
3. Former residents – eighteen individuals (nine men, nine women) who joined the community in its early days, lived there for several years (mean = ten years), and then left it and lived elsewhere, like Charlotte, a certified midwife who advocated legalizing lay midwifery and now serves as an "end-of-life doula," and Jeff, one of the most influential scientists worldwide exploring the medical qualities of cannabis.

Study participants' ages at the time of the interviews ranged between 66 and 78 (mean = 72.1), and the majority (32 out of 40) were retired or semi-retired. Thirty-three were married or in steady relationships, but as many as 24 interviewees had been divorced at least once (eight had been divorced two to four times). All study participants but one had biological and/or adopted children (mean = 2.88), and some also mentioned involvement in raising their partners' children. The majority (33 out of 40) had at least some higher education; five of these had MA degrees, and five had MD or PhD degrees. A comparison among the three groups suggests that they share very similar backgrounds. Still, those who left The Farm reported a higher incidence of divorce and consisted of a somewhat higher number of individuals with master's or MD/PhD degrees. For more details about the study participants, data collection, and analysis, see the Appendix.

To protect study participants' privacy, I changed their names to pseudonyms and deleted many details that might have indicated their identity. However, when reporting about specific businesses and non-profit organizations that they established, titles of books they wrote, and the like, I used their original names. For example, when I wrote about Nancy Rhine, a former Farm resident who became one of the most influential women in internet history, I used her name, but I used her pseudonym in other parts of the book. By so doing, I protected the more sensitive information that she and all other study participants provided during the interviews.

Several sources of information were used to support and add to the insights arising from the in-depth interviews:

1. *Participant observations.*[4] During my stay at The Farm in February 2020, I had numerous opportunities to observe daily life and participate in formal and informal community activities (Figure 1.3), including two sessions of Dance of Universal Peace, a yoga class, two-hour Zazen meditation, drum circle, potluck, campfire, community meeting, and board meeting of one of the non-profit organizations operated by The Farm. I also had dinner with one of the couples I interviewed, visited one study participant at his workplace, and was given a private tour of The Farm by another. In addition, I had many conversations with my hosts and other community members (including younger and new members, as well as candidates for membership). My impressions were documented in a journal using thick description.[5]

2. *Online observations.*[6] As soon as I heard about The Farm, I registered for its monthly newsletter and reviewed its contents for a year and a half. Later, I joined one of the community's Facebook groups called "Friends of The Farm Tennessee," which has more than 6,000 members, and visited it weekly for a year. In August 2020, I also participated in an online Sunday Service led by two study participants. All online observations taught me a lot about the community, but I mainly documented content related to later life in and outside The Farm.

**1.3** The gazebo in The Farm's central meadow, where some community activities take place.

3. *Review of materials shared by study participants.* Some study participants shared with me books and articles they had published, photos and videos, print materials (e.g., brochures, copies of newspaper articles), and links to websites related to The Farm or to organizations in which they were involved. In addition, during the interviews, many of them mentioned events, books, films, and even terms I had never heard before. To complete my understanding of their world, I read everything they shared with me and watched quite a few films (e.g., *American commune, Fantastic fungi, Crip camp: A disability revolution*). I also looked up every term they mentioned that I was unfamiliar with (e.g., "nutritional yeast").

Applying a triangulation[7] approach, I integrated the findings yielded by the various secondary sources with the results stemming from the primary one (i.e., the in-depth interviews). This integration enabled the creation of a consistent, reliable, rich, and hopefully clear and inspiring report of the study's insights.

## THE BOOK

After twenty years in academia, I was clearly "programmed" to academic writing and was comfortable writing for a small audience of scholars and students interested in my work. While conducting the present study, however, I felt that it would not be appropriate to restrict its insights to academic circles. The reason for this is, first and foremost, the fact that there is an entire generation in the U.S. and many Western countries that identify with the hippie movement and its values or at least sympathize with them and may be interested in the study's results. Second, even without any personal connection to the hippies, I think that we all have a lesson or two to learn from them about aging well physically, psychologically, socially, and spiritually. Accordingly, I decided to write this book in a reader-friendly style that will make it accessible to academic and general audiences alike. While the content remained the same, I have tried to use easy-to-follow language. I have also added many notes to clarify various terms and provide more information about events mentioned in the text. Moreover, I have tried to limit all theoretical discussions to the introduction and summary of each chapter.

The two post-Introduction chapters of this book set the stage for the present study. Chapter 2 briefly reviews the hippie movement's history and ideology. It also summarizes the literature exploring where all the hippies went and what legacy they have left the world. Chapter 3 offers a brief history of The Farm community. Using published books about The Farm and materials posted on various websites, this chapter also relies on the stories shared by the study participants. It thus provides a somewhat hybrid version of The Farm's history that enables understanding of what it was (and is) all about from the perspective of the people who were there from the very beginning.

Chapter 4 deals with matters of identity, one of the central research foci. Specifically, I was interested in learning whether older hippies still consider themselves hippies. If so, how do they negotiate the seeming contradiction between being a hippie – a term commonly associated with youth (as reflected in its synonym "flower child"[8]) – and being old.[9] Distinguishing between *essence, behavior,* and *look* and suggesting various continuums of hippiedom, this chapter sheds light on the identity work done by older hippies regardless of their current circumstances and lifestyles.

Chapter 5 focuses on the hippies' ambition to change the world. Relying on the concept of "generativity," namely, the concern to guarantee the wellbeing of future generations, this chapter differentiates between the hippies as a collective, The Farm as a distinct community, and the individual level. Referring to past and current activities, the findings presented in this chapter suggest that the ambition to change the world, the behavior it yields, and the appraisal of its consequences offer a significant source of meaning and satisfaction among aging hippies.

In line with their rejection of mainstream society and values, the hippie movement adopted aspects of Eastern philosophy, promoted sexual liberation and the use of dope and psychedelic drugs, and turned to alternative arts, rock music in particular, as a means for expressing their feelings and worldview.[10] Departing from the ethics of sex, dope, and rock, Chapter 6 discusses the daily activities of older hippies. By exploring what they currently do for fun and comparing it with their past leisure activities, this chapter explores patterns of continuity and change and their contribution to hippies' wellbeing in later life. Similarly, Chapter 7 explores whether and how their spirituality changed with time and points out unique patterns that could only occur among people who had had an eclectic spiritual philosophy early in life. It also suggests that among aging hippies, the spiritual sphere is like a playground full of possibilities.

The ethics of community – another dominant value of the hippie movement – lies at the heart of Chapter 8, which examines The Farm as a case of a "maturing community." Here, more than anywhere else, the differences between the people who live at The Farm and those who left it are most notable. Notwithstanding, this chapter reveals the power of what may be described as the "cement" of powerful shared experiences in early life in forming a lifelong bonding that remains stable and offers a sense of community regardless of physical distance and frequency of contact. This chapter also highlights the challenges of community life and examines them vis-à-vis perceived advantages.

Chapter 9 considers end-of-life matters and reports the efforts made by The Farm and its members to make their own and their loved ones' final years and death as peaceful and comfortable as possible. Discussing issues such as advanced care planning, facilities for the aged population, and alternative burials and commemorations, this chapter demonstrates, once again, the hippie tendency to do things somewhat differently. It also suggests that their lifelong values and beliefs has made them slightly less fearful of death than older adults who were not part of the hippie movement.

The final chapter of this book is where I discuss whether or not hippies age differently or better than other older adults, basing my arguments on two complementary perspectives. The first is the viewpoint of the study participants and the second is my own. I then summarize the study's conclusions and take-home message for all of us, whether we were/are hippies, adore them, or completely oppose their values and lifestyle. We are all aging, and there is probably nothing we can do about it, but I believe that we and others may benefit if we make our later years meaningful, satisfying, and "hippie" to an extent.

# CHAPTER 2

# The Hippies

THERE IS NO OTHER GROUP OF INDIVIDUALS associated with the 1960s counterculture more than the hippies – the long-haired colorfully dressed youth who rebelled against mainstream societal values, preached and practiced love and peace, explored psychedelic drugs and Eastern spirituality, experimented with communal living, and generally sought more meaningful and authentic lives. Numerous books, articles, and films have described the hippie movement's history and ideology, and any attempt to present a brief review of them is inevitably superficial. Nevertheless, familiarity with the hippies' origins, history, and ideological tenets is vital for understanding the lived experiences of aging hippies described in this book.

## A BRIEF HISTORY OF THE HIPPIE MOVEMENT

Initially suggested by Theodore Roszak,[1] the term "counterculture" refers to a host of movements that emerged in North America and Europe in the 1960s and early 1970s – predominantly of teens and people in their twenties who rejected the traditions, values, and lifestyles of the hegemonic society. Such movements in the U.S. were quite diverse and included anything from artists, communards, and users of psychedelic drugs to political radicals and activists. Many of them, however, could be classified as hippies at one time or another as they shared an aspiration to create a new, superior society based on alternative culture and institutions.

Historical reviews of the hippie movement[2] tend to relate to four periods: its antecedents and origins from 1945 to 1964; its emergence in

13

1965 and 1966; its development from 1967 to 1969; and its peak and decline from 1970 through 1973. Borrowing from the "flower children" metaphor often used to describe the hippies, these periods are labeled here as *seeding, sprouting, growing,* and *blossoming and withering.*

SEEDING (1945–1964) The oldest hippies were born roughly between 1935 and 1945, while the majority was born between 1945 and 1955. Still, all experienced common events and developments that promoted their alienation from mainstream America. Shortly after the Second World War, the U.S. found itself engaged in an ongoing strategic, economic, and ideological struggle with the Soviet Union – the Cold War. To protect the American people, allies, and interests, the U.S. invested billions in military buildup. In addition, they developed policies and programs aimed at hunting communists at home in a manner that trampled individual liberty.

Paranoia and hysteria reached an apex between 1949 and 1954. It became illegal to belong not only to a communist party but to any organization that advocated a violent change in government. Many states even had laws prohibiting criticism of the government, the use of rebellious language, and the execution of any "un-American activities." The enforcement of such policies often involved accusing American citizens of betrayal without proper evidence – a practice named McCarthyism, after the Republican senator, Joseph McCarthy, who argued that numerous communists, Soviet spies, and sympathizers had infiltrated the U.S. federal government, universities, film industry, and the like. Both the policies and their enforcement hampered social progress, discredited civil rights, and constrained individual freedom. People had to think twice about their beliefs, activities, the friends they associated with, the books they read, etc.

The great fear declined in the mid-1950s after Stalin had died, the Korean War had ended, and McCarthy had fallen into disgrace. By that time, however, conservatism already ruled. The post-war baby boom and the growth of suburbanization were at a peak, and the economy was prospering. About one-third of the American population – mostly white, young, middle-class families – lived in suburbia and exhibited rather conformist lifestyles. The men were expected to provide and the women to be homemakers; belonging to a church, club, or any other organization seemed mandatory, and expressing skeptical thoughts put one at risk of social exclusion. The "conservative consensus" was a prominent feature of the culture and prevailed on nearly every issue, from political views to sexuality.

In the early 1960s, the vast majority of young adults, who had grown up in suburban families, prepared for the conservative life their parents prescribed to them. However, some of them did not look forward to living such lives. They thought that the time for a profound transformation of the American culture and the world at large had come. Most scholars agree that the seeds of these thoughts were sown by the "beats" (or "beatniks") – a movement of a few thousand people started by a group of authors whose work was published and popularized throughout the 1950s, such as Allen Ginsberg, William S. Burroughs, and Jack Kerouac. Inspired by the mid-nineteenth-century romantic countercultural movement against the onset of the American industrial revolution, as well as by the world of 1930s and 1940s black hipsters, the central elements of beat subculture were the rejection of materialism and traditional values, making a spiritual quest by exploring Native American and Eastern religions, experimentation with psychedelic drugs, and sexual liberation.

The beats had a most significant impact on the younger baby boomers, acting as participants, mentors, and leaders. Bach,[3] however, noted that parallel to the beats, there were other writers (e.g., J. D. Salinger, Joseph Heller), humorists (e.g., Lenny Bruce, Mort Sahl), and filmmakers (e.g., Nicholas Ray with *Rebel without a cause*, László Benedek with *The wild one*) who dented the conservative status quo. Moreover, he argued that many in the younger generation did not hear of Lenny Bruce, nor did they read much. The two elements that seemed to impact them most and facilitate the transformation from beat to "hip" were rock music and lysergic acid diethylamide (LSD). Unlike the beats, who favored jazz, the hippies' music was rock, which represented something new, exciting, and sexual, and symbolized a protest against the adult world. Marijuana and even more so LSD were indulged by the hippies significantly more than among the beats. Somewhat inspired by Timothy Leary's studies on psychedelics in the early 1960s, the hippies regarded these substances as having the ability to open the mind to new sensations and spiritual experiences. In contrast to the beats, however, they did not hide in dark cafés and jazz clubs, but rather celebrated such mind-altering drugs out in the open.

Some of those who became hippies were initially engaged in New Left activism and joined the Students for Direct Action or the Student Non-Violent Coordinating Committee. Overwhelmed by the Kennedy assassination in November 1963 and anxious about the Cuban Missile Crisis, they protested against the arms race, read underground newspapers that posed a deliberate counter to the establishment-supporting mainstream press, and started to become aware of various civil rights matters.

The most prominent indication of mid-1960s student unrest occurred at the University of California at Berkeley in the fall of 1964. Following the banning of political material dissemination near the campus entrance, the students demonstrated for nearly four months. They held rallies of thousands of participants, gave exciting speeches, and even occupied the administration building at some point. Their activities led to almost 800 arrests before administrators and students finally resolved the conflict. Notwithstanding its success – which served as an example to many students' riots that followed – something more profound unsettled the demonstrators: They started to realize that rather than encouraging a critical perspective and creative solutions, the university represented the establishment and the conservative status quo. They perceived the universities as old-fashioned factories, where they constituted mere numbers, required to take irrelevant courses, read incomprehensible books, and had little to no personal contact with the faculty. Instead of struggling with the university officials and trying to change the system from within, some students decided to drop out of school and out of the mainstream, liberate themselves from the issues distressing others, and adopt an alternative lifestyle and culture. More than any other, this act symbolized the separation of the hippies from the New Left activists.

SPROUTING (1965–1966) From 1965, the alienated dropouts attempted to create a new culture, a new society, and even a new civilization. The onset of the Vietnam War in the summer of that year further alienated those who had experienced the turmoil of the 1950s and early 1960s and produced many new counterculturalists.

The opposition to the war had diverse reasons: Some opposed war on principle, others thought America had no rightful place in Southeast Asia, and many believed that preserving an independent, noncommunist South Vietnam would not impact the world's security. Regardless of the reason, none of them accepted the American leadership's arguments regarding the necessity of the war and thus gradually lost their trust in authority.

Another crucial alienating factor was the draft, since the government was forcing young men to commit violence and even die in a war they did not support. In addition, although many young people chose to acquire higher education – either because they were going through the motions, doing what their parents expected of them, or because it was the only legal way for healthy young men to avoid the draft – they found the universities repressive. Moreover, the authorities increasingly harassed and intimidated young adults by searching for marijuana and LSD, restricting music playing, and interrogating antidraft organizers. While the war, draft, oppressive universities, and intimidating police served as factors pushing the youth away from the mainstream, music acted as a "pull" factor attracting them to the counterculture. During the sprouting period, leading musicians such as Bob Dylan, the Beatles, and the Rolling Stones assumed a hippie persona. Spreading revolutionary ideology and style, they became the role models for many young people who followed them right into the counterculture.

From 1965 to 1966, the counterculture's core values materialized, and the differences in philosophy and style between the New Left and the counterculture became apparent. Separated from the New Left that vigorously protested against the escalating war in Vietnam, the counterculture started to grow. Hippie[4] communities emerged all over the U.S. as an increasing number of young adults dropped out of the mainstream, attended happenings, and practiced the unconventional hippie values. Such communities developed in and outside major universities and counterculture institutions such as the "free universities" that offered an alternative to traditional academia. In addition, intentional communities and communes started to appear in urban settings and even more so in rural areas.

New York, Los Angeles, and San Francisco were the largest centers, and the most notable hippie scene was undoubtedly to be found in the

Haight-Ashbury district of San Francisco. Populated by ex-beatniks, Berkeley dropouts, artists, and musicians, and offering an abundance of spontaneous and organized musical, cultural, and spiritual events, this racially integrated district of forty-four square blocks adjacent to the Golden Gate Park turned San Francisco into the center of the hippie movement. San Francisco was also where hippie milestone events such as the Ken Kesey and the Merry Pranksters' acid tests[5] and the Love Pageant Rally[6] took place, as well as legendary dancehall concerts.[7]

Most Americans did not differentiate between political activists and the counterculture, believing that those who wore long hair, beards, beads, and outrageous clothes[8] belonged to a monolithic movement. In reality, significant tensions existed between the New Left – whose members engaged in overt political activism – and the hippies, who thought that conventional America could not be changed or reformed through the existing political process. Leaning Left, they were apolitical, antiauthoritarian, and anti-institutional. Accordingly, they rejected engagement with mainstream culture in any capacity, including protest. Instead, they chose withdrawal, cultural radicalism, and a quest for personal liberation.

GROWING (1967–1969) As 1967 began, the counterculture population was growing exponentially. Spreading across the country and taking root in nearly every city and university, it increased from tens of thousands in 1965 to about 400,000–500,000 in 1968. By the turn of the decade, it was already estimated to be in the millions. Although the counterculture and New Left remained separate and distinct branches of the youth rebellion, a partial blending of the two occurred as more hippies joined antiwar protests and more New Leftists embraced hippie practices and styles. From that point, the hippies could be classified as either "purists" or "hybrids," who were both hippies and New Leftists.

What seemed to bring the two streams together was a series of outdoor hippie gatherings ("love-ins" or "be-ins") that took place all over the U.S. in 1967, starting with the "Gathering of the Tribes for a Human Be-In" held in San Francisco in January, where Timothy Leary delivered his "Turn on, tune in and drop out"[9] speech in front of 25,000 attendees. However, the activists also made significant efforts to convert the hippie ideals of peace and love into political action. They perceived the hippies as a substantial available workforce and used a variety of tactics to attract them: from claiming that the children of Vietnam needed their love to scheduling rock concerts and light shows in the antiwar movement's fundraising events. Their efforts were pretty fruitful, as more and more hippies joined antiwar protests. On April 15, for example, about 50,000 people demonstrated in San Francisco while 200,000 marched with Martin Luther King, Jr. and other notable figures in New York City.

Meanwhile, be-ins continued to grow, underground newspapers proliferated, and the counterculture expanded rapidly. Be-ins thrived all over the U.S. throughout the spring and summer of 1967, known as the Summer of Love. Some even had a political orientation, such as the one staged in Newark following the July 1967 race riots.[10] Still, the scene in Haight-Ashbury was the largest and most vibrant of all. The area was already packed with counterculturalists, new businesses opened quickly, and the national and international media constantly covered it using descriptors such as "flower children" and "love generation." The news coverage led about 75,000 runaway middle-class teens from all over the U.S. to Haight-Ashbury during the Summer of Love.

Whereas this summer began with great hopes inspired by the release of the Beatles' album *Sgt. Pepper's lonely hearts club band* and the first rock festival held in Monterey, the numerous individuals that filled the Haight-Ashbury district eventually led to its decline. Many of these so-called "plastic hippies" were mainly interested in drugs and sex and were not seeking spiritual awakenings nor did they aspire to form a new and better world. The majority did not stay long, just long enough to say that they had "been there," and most of those who did stay only played at being a hippie. Having no place to live and no means of supporting themselves, many quickly turned to begging on the streets and sleeping in doorways. Soon after that, addictive drugs made their way to the district, and it turned to an area of homeless and hungry addicts, who often became violent. By the end of the year, seventeen murders, 100 rapes, and nearly 3,000 burglaries had been reported. This negative turn led the veterans of the Haight-Ashbury to declare the "death of hippie," a step quickly followed by the national press. Both, however, were fundamentally wrong.

As 1968 approached, the counterculture's numbers kept growing exponentially, and the hippie movement was about to enter its most monumental year. Several processes and events shook American society during that year, including the loss of faith in Washington officials, who had been assuring the public that America was winning the Vietnam War, the assassinations of Martin Luther King and Robert Kennedy, and the ensuing students' riots in American universities. The New Left and counterculture moved closer together and even converged somewhat. The students that occupied Columbia University, for example, smoked dope, made love, and referred to occupied buildings as "communes." Combining political activism with hippiedom was also the basis for forming the Youth International Party (Yippie) and the White Panther Party in 1968. As the hippies and the New Left perceived themselves as profoundly different, however, both harshly criticized these parties, and most hippies wanted nothing to do with them.

Overwhelmed by New Leftists and hybrid hippies, the purists became even more determined to "do their own thing." Although be-ins waned in frequency after 1967, they continued to be held, as well as what could be described as cultural activism, such as the protest against public nudity laws. However, complete evasion of the era's social, cultural, and political upheavals was not possible. Moreover, as most Americans made no distinction between antiwar activists and hippies, they were all perceived as traitors. Newspaper articles and street billboards publicly marked them as such; they were banned from workplaces, restaurants, and the like (Figure 2.1), and even experienced actual violence from both citizens and the police.

The counterculture, however, survived the establishment repression. In fact, the hippies' numbers continued to multiply as 1969 started. Multitudes of young people adopted the hippie lifestyle, and alienation increased, especially as Richard Nixon moved into the White House and the outlook on the antiwar front appeared hopeless. In addition, the hippie rock festivals, which took over the be-ins as the counterculture's primary gathering events, attracted thousands of American youth to concerts in every region of the country. Numerous multiday shows were held in 1969, the "year of the festivals," but the Woodstock festival held in August, which attracted an audience of more than 400,000, was by far the

**2.1** "Hippies use side door" signs were used by businesses in the 1960s to direct hippies away from the main entrance to avoid upsetting the regular customers. Such signs today are humorous memorabilia of that time.

greatest and most important. It was and still is considered the supreme moment in the history of the counterculture.

Woodstock encouraged the notion that America was on the edge of a cultural revolution and fueled the hippie claim that the world was entering a new age – the Age of Aquarius – characterized by faith, peace, and love. Meanwhile, the New Left continued their massive antiwar demonstrations. Millions, hippies included, participated in protests such as the Vietnam Moratorium Day in October and Washington for Mobilization Day in November. Two events that occurred during that year – the brutal murder of Sharon Tate and three of her friends by Charles Manson and his group, and the violence between Hell's Angels and hippies at the Altamont rock festival four months later that ended with the death of eighteen-year-old Meredith Hunter – cast dark shadows on the bright hippie future. The hippies, however, did not consider Manson one of their own, and most did not attend Altamont and dismissed it as a singular incident. Therefore, at the start of the 1970s, they still had great faith in the new society and the new age.

BLOSSOMING AND WITHERING (1970–1973) In the early 1970s, the counterculture thrived, but it had undergone a drastic transformation since its inception, hardly resembling the counterculture of 1968 and even less so the counterculture of 1965. After the tragic killing of four students at Kent State University,[11] nearly all the lines dividing the New Left and hippies faded. They became a rather integrated, dissident youth culture dedicated to creating a new America while opposing the Vietnam War, Richard Nixon, the silent majority, and the establishment. Believing that a new society could be formed only when the young united, this culture viewed itself as one "counterculture," "tribe," and "people" standing together as Us against Them, Left against Right, Hippies against Straights. Many, if not most, of the 36 million Americans aged fifteen to twenty-five (18 percent of the total U.S. population at that time) participated in, or at least sympathized with, some aspect of the counterculture, leading to its peak in 1971.

Simultaneously, after a series of ecological disasters spiked the American public's awareness of environmental problems, the dissident youth also discovered environmentalism. Like war and racism, they saw the degradation of the environment as another symptom of a sick establishment. Many of them joined environmental organizations protesting against chemical companies, air pollution, deforestation, and the like.[12] These efforts, however, were harshly criticized by the more radical New Leftists, who saw environmentalism as a phenomenon that takes the public attention away from the more crucial issues such as the Vietnam War, racism, imperialism, poverty, and police repression. Some hippie purists also endured. They opposed violent radicals, refused to participate in demonstrations, advocated cultural revolution, and built the new society in secluded rural communes. However, most of the new society builders did not differentiate between politics and environment, nor did they make distinctions between political and cultural radicalism.

As Nixon began to wind the war down, the antiwar movement started to fade away. April 24, 1971, marked the last major national demonstration, after which the antiwar movement gradually diminished. Future protests attracted a significantly smaller number of protesters, and the burning campuses became peaceful. The Left fragmented into several autonomous movements seeking individual empowerment: women, gays, Afro-Americans, Native Americans, and Hispanics campaigned and demonstrated for their rights. In addition, some activists sought to put their lives back together after years of activism. Such activists, like hippies, turned inward, striving for personal awakenings and self-realization, and headed back to the land for peaceful and rewarding personal revolutions.

The hippie purists, too, declined in numbers. After the overdose-induced deaths of Janis Joplin, Jim Morrison, and Jimi Hendrix, individuals lost faith in a cultural revolution that would be achieved with the use of dope. In addition, while most dissident youth kept attending rock festivals, law enforcement officials aimed at preventing further rock concerts from taking place by imposing court injunctions and health and sanitary regulations. Gradually, rock festivals and record production became a large, regulated industry, further damaging the hippies' faith in a cultural revolution.

However, the counterculture remained at its peak a bit longer, and its values continued to evolve. Closely related to the emerging orientation toward environmentalism was the dissident youth's tendency to disapprove of industrialization and technological progress alongside their new-found appreciation of the outdoors, organic food and vegetarianism, and back-to-the-land commune building. Love of the outdoors also triggered the popularity of hitchhiking, backpacking, and camping, with about 20 million Americans aged eighteen to thirty-four traveling in that manner in 1971. Like their communard counterparts, backpackers and campers sought to escape society and find peace of mind. The music of the early 1970s exemplified the inward-turning characteristics of the counterculture as singer-songwriters (e.g., Joni Mitchell, Paul Simon, Carol King) wrote and performed apolitical, personal, and introspective songs. Similarly, the hippies' back-to-the-land orientation coincided with the increasing popularity of country-rock. Numerous books and catalogs published in that period also celebrated nature, the natural, and simple living.

Many hippies did not limit their travels to America and toured the world. While some roamed Europe, making certain cities such as Amsterdam and Rome hippie centers, others traveled to Southeast Asia, India in particular, congregating in Bombay, the foothills of the Himalayas, and the beaches of Goa. Seekers also visited or lived in the

Middle East and Africa, and closer to home they traveled to Mexico. However, they were not warmly welcomed everywhere. Mexican authorities, for example, deported or arrested them, and Thailand instructed its embassies to refuse visas to the flower children.

In the early 1970s, at the same time that hippies were hitchhiking in the U.S., traveling the world, and marching in the last major antiwar demonstrations, the counterculture's institutions significantly grew in number and diversity. They included food- and nonfood-related co-ops, hip businesses, headshops (selling bongs, pipes, and rolling papers for smoking marijuana and hashish), free stores, free universities, free clinics, legal services, "churches," underground newspapers, radio stations, community switchboards, and shelters for street people and runaways. Rock festivals were also held throughout the early 1970s, but from 1972 onward, the hippies gradually disappeared from the headlines, and the counterculture started to fade away.

Several factors led to the counterculture's decline. On the one hand, counterculturalists became increasingly involved in mainstream America. In 1972, they lined up behind Democratic presidential candidate George McGovern, who promised to end the war. They were also obsessed with presidential politics when Nixon became embroiled in the Watergate scandal. In addition, as the war in Vietnam caused huge deficits, the U.S. was experiencing a significant economic downturn reflected in unprecedented inflation rates, productivity stagnation, increased unemployment, decreased income, and a declining standard of living. Under these circumstances, it became more challenging to live on society's economic margins. Moreover, the flower children were growing older, and many decided to settle down, marry, obtain stable jobs, and raise families.

On the other hand, mainstream Americans increasingly adopted the counterculture's style and values. These were increasingly present in the mainstream culture through language, film, and theater and gradually diffused into the mass consumer culture. For more and more young people, the counterculture became a fashion statement. These individuals did not adhere to authentic hippie values but were seeking a good time. The more mainstream the counterculture became, the less "counter" it was. Accordingly, the counterculture's immense popularity, which had caused it to peak, eventually caused it to fade.

On January 27, 1973, North Vietnam and America signed a truce, and by spring, the war was over. The counterculture held its last collective event on August 4, 1973, at the Watkins Glen Summer Jam – a one-day event in New York, which surpassed Woodstock's attendance. Hippies continued to drift around campuses and hip urban neighborhoods and live communally through most of the 1970s. Still, the counterculture no longer existed as a significant opposition to mainstream America as it had already, to some extent, transformed it.

## THE HIPPIE IDEOLOGY

The hippies first identified themselves by what they were not. Protesting against and refusing to cooperate with mainstream America, they were against traditional values, against war and any other form of violence, and against capitalism and the American liberal ethic that sustained capitalism's power. Then, they defined themselves according to the alternative philosophy and way of life they proposed, which stressed the need for peace, love, spirituality, creativity, community, environmentalism, and a simple, less materialistic life. Many aspired to replace hegemonic culture with an entirely new society. Others, however, took a more realistic approach, regarding hippiedom as representing an alternative lifestyle that could only set an example for the world.

The triad "sex, drugs, and rock-n-roll" usually comes to mind when reflecting on the hippies. Indeed, the hippies' apparent behavior included celebrating free love, smoking marijuana and using LSD, and promoting alternative arts and music as well as unconventional fashion. However, their particular lifestyle was only an external expression of numerous, complex, and diverse ideological principles that cannot be easily summarized. Timothy Miller brilliantly met this challenge in his 2011 book *The hippies and American values*, where he described the complex hippie ideology according to five dominant ethics, as follows.

THE ETHICS OF DOPE "Dope" was a term used by the hippies to describe what they perceived as good substances that turned one "on" and gave vision and clarity (e.g., marijuana, hashish, LSD, psilocybin, and peyote). It stood in contrast to bad, addictive, and harmful drugs that dulled the senses (e.g., amphetamines, methedrine, and opiates but also alcohol and nicotine). Dope was probably the most significant symbol differentiating between the counterculture and mainstream America. As the counterculture was unabashedly hedonistic, fun was a motivation for using dope. Still, there was also a rebellious dimension in the hippie pleasure ethics because drug use was condemned by hegemonic society. Moreover, the counterculture overall agreed that dope could erase old behavioral and mental conditioning and fundamentally expand one's consciousnesses. This change, they thought, was crucial for forming a new culture. Dope was perceived as a tool that provided healing and insights, often described as answering the most challenging existential questions and offering a path to spiritual enlightenment.

The hippie "drop out" and "do your own thing" ethos also meant "seeking," which paved the way for spiritual awakenings and the exploration and embracing of various Eastern religions and mysticism, the most notable being the Hare Krishna movement, Buddhism and Zen Buddhism, Taoism, and Sufism. Many hippies believed that dope could be a key to spiritual experiences and help foster spiritual communities. They spoke about it as a sacrament and argued that it should be used ritually with great intention. Similarly, they advocated using dope as a means of communing with nature and gaining a deeper understanding of societal and cultural evils.

While understanding that dope can be used for evil purposes, especially for controlling others, and strongly opposing such abuse, the hippies also claimed that dope provides creative inspiration. Many amateur and professional hippie writers, artists, and musicians testified that what they sensed and saw while "high" influenced their artistic outcomes (Figure 2.2).[13] Similarly, and with a strong connection to the following ideological tenet, dope was valued for its ability to facilitate interpersonal interaction, intimacy, and better sex.

THE ETHICS OF SEX As opposed to conservative America, the hippies believed that people should not restrain their sexual desires and should feel free to enjoy sex at will. Comprising a range of feelings and activities, sex was perceived as fun and healthy, and thanks to the contraceptive pill – licensed in 1960 – it was also regarded as safe. To a lesser degree,

**2.2** Hippie art, created by former Farm resident Linda Speel in 2020.

sex was also considered revolutionary, as the hippies enthusiastically smashed sexual taboos. They endorsed masturbation and nonmarital sex, promoted nudity as an expression of one's freedom, and gave space to what was commonly perceived as deviances (e.g., homosexuality, BDSM). Moreover, whereas for most hippies liberated sex remained a spontaneous one-on-one experience, some advocated organized free sex and orgies.

Not everyone, however, celebrated free love. In addition to being a fun, pleasurable activity, sex was perceived by some hippies as having a deeper and even spiritual meaning. Typically, such hippies thought that sex within the context of love and concern for the partner is better and more significant than casual sex. Others opposing casual sex stressed the potential risks of sexually transmitted diseases (STDs) and unwanted pregnancies. Furthermore, some spiritual movements, such as Hare

Krishna, endorsed celibacy, and certain hippie writers and known figures (men mostly) such as Ken Kesey and Stephen Gaskin – the founder and leader of The Farm – strongly opposed abortion. Presenting abortion as a violent act that contradicts the hippie aspiration for nonviolence and peace, these persons questioned the free love practices that could still cause them, despite the widespread use of the contraceptive pill.

In this regard, it should be noted that the heyday of the hippies came before the widespread dissemination of contemporary feminist thought. Thus, the counterculture often preserved traditional gender roles, and the hippie sexual liberation was primarily oriented toward male pleasure. Equating sex with masculinity, a fair share of misogynistic, chauvinist hip men took advantage of hippie women and treated them as sex objects. Eventually, however, the counterculture played an essential role in the rise of the new feminism – a trend that put some sticks in the spokes of the sexual revolution.

THE ETHICS OF ROCK Rock, more than anything else, formed and shaped the hippie movement. The hippies lived it, breathed it, and believed that it was key to their rebellion against the mainstream. Before 1966 and even later, folk music (e.g., Bob Dylan, Joan Baez) was the dominant music of the rebels. Expressing distrust of the establishment and loaded with themes of peace and justice, folk music bridged the 1950s and the 1960s. When the Beatles started their rise to fame, however, new hip rock bands (e.g., the Grateful Dead) began to appear, Dylan incorporated rock into his music, and rock became the language of the counterculture.

Whereas dope was usually an individual experience, and sex was typically interpersonal, rock was communal – mainly thanks to the be-ins, concerts, and festivals, where it was the main attraction and led to collective identity formation. The 4/4 beat demanded dancing, so rock was physical and sexual, high amplification was mandatory, and the lyrics reflected and shaped the counterculture's values. Rock, therefore, was a totality. It was a liberating force, and thanks to mass media and the affordability of vinyl records, it reached the hearts and minds of millions. Carrying messages promoting alienation from mainstream society, dropping out of it, and joining the cultural revolution, rock music affected the entire generation and constantly attracted young newcomers to the counterculture.

After the Beatles' *Sgt. Pepper* acid rock album was released, rock and dope ethics intertwined. Dope affected the musicians and their audiences alike, and because being "stoned" has a lasting effect, the messages against contemporary culture and in favor of peace, love, and being yourself permeated listeners' everyday lives. Thanks to its ability to expose the deception of Western culture and to change its listeners' life orientation, politically and otherwise, rock was described as revolutionary and as having the power to change and eventually save the world.

**THE ETHICS OF COMMUNITY** Intentional communities have a long history in American culture. Most early communes were based on either religious or radical political and social ideologies and had a strong structure and sense of purpose. Most hippie communes, in contrast, endorsed freedom, hedonism, and even anarchy. Embodying the hippie ideals, such communities flourished, and in the early 1970s, it was estimated that there were thousands – probably tens of thousands – of communes all over the U.S. with hundreds of thousands – perhaps 1 million residents and even more visitors.

The idea of communes (or "tribes") of hippies sharing their lives was suggested by the movement's philosophers, Timothy Leary, Allan Ginsburg, Alan Watts, and Gary Snyder, in a meeting[14] documented by the *Oracle* newspaper. This idea was inspired mainly by the Native American way of life that the counterculture admired. Still, the proliferation of communes was often ascribed to the rock festivals, which functioned as short-lived communes to an extent. Festival attendees were overwhelmed by the instant sense of community they provided and wanted to have such an experience regularly. In addition, the music fed the communal impulses by creating a sense of oneness, and the rock bands themselves were models of communal living. Dope, too, played a role in communalism by engendering a sort of community of its own and encouraging the transition to rural areas for closer contact with nature and the relatively smaller chance of being detected by the authorities. Yet, the primary purpose of the communes was to pose an alternative to the mainstream lifestyle, in which affinity and solidarity between self and others ruled. In the case of rural communes, the same solidarity also applied to nature.

The numerous communes varied in location, size, structure, and orientation. Whereas some had a more spiritual, ideological, or therapeutic nature or simply allowed lonely (and often financially constrained) young people to live together, others were utopian communes that tried to demonstrate a new and better way of living. The daily reality in most communes, however, was far from utopic. Reported downsides included difficulty maintaining rules and agreements, oppressive behavior toward women, and attracting individuals who failed to function in conventional society who also had poor skills for group living. Consequently, most communes did not last more than a year or two, and relatively few, no more than a couple of hundred, have survived to this day.

THE ETHICS OF CULTURAL OPPOSITION Dope, sex, rock, and community were not the only categories of hippie ethics. An overarching theme encapsulating all previous ethics and the entire history of the hippie movement was the opposition to establishment culture. This opposition was not merely rejection, as it also had a vision, an alternative. Promoting peace and love was thus, from the very beginning, a cultural conflict. It touched nearly all parts of life and offered broad goals for humanity.

"Love" meant several things to the counterculture: an emotion, a state of mind, and a way of life. Love was considered to embody an ethical conviction and thus could become an action that, if indeed performed, would change the world. For most hippies, love also meant nonviolence. This meaning bridged them with the New Left and led to the aforementioned occasional overlaps between the two streams, despite the hippies' apolitical approach. Finally, based on Eastern metaphysics and Native American tradition, love also meant respecting, appreciating, and preserving nature. The latter, combined with the aspiration for simple happy living not controlled by capitalist forces, also served as the basis for the hippie anticonsumerism.

To a country built on a Protestant work ethic, the hippies proposed the ethics of play. They believed that play – as practiced in any informal leisure activity – enabled one to experience freedom and live life to its fullest. It is important to note, however, that having strong play ethics did not rule out work. Work could actually be enjoyable and even playful when it was meaningful. Work was only condemned when it was purposeless and stemmed from need. To conclude, everything that caused pleasure, be it play, dope, sex, and even some types of work, served the ultimate goal of hedonism. This ideal was not only morally valid but also stood in sharp contrast to Judeo-Christian ethics.

## THE HIPPIE LEGACY

Whereas most components of the hippie ideology were not innovative and originated in other times and places, from ancient India to contemporary Native America, their integration and intense promotion were relatively new and had a significant impact on American culture and society in the 1960s. Moreover, it was argued that the hippies' influence virtually reached every corner of the world and has lasted in some manifestation or another into the present through fashion, behavior, and attitudes.[15]

Determining if the hippies' impact was positive or negative depends on one's perspective.[16] Conservatives, for example, typically perceive the 1960s as a poor decade in which American values began to decline. Liberals, however, see those years as a time of idealism, optimism, and promise. They value the antiwar, civil rights, women's, and environmental movements, the loosening of traditional social and cultural restraints, and the enhancement of the ethics of fun and play. Regardless of their perspective, all agree that the hippies had a tremendous influence on the popularization of recreational drugs, sexual liberation, casual clothing, certain linguistic idioms, and so forth. Some argue that these changes would have occurred anyway, but the counterculture definitely accelerated them.

The hippies' esthetic and fashion have had a lasting impact reflected in greater freedom to dress as one pleases, as most individuals in the U.S. and elsewhere now wear informal clothing. Rock-n-roll became popular and mainstream, sexual habits have generally become more permissive, and attitudes toward drugs such as marijuana have changed so much that its use has even been legalized in some states in the U.S.

and elsewhere in the world. Similarly, hippie movements (e.g., environmentalism, natural foods) continue to thrive, as do what may be considered as their "offspring" – movements that emerged in post-hip times but reflect some of the hippie ethics such as the New Age movement, the Slow movement that advocates a cultural shift toward slowing down life's pace, the Polyamory movement endorsing intimate relationships with more than one partner, the Rainbow Family, and the recently flourishing intentional communities. Furthermore, questioning authority is now considered good citizenship. People in Western countries are generally more aware of issues such as war and peace, the environment, and individual rights, and express skepticism and suspicion of their governments and political leaders.

Despite all that, America today is far from being the realization of the hippie dream. On the contrary, the aspiration for peace and love is regarded as naïve, race tensions are at peak, and American conservatism (as reflected, for example, in the New Right) seems more vital than ever. Other drugs and musical genres have largely replaced dope and rock, and some even blame the hippies for current drug issues and the prevalence of STDs. In addition, while cynical, materialistic self-indulgence rules, environmental forecasts pose an actual threat to humankind's future. Overall, the hip ideology does not dominate the world as some hippies had hoped. Still, while no scholar can determine whether the counterculture succeeded or failed, it is clear that certain aspects of its legacy have remained and continue to resonate with the larger culture.

### SCATTERING: THE HIPPIES' LATER YEARS

To understand where all the millions of hippies have gone, one must first realize where they came from and what types of hippies existed. The hippies were predominantly young people from white, middle- to upper-class, urban, and suburban families. The majority had at least some higher education; only a few came from blue-collar families, and even fewer were Afro-Americans. Yet, despite their similar background, the hippies were far from being a homogeneous group. Using terms common among the hippies, Howard[17] differentiated between the "visionaries," the "plastic hippies," the "midnight hippies," and the "heads and freaks." The visionaries were the idealists who aimed at posing an alternative to existing society. Plastic hippies were young people who adopted the hippie look and some lifestyle elements but had only the most superficial understanding of the ideology. Midnight hippies were older people, mostly in their thirties, who were already part of mainstream society but were sympathetic to the hippie lifestyle and ideology and partly adopted them. The heads and freaks were the more drug-oriented hippies, but there was a significant difference between the latter two:[18] Heads used drugs (typically LSD) as a means of self-realization or self-fulfillment, while the freaks' use of any drug (be it methedrine, LSD, marijuana, or even alcohol) was purely hedonistic, tended to be excessive, and caused them to become disoriented and behave erratically or even violently. This typology, therefore, represented value tensions in the counterculture.

A survey[19] conducted at the end of the 1970s with 1,005 "true veterans of the Sixties" reported that by that time, most of them were married or in steady relationships and had jobs, mainly in the free professions (e.g., educators, doctors, lawyers) or in clerical work and sales. Such data may explain why the hippie movement was often described as a temporary phenomenon, and the hippies as deluded youngsters who later woke up, realized they could not change the world, and decided to rejoin the same mainstream they had previously criticized. This portrayal, however, was not the case for everyone.

In an interview[20] for *60 minutes* held in 1977, Dr. Steven Patel of the Haight-Ashbury Research Project suggested that the hippies were "no longer dropouts, but they have dropped down to a marginal participation in mainstream society." According to his research, only 40 percent fell into the "re-entry group" that returned to the conventional society from which they came. An additional 40 percent were in the "semi-re-entries," who, while turning to a more traditional lifestyle, retained substantial hippiedom (The Farm was mentioned as an example), and 20 percent were "nonre-entries," who were still heavily committed to drugs. Using Howard's typology,[21] it is quite probable that those who fell into the re-entry group were the midnight and plastic hippies, and that while the freaks were those who were more likely to be nonre-entries, the visionaries were those who tended to be semi-re-entries.

Petal's equal distribution of re-entries and semi-re-entries was challenged decades later by Moretta,[22] who claimed that some hippies "re-entered mainstream life on a grand scale, becoming over time ice-cream moguls, media magnates, and triangulating politicians. Yet, for every ex–flower child who 'sold out' to the post–1960s establishment, thousands more, in some form or another, have remained true to the hippie spirit." Most of them also look back fondly at their experiences in the 1960s. A study of former hippie commune members,[23] for example, demonstrated that nearly all of them believed that their time as communards was a significant period in American history as well as in their own lives. They were also entirely unapologetic for the 1960s and their part in the counterculture, as they believed that hippiedom had altered America for the better.

The survival of the hippie movement is evident in the communes founded in the 1960s that still exist in one form or another (e.g., Hog Farm, The Farm, and Twin Oaks), and in scattered enclaves, primarily in college towns and rural areas, where the original hippies keep "doing their own thing" away from the spotlight. It is also manifested in the aforementioned hippie offspring movements (e.g., New Age movement, the Slow movement), and some countercultural qualities can be recognized among attendees of rock festivals and fans of alternative music, various subcultures with alternative identities (e.g., goths, Rastas, and ravers), and online communities focusing on music, psychedelics, conspiracy theories, and so forth. However, it is unclear to what extent the original hippies participate in such hippie offspring movements and activities.

The sole topic that has been systematically studied among maturing hippies was their parenting styles and their children. Such studies[24] found that many counterculture parents reported a monthly income lower than the average, had a high rate of divorce and remarriage, and tended to move a lot. Although their parenting style emphasized respect, emotional expressions, and physical contact with their children, many of their children described their childhoods as unhappy, said they did not have a good relationship with their parents, and reported difficulty adjusting to mainstream culture as they grew up. In an eighteen-year study, however, Weisner[25] demonstrated that parents who remained committed to the counterculture's ideology produced children who did better in school, had fewer behavior problems, and wanted to contribute to society more than conventional children. Poorer outcomes were reported for children whose parents were less committed to the counterculture or who experienced unstable childhoods. Yet, they were not associated with so-called harmful counterculture practices such as single parenthood by choice or drug use.

Hardly any studies have explored the hippies in their later life, and most of them presented a medical perspective. Such studies suggested that "ex-hippies" who have a long history of illicit drug use are at greater risk for acute and chronic comorbidities.[26] In addition, they tend to be involved in unprotected sex more than their younger counterparts, a behavior that puts them at greater risk for HIV and other STDs.[27] In a rare psycho-social study, Adams and Harmon[28] explored the significance of music in the lives of old hippies. Focusing on a community of "Deadheads," namely, fans of the Grateful Dead, they found that many of them still consume relevant content via online, recorded, and print media and attend performances of bands including surviving members of the original band, cover bands, and other jam bands. Such engagement seemed to be an essential component of their identity and preserved a sense of both self and group continuity.

Lastly, in her book of interviews with ex-hippies, Sandra Gurvis[29] described herself and her close ex-hippie friends as typical middle-class Americans, with jobs, children, and grandchildren, like "the people next door, in line in the grocery store." She summarized: "It is hard to visualize the graying, prosperous-look men in a golf cart at the country club or the overweight, aging couple making their way through the buffet line as fresh-faced youths who once stood on the college commons chanting 'Hell no, we won't go!'" So far, however, no study has presented an in-depth investigation of the identity, daily activities, and wellbeing of such re-entrees, nor of their semi-re-entry counterparts. Other than the fact that the flower children of the 1960s are now over sixty, little is known about their later years – a lacuna that the study presented in this book aims to fill.

# CHAPTER 3

# The Farm

S CHOLARS STUDYING THE COUNTERCULTURE of the 1960s agree that The Farm represents the archetypical hippie commune. Miller,[1] for example, argued that "if one had to perform the impossible task of picking the one commune that most perfectly epitomized the spirit of the communal 1960s era, The Farm would be a leading candidate," Bach[2] claimed that "The Farm, probably more than any other single commune, exemplified the spirit of back-to-the-land living," and Moretta[3] described it as "one of the most emblematic, intriguing, and successful hip 'collective' endeavors of the era." Such descriptions may explain why The Farm was, and still is, the focus of numerous studies, books, journal articles, documentaries, news reports, and the like. The brief review of The Farm's history presented here is based on some of these books[4] as well as the forty interviews I conducted with the community's founding members.

## FROM HAIGHT-ASHBURY TO RURAL TENNESSEE

The Farm was founded in 1971 near Summertown, Tennessee, but it originated in the Haight-Ashbury scene in San Francisco, or even more accurately in the mind of one person who was fascinated by that scene. Born in 1935 in Denver, Colorado, Stephen Gaskin was a little older than the average hippie. After serving in the Marines during the Korean War, he spent some time running cafés and drinking heavily in North Beach, San Francisco's "beat" enclave. Although he identified with the beat ethos, he eventually decided to go to college, earned a Master's degree in English and Language Arts, and then worked as an instructor at San Francisco State College, teaching basic composition and creative writing classes.

By 1966, after seeing his students drop out of school one by one to live an alternative life, he followed them to see what was happening and quickly found himself engaged in the counterculture. Experimenting with marijuana opened new doors of consciousness to him, and soon after that, he was already tripping on LSD. Like other countercultural-ists, he grew his hair and beard long, and by the end of the Summer of Love, he became "too wired" to be rehired and found himself without a job. As he wanted to keep talking to young people, Gaskin decided to teach at the college's Free University – after-hours classes on nonaccred-ited subjects – and took the Monday night slot.

In the first year, his classes drew only several dozen students, with whom he held discussions that aimed at gaining a better understand-ing of the shift in consciousness following the use of mind-altering drugs. Gaskin and his students talked about their own experiences in light of ancient and modern philosophers, mainstream and esoteric religions, Eastern mysticism, parapsychology, psychology, and sociology. Eventually, they concluded that all wisdom shares the same threads of truth and that along with peace and love come values of honesty, com-passion, and justice. That simple truth suggests universal life lessons, according to which life is a trip guided by individuals' responsibility for their actions, attitude, and energy.

The "Monday night class" became a testing ground for ideas and energy perception. Gradually, the word about them spread throughout San Francisco's Bay Area, leading to an increasing number of attend-ees every week. As the audience grew, larger venues were needed, and the classes had to move off campus. They were first held in a church basement in downtown San Francisco, then at the Straight Theater on Haight Street, and finally at the Family Dog rock hall near the beach, which hosted between 1,000 and 1,500 people every week. Shirley, who moved to San Francisco in 1969, recalled her first days in the city:

> I asked some people, "Well, what's happening on Monday night?" and the people say, "Oh! it's Monday night classes." So, I said, "How do you get there?" "Just walk out front and go like this" [showing thumb up – i.e., hitchhiking] he said... And so, I did. The first car that came along said, "Well, where are you going?" I said, "Monday night class," and they said,

"We are too. Jump in!" So, I got a ride, and it was such an amazing experience... I went every week, and I always hitchhiked because it was really easy. Everyone was going.

Like Shirley, half of the study participants attended the Monday night classes in San Francisco, and all of them described the meetings as an extraordinary experience. According to their testimonials, several factors made the classes stand out in what Dennis labeled the "soup of spiritual paths" characterizing San Francisco at that time. The first was Gaskin's comprehensive knowledge ("His lectures were way above almost anything I'd ever heard at Harvard" – Daniel) and his ability to simplify and integrate various sources of information into coherent themes, as described by Bill:

> I liked what he was saying in a broad sense and felt that it would maybe give me a little bit of guidance because, at that time, I was like, "What do I do with all of this sudden influx of new information about so much that had great meaning that I was reading out of Huxley and other Eastern religious people?" So, this was a chance that somebody could maybe pre-digest some of it, and then I would be able to apply it to my life.

The second factor was Gaskin's way of communicating with his audience. Gordon, for example, said, "He had a unique way of talking that was at once very erudite and highly informed, and at the same time it was this sort of beatniky street language, you know, all mixed together." Similarly, Bill recounted, "It was a language – he spoke a language that we all could relate to. It was much like Eastern religion but an Americanized Eastern religion." In addition, Gaskin's hippie persona made the large crowd of young seekers identify with him, as Dennis explained:

> Stephen Gaskin was only one of many people [spiritual teachers]. The thing that attracted me to him was that he was a hippie, and I was a hippie. He smoked grass. I smoke grass. He talked about his ideas of the world, his worldview, and I could totally relate to him: "Yeah. That sounds like what I want to do."

Another source of attraction was the atmosphere in the classes. Shirley reported that every class started with twenty to thirty minutes of meditation, after which Gaskin used a conch shell to form a tone "so that everybody could om at the same time. And we have a thousand people oming in this rock-n-roll hall which had really good acoustics... It was extremely unusual, and I thought, 'I'll never see anything like this again.'" After the classes moved to the Family Dog rock hall that was in "a beautiful spot right next to the ocean" (Jane), Gaskin also started holding "Sunday morning services" dedicated to meditation in the nearby park. James testified, "Stephen felt like we were kind of a church, and he wanted to establish Sunday's service so we would have it." Gordon added, "We'd go out to Central Park and watch the sun come up on Sunday mornings, and then [after meditating] we'd have a little spiritual talk. He would give a talk, and everything would be good."

Within three years, Gaskin became the counselor, role model, and minister – or, as he described it, a "spiritual teacher" – to an evolving community of mostly young adults. Powered by the highest hippie ideals and drawing on tenets common to all religions, the community's philosophy developed and was refined over time. Most simply put, this philosophy asserted that "we are all one": We are all part of the same system, referred to as "the universe," and thus, whatever we do affects the world around us. The universe is too vast to comprehend, but any effort to relate to the "All" could be called "spirituality," and there is ultimately only one big church in which we are all members. Each of us has a "higher self," and any church services, be it prayer, meditation, lovemaking, or tripping, are all supposed to help one be in touch with that self. An actual change can only come from the spiritual plane, and although people can make agreements at different levels of consciousness, a spiritual agreement is the most effective when trying to better the world. The keys to raising the level of consciousness are telling the truth in everyday life (because it is only when real feelings and hidden agendas are brought out and resolved that one is free to thrive), and understanding that "attention equals energy," and thus "what you pay attention to, you get more of." Monday night class and The Farm community that followed it were committed to raising the level of consciousness in the world by practicing these principles and sending out a strong signal of love, intelligence, tolerance, and hope, in as many ways as possible.

While acting as a spiritual teacher to a growing audience of young people, Gaskin had also gained a reputation as someone who could explain the social and political changes among the youth. For that reason, in 1969, he was invited by the progressive American Academy of Religion to travel the U.S. and speak at local churches and colleges. James explained that the primary purpose of the tour was to interpret the counterculture to the worried mainstream America:

> The parents were concerned about their young people growing their hair long, looking different, taking cannabis and psychedelics, and seeming not to be interested in the traditional way of American life very much. It was not easy, so they [academy members] wanted to find out what could be done about that. They had Stephen talk in a convention of ministers, and they liked what he said because he gave them hope that the kids are just experimenting and trying to figure out how to live in the world they inherited. So, they invited him to come to speak personally at their churches.

Gaskin, who was living in a school bus at that time, decided to make the tour – later known as the Caravan – in his home on wheels and invited his students to join him. About 250 of them accepted the invitation ("Everybody wanted to go with him" – Jane). After a period of preparations in which they collected money ("We sat in a circle and we decide we put all our money together" – Shirley), purchased old school buses, and converted them into living spaces, Gaskin and company hit the road. "We got busses, and we've fixed them up little by little basically and bought some rice and some beans and peanut butter, and we went on the Caravan around the country" (Gordon).

Between August and December 1970, the Caravan traveled across forty-two states and drew considerable attention. Bill recalled, "People were fascinated, 'why are you doing this?' Well, peace and love, brother. Our friends were dying in Vietnam, and we were saying this is the wrong direction. Society is moving in the wrong direction." The interactions with local people led some of the latter to join the Caravan. Ben, for example, joined it after attending Gaskin's talk in New York ("He was doing this question and answer repertoire, and it sounded very inviting at the time"). Andrew became part of the Caravan after running into it

on the way to Boulder, Colorado, because "these seemed like such interesting people and so nice that I wanted to be a hippie too... so I got on
a bus and stayed." Consequently, the Caravan grew to about 100 vehicles
at its peak, of which sixty were full-length school buses accommodating
ten or twelve young people.

The Caravan was the staging ground for The Farm community. While
on the road, the group started to feel that they were not merely passen-
gers and that strong and meaningful ties were forming among them.
After heading back to San Francisco, which by then had degenerated
into a cesspool of crime, hard drugs, and violence, they realized that they
were already a "community on wheels." They decided that the time had
come to move from talking about their ideals of a new society based on
spiritual values to forming such a society. Jane shared:

> We came back, and we all lived in our buses, and we were on the beach
> right where we used to do Monday night class. We gathered and kind
> of debriefed from what we had just done, and Stephen said, "We have
> become a community on the road, and we need to take the energy that we
> have built and actually do something with it instead of having everybody
> going our separate ways."

Forming a new society could not be done in California because land
prices were too high and there were already too many gurus and spiritual
teachers active there, or, as James put it: "California was too expensive
and had too much political upheaval going on." Therefore, in less
than two weeks after returning to the San Francisco Bay Area, Gaskin
announced that the Caravan would be leaving for Tennessee – where
it had been warmly welcomed a couple of months earlier – to look for
land.

In February 1971, Gaskin and 300 of his followers hit the road
again for a second Caravan. By May, they had parked near Nashville,
Tennessee, and went searching for land. While visiting a guitar store,
Bill met a woman who owned a property called the Martin Farm in
Lewis County, one of Tennessee's poorest and most undeveloped rural
counties. She was willing to rent the group her land for 1 dollar a year
until they could find a permanent spot. Soon after that, the Caravan
headed for Lewis County, about sixty-five miles south from Nashville.

**3.1** Buses used during the Caravan can still be found on The Farm today.

After spending several months at the Martin Farm, they were offered an opportunity to buy the nearby Black Swan Ranch – 1,000 acres of land covered by hardwood forest mostly and home for one family and seventy-five cows – for 70 dollars an acre, and "so, we put together our resources, and we had enough money for a down payment on the land… and just drove our buses down, found a place, backed it in, jacked the buses up off the ground, and got to work" (Dennis) (Figure 3.1). Two years later, an adjoining 750 acres were purchased for 100 dollars per acre.

## THE COMMUNAL PERIOD (1971–1983)

In the early years, Farm members lived under more primitive conditions than any other hippie commune. Members signed a vow of voluntary

**3.2** An old building currently used as an office.

poverty, turning over to the community all cash and possessions to be used according to need. The needs, however, were many. Other than one house and a couple of barns, there was practically nothing on the land. Everything – from basic infrastructure and housing to food and income sources, an education system, healthcare, and the like had to be built from scratch ("All the roads, the doctors, the houses, the projects, the gardens, none of that was here. It was all brought and manifested by us hippies" – Sam). Quickly, therefore, the community formed task forces, or "crews," to meet the numerous challenges. Depending upon the job, the crew could be one person or fifty. The main ones were the farming crew, who grew a significant portion of the community's food for the first several years, the canning and freezing crew, the construction crew (Figure 3.2), the motor pool crew, the horse crew, and the medical crew. There were also the gate crew, various cooking crews, a radio and electronics crew, and crews to install and operate the flour mill, water system, and public laundry facility.

As most community members had grown up in white, middle-class families and the majority had at least some college education, many could teach at The Farm school, which, at its peak, had 365 students from kindergarten through 12th grade and ran on shifts. Some members had a degree in education and thus could guide the others regarding pedagogical methods ("I said, 'Let's take the summer hay and create a curriculum,' because I'm looking at these people who don't know how to teach school and they need some guidelines" – Stephanie). Similarly, people with relevant backgrounds trained the medical crew, as Cindy described:

> We had a lab. We had a pretty big crew… and we had the guy that started the clinic and another lady who had medical technology training… and she was really good at having classes, and we had a real school, it was a real apprentice program. And we practiced blood drawing on each other, and we were taught how to do cultures. I mean, it was – it was very technical and really done right.

Sometimes, a visitor, a friendly neighbor, or someone in the area taught community members various skills. Many, for example, mentioned Homer Sanders, a local sawmill operator that "hired a bunch of us" and "it was like going to a vocational-technical school because he knew everything, he knew plumbing, he knew electric, he knew this and that" (Dennis). Likewise, women who practiced midwifery said that they had learned a lot from Dr. Williams, who was a "local doctor that had been delivering Amish babies for years and came to The Farm once a week to help us with the baby clinic and if we had a problematic pregnancy" (Laura). Similarly, Chris, who served as the commune's "barefoot dentist" even though he was not licensed to do so, learned the job by watching a visiting dentist ("And I did root canals, impacted wisdom teeth. I'm this oral surgeon without a license. Nothing was legal… It was really under the radar, but I learned. I'm pretty good at it"). Later on, he even trained health workers in western Africa and Haiti to do various dental treatments.

Commune members who had no background in the job they were supposed to perform nor someone that could teach them often learned by trial and error. Tim said that he learned to do carpentry work from a book and argued that "construction is not that hard. You just go on the job… You learn by doing. That's how it works." Sometimes, however, that did not work too well. Bill, for example, built the commune's shower house, and one morning, after a freezing night, he found that all of the pipes had burst because the water in them froze and ice expands: "Well, that was my first lesson in winter – nature works its wonders... and suddenly, we had no shower house."

As the commune was supposed to set an example to the world, a promo crew was formed to handle The Farm's public relations, and the Book Publishing Company (BPC) – the first business on The Farm – was founded. The first published books included *Monday night class* and *The caravan*, which were based on transcriptions of Gaskin's lectures, and *Hey beatnik! This is The Farm book* that described life at The Farm. Starting in the fall of 1972, Gaskin also frequently went on speaking tours around the U.S. and abroad. For that, he assembled a traveling group of Farm members that included a bus driver, mechanics, radio and sound systems technicians, and a rock-n-roll band called, how not, The Farm Band. These efforts seemed to be successful, as a growing number of young adults heard about The Farm and learned about its philosophy. Many also decided to visit and check it out and ended up joining the commune. Nicholas and his spouse, for example, joined The Farm following a visit triggered by Gaskin and his team's presentation in Kentucky, and Henry and Sarah first heard about The Farm when Sarah bought a copy of *Hey Beatnik!* at a local health food store. They became curious about The Farm, came to visit, and eventually were "just so impressed by everyone's integrity and warmth" that they decided to stay.

The convincing promotion resulted in rapid expansion. From an initial population of about 300 in 1971, The Farm grew to about 600 in 1974, 1,200 in 1978, and a peak of close to 1,500 in 1980. Gaskin's speaking tours also motivated people in different parts of the U.S. to start similar communities in their areas. Gaskin invited such individuals to come to The Farm to learn how it was done and offered to send people from The Farm to help them start theirs. In the first ten years of The Farm's existence, such satellite Farms and projects emerged in Wisconsin, Florida, Missouri, California, New York, Virginia, Michigan, Louisiana, Alabama, Kentucky, and even in Canada and Ireland ("We had hippies from all over Europe come live with us and experience community living. It's a highlight of my life" – Brian). Besides these settlements, Farm people also started projects and sent volunteers to Guatemala, the Caribbean, Lesotho, and Bangladesh. For some community members, this meant a pretty dynamic decade. Joan, for example, shared:

> Smaller farms were sprouting up all over the place. And so, we went to a farm in Kentucky... we stayed there for a couple of years. Then we came here for a few years off and on because we would come here, we would go to a small farm in Florida, and then we go to a small farm in New York, and back here, and then back to Florida, and we just bounced around, we didn't have children.

The satellite Farms had an average life of about five to eight years, ending in the early 1980s, when they either folded back into the main Farm, ceased to exist, or evolved into something else.

Population growth did not stem from newcomers only. As the settlers were mostly in their early twenties, many couples were getting together and starting families. Within a year of its establishment, the first wave of The Farm's "baby boom" was taking place, and within four years, the population of The Farm was about one-half children. The Farm also attracted many new members through its spiritual midwifery program established by Ina May, Gaskin's spouse, and her team (see Chapter 5). Many members of The Farm joined the community first as single women or couples going there to have their babies. Tim and Debbie, for example, spent several weeks at The Farm while waiting for their son's birth. During that time, they made a lot of friends and started thinking about moving there. Because The Farm was already quite crowded, Gaskin encouraged them to establish a satellite Farm, which they did. They convinced a couple of friends to move in with them and "tried to keep The Farm's agreements," but then they "just realized it wasn't the same," sold their Farm, and moved to The Farm in Tennessee.

Aiming to prevent abortions, the midwifery program offered young single mothers to take care of their babies for as long as needed and that if they ever decided they wanted them back, they could have them. This offer was embraced by quite a few single women who came to The Farm to give birth and went away, leaving The Farm with many foster children to raise but without additional working adults. Moreover, "The Farm had a couple of kids who were dropped off by their parents, and we never saw the parents again. They were like the age of 11 and 13 or something" (Bill).

To feed its growing population, The Farm needed more sources of income, and new businesses opened. The Farm Building Company supplied as many as sixty construction workers every day to building sites in the surrounding area. Farm Foods, which started as the marketing wing of the farming crew, grew into a most successful business, much of that involving the production and marketing of soy products.[5] The Farm's electronics crew started a company called Solar Electronics that designed and installed alternative energy systems in various parts of the country and later produced Geiger counters to measure radiation levels. While being a source of income in itself, the BPC supported these efforts by publishing vegetarian cookbooks and books about nuclear power versus solar power, electronics, spiritual midwifery, natural birth control, Native American issues, and other topics. In addition, many individuals were working full or part time outside The Farm, handing their salaries over to the community. Paul, for example, was sent to Southern Louisiana to work in a shipyard, and Evelyn started working at the hospital in Columbia, about twenty-five miles from The Farm: "We wanted to send some people to town to work and sort of that's goodwill, and we wanted to make money. I made two dollars an hour and handed my check to The Farm's bank lady."

The crews worked six days a week, twelve hours a day in their peak seasons, and in their off season, their members held other jobs. Others juggled between on and off Farm jobs. In addition, the commune "had something we called Farm Hands, which was offering our services to the local community, and everyone on The Farm was required to spend one day a week on Farm Hands" (Bill). By the time everyone got back home in the evening, there was always more work to do. Most members lived in school buses and tents, and when the first houses were built, they accommodated twenty to thirty and even up to sixty people each. Taking care of such households' basic needs required as much effort as building the community or bringing income ("I did a lot of farming, plus raising my kids. We lived in a household with 50 people, and that took a lot of my attention in keeping it clean, keeping it together" – Jane). Cooking, cleaning, and laundry shifts took a tremendous amount of work, especially during the first few years when there was no running water in the houses and electricity was just a car battery charged by a trickle system (direct AC power was run only to the public workplaces). Members of both sexes covered for each other, took care of the kids in shifts to allow others to work, and built housing additions and improvements, and sometimes whole houses, in their "spare" time ("You had to build your house when you got home from work" – Tim).

Despite the fairly extreme work ethic, community members still had some leisure time. With no electricity, no television, and hardly any radio, they spent their free time socializing, playing music together, and dancing. Charles shared: "There was a swimming hole where we would go swimming, and there were dances. People played music, and we had square dances. Later we had rock-n-roll gigs, and it kind of expanded... otherwise, we were just following Stephen all the time." Cindy added that "the kids didn't have afterschool activities and sports teams, but they did have sports though, we had the local baseball, soccer, and basketball." She also described some family fun time: "There is a nearby waterfall just outside of Summertown, and we would go there and take the kids and swim on a Saturday or Sunday and just be out in nature." Lillian commented, "Oh, well, the idea was you were always supposed to be having fun, so we would take a smoke break whenever we had it," and Carolyn explained:

> You know celebration, there's a lot of those celebrations implied in being a hippie. It's wonderful to celebrate life and have fun, and our culture just taught us to be so serious, so focused on academics and getting through college instead of being more playful and more celebratory. Everybody was in a band, everybody got a chance to sing or dance, just more free form.

Yet, the activities that brought everyone together were the Sunday morning services and the community meetings. The Sunday services were the center of the community's spiritual life and, for many individuals, the highlight of the week. All community members attended services except for those whose turn had come to stay home and babysit. Initially, the services were held at sunrise, just like in San Francisco, but that had changed to a later hour to give people who rose early every day a chance to rest. Whenever possible, the services were held outside in a designated meadow. They started with one-hour meditation ending with a long "om" chanting, after which Gaskin would stand up and talk for about two hours and, if there was a wedding to perform, this was also the time for marriage ceremonies.[6] Gaskin's lectures were typically on some spiritual matter, but he also used this opportunity to update the community members on the global aspects of The Farm. Members were encouraged to comment, add to the discussion, and bring up additional topics. To avoid interfering too much with the spiritual state of mind, purely material matters were discussed in meetings scheduled for weekdays. Like others, Evelyn described the Sunday services as an "exquisite" and "incredible" experience. She even said that if she had to name her most favorite thing on The Farm, then "that meditation with that many people in that meadow" would be it because "I'm sitting here going wow, you know, this is a heavy community, right?"

Although building the community took tremendous efforts, the commune was committed to bringing love and hope to people whose needs were greater than their own. So, as early as 1974, it formed Plenty International – a not-for-profit organization aiming to protect and share the world's abundance and knowledge for the benefit of all. Plenty started locally by serving nearby neighbors who needed some help, be it fixing a leaky roof or providing free medical care, and by collecting and transporting food, blankets, and clothing to tornado and flood victims in Mississippi, Alabama, and Tennessee. Its slogan at that time was "Next time you need help, call a hippie" (Gordon). Soon, however, Plenty expanded to national and international projects, among which the most notable during the commune period was a four-year project assisting villages in Guatemala after an extreme earthquake in 1976. Plenty volunteers built over 1,200 houses, twelve schools, and several public buildings during that period. They also helped install portable water systems, sanitation, and communications technology and introduced Mayan people to soybean foods and agriculture. Nicholas, who spent a couple of years in that project, said, "It was peak life experience, there was heaven, paradise, the people were just so wonderful and so close to nature and the divine and a richness of culture that is missing in most of the world." Another major project was the formation of emergency medicine services in the South Bronx, an area with such a high crime rate that emergency responders and ambulances refused to go there. After negotiating with the city, Plenty also renovated abandoned apartment buildings in that area and populated them with people who assisted in the renovations of inexpensive rentals. Plenty's motto was, and still is after almost fifty years of numerous successful projects carried out in nineteen countries: "Because in all fairness, there is enough."

## A HIPPIE COMMUNE?

Reading the books, watching the documentaries, and especially talking with forty of the founding members of The Farm made me wonder how "hippie" this hippie commune was. Its work ethic and pretty spartan lifestyle reminded me of the Kibbutz in Israel (minus the Zionist component) more than the anarchist and hedonistic community I had expected it to be. To an extent, it was even conservative, as Cliff described:

> So, you think hippies, obviously free thinkers, liberal, live and let live kind of stuff, except that we did have what we called a set of agreements and part of the agreement as it evolved meant living in these big households, living in voluntary peasantry and not smoking [cigarettes], not drinking. We had lots of agreements. It was an experiment, and to me, we had a lot of data showing that many of our ideas weren't workable. Yet, we refused to change and adjust to what the data was. Many people were ready to change, but there were cult-like aspects. Even though we denied it and worked hard not to be that way, it still was in some respect. Our instinct as a group was to be liberals, but we kept being turned back to "no, no, no, that's not the vision, we have got to do it this way."

Despite such reservations, examining The Farm's characteristics vis-à-vis the hippie ethics[7] suggests that it was indeed a prototypical hippie commune.

The *dope ethics* of the community consolidated during the first Caravan. After celebrating psychedelics in the early days in San Francisco, Gaskin banned the use of LSD because he was worried that people who could not handle it would try it just because they knew that he and his

community were users. Similar to other hippies, he also objected to nicotine and alcohol. Therefore, the use of these three substances was not
allowed on The Farm, whereas natural psychedelics (such as peyote and
psilocybin mushrooms), which were hard to find, and marijuana were
considered legitimate.

Farm members used dope for insight, for ceremonial value, and for
lovemaking enhancement. They used it during work breaks, at Sunday
services, and even during birth-giving ("Two-thirds of the women were
cannabis-using during their pregnancies, and I saw the wonders of it
being so valuable for labor and delivery" – Jerry). Moreover, The Farm
had a "pot crew" responsible for growing marijuana for community consumption, but this led to some trouble, including Gaskin and a couple
of members spending almost a year in prison in 1975. Another incident,
in which the police searched The Farm for marijuana, ended better:
The plants the police considered cultivated marijuana turned out to be
simple ragweed (Figure 3.3). The day of this incident – July 10, 1980 –
is celebrated to this day as an annual Ragweed Day, in which reunion
gatherings of several hundred people are held both at The Farm and in
California.

The *sex ethics* at The Farm was far from supporting free casual love.
Instead, following the tantric sexual path, where lovemaking is an
important healing exercise for body and soul, sex was perceived as having deep spiritual meaning, as a holy sacrament to be practiced with
great intention and commitment. Accordingly, the rule was, "If you're
sleeping together, you're considered engaged, and if you're pregnant,
you're considered married." This policy lessened the amount of casual
sex, unwanted pregnancies, and hassles, but it also yielded marriages of
people who hardly knew each other, leading eventually to high divorce
rates. Anna testified:

> There was a lot of pressure to get married on The Farm. That was one of
> the things about being in Tennessee; they didn't like you to just live with
> people. No, no, we had to become kind of square to survive there... The
> ironic thing is that Stephen in his shadow-side would say, "Well, the peo-
> ple that I married, none of them have gotten divorced." He used to brag
> about that. Well, it turned out 80% of the people he married got divorced.

**3.3** A caricature from "Ragweed days" by former resident William Gross.

In contrast to this somewhat conservative policy, The Farm was famous for its "four-marriage" – an agreement taken by a few members only, as a serious attempt at a new inclusive type of family. The four-marriage was like a two-marriage, but with four people who considered themselves married to each other in all ways, including raising their children together and being sexually faithful to each other. Gaskin, for a period, was even in a "six-marriage" of three women and three men. Causing tensions and conflicts and requiring too much energy to sustain ("I don't know if you have ever taken psychedelics, but it was like being on a psychedelic 24 hours a day, seven days a week" – Harold), none of these marriages lasted more than a few years. Moreover, such marriages were harshly criticized by some community members, as Gordon stated, "You know, Stephen was the leader and the four marriages, which I think was a lot of baloney. He tried to make wife swapping a spiritual practice, and I don't agree with that at all."

In addition to the four-marriage, communal living caused sexual tensions, sometimes leading to infidelity and underground partner swapping. For example, one study participant told me that he and his spouse "lived on and off with one couple." They became very "tight" to the extent that "for five years, you know, we had an open sexual relationship with the couple that we'd already had years of history with. We have raised our kids and traveled; been a family." Another participant said that his spouse "ended up having an affair with some guy and then they went off," and a third one shared that he had been married to his spouse for over fifty years but also "had a relationship with another woman and we had a daughter together." Among the nonmarried (single and divorced), there were even more sexual happenings, as Bill said:

> We were always kind of loose about sex, but not to the extent that so many other hippies were. We used to call ourselves as a "family monastery," and there were ways that we wanted to be with each other that were respectful of that. Now, that wasn't always the case either. I don't want to rose and cover this up with any – give you the wrong idea, because after my wife and I broke up and I entered the single market, I suddenly found there was a lot of hanky-panky going on.

The Farm did not have an explicit "agreement" regarding gender, and it maintained rather traditional gender roles: While the men were typically out working, many women had "feminine" jobs (educating, midwifery, bookkeeping) and took care of the kids, cooked, and cleaned. Some study participants, mostly men, argued that this division was the women's choice and that some women, who were so inclined, had important, influential, and powerful positions. According to Bill, the midwives in particular "had an increasingly large role in decision-making and were given lots of authority." In addition, some desired jobs were preserved for women only, as Charles described: "The bookkeeping was always considered a woman's job, so I always couldn't do it even though I wanted to." Moreover, the men "usually tried to do their share of the babysitting, diaper changing, laundry, and dishes" (Traugot[8]). Those exhibiting chauvinism were told off and even punished: "He [spouse] was kind of chauvinistic, and people got together and told him he needed to go off The Farm for a mission of some kind and just think about being chauvinistic" (Charlotte).

Some women, however, stressed that The Farm in its early years was pretty paternalistic and sexist. This view was reflected in harsh statements such as: "In such a sexist sort of self-environment, women would kind of keep all of the things going on The Farm... whereas the guys went off The Farm to make money" (Anna), and "Men on The Farm were very paternalistic and very condescending toward women, especially if you were single" (Shirley). Arguments about gender inequality were also expressed incidentally. Cindy, for example, disclosed imbalanced home responsibilities: "In most of the places we lived we got into scheduling things, and so everybody took turns, everybody had – well, the guys didn't have a dinner night, but they might have a cleanup night." Sex, too, was directed at men's pleasure. In fact, at one point early in The Farm's existence, Ina May Gaskin called a women's meeting to encourage them to try to satisfy their men because this would make for happier families and a more harmonious community.

The *rock ethics* at the commune also seemed to align with the hippie ethos. In the early days, The Farm was somewhat conservative about music, as Gaskin argued that sexist or violent lyrics stayed with the listeners and affected their consciousness. Unable to rely on existing materials, some individuals started writing original songs with spiritual and love themes, and pretty quickly, The Farm Band had its own repertoire. Similar to rock-n-roll musicians of the era, The Farm Band had a powerful status in the community, second only to Gaskin and his family: "There was the 'royal family,' and then the band was way high up there because they traveled with Stephen" (Laura). Albert mentioned that "The Farm band was the best – it had the best equipment, the best musicians... it had a lot of position, they would be practicing when everyone else was out in the field sweating." Gordon, who played in the band, agreed:

> Music sort of began when The Farm began... one of Stephen's closest students was very much in the music, and he was writing, you know, very nice, very lovely, very spiritual songs. So those were okay, and so those of us who played instruments all congregated around him and... I got ahold of a lap steel guitar kind of a Western Country sound... and they really liked the twang of the steel guitar even though I didn't really know how to play it, but I could make it sound like I did, so I was "the man" for that moment.

The Farm Band, however, was not the only band active in the commune. Musical instruments were among the only personal belongings allowed, and they were played at home and in community gatherings. Several bands were formed, got together to practice, and performed at parties, on holidays, and the like, including the large seasonal canning and freezing parties that lasted into the night. Some of the bands were also involved in outreach concerts. For example, a band called Heart Beast performed in prisons: "We wanted to influence them [the prisoners] in an uplifting, positive way. Bringing the music that we chose to play would be a very positive message kind of songs. They always wanted to hear 'Free bird'" (Sandra).

The Farm also had its own FM radio station, WUTZ (UTZ means "good" in Cakchikiel, a Mayan dialect), which was licensed and operates to this day. Music was thus always in the background while working and when the households got together at the end of the day. Moreover, all children were encouraged to participate in music and art classes and were taught how to play various instruments by The Farm's adult musicians. There has also been a strong tradition of child bands on The Farm that continues to this day. Some of the adult and child bands formed on The Farm still play together elsewhere.

The *community ethics* was the basis of the commune. The Farm was a spiritual, ideological, and utopian commune that tried to demonstrate a new and better way of living. Members shared their lives in all ways one can imagine and operated as a large extended family, like a clan or tribe. The community's goal was to help each individual to "leave their ego at the gate" and unite in body and spirit with the larger community. Members assumed each other's goodwill and, for the most part, took for granted each other's commitment, honesty, and reliability. Sometimes mothers would nurse each other's babies ("We took care of each other's babies, nursed each other's babies and stuff so we could go work" – Cindy), and children were cared for in groups known as "kid herds," having different adults taking turns watching them ("The women would have little herds of kids, you take one day a week... but you also had your days when someone else had your kid" – Carolyn). Thus, the children grew up with a sense of having multiple parents and bonded with each other like siblings. Accordingly, many of the children who grew up on The Farm are still connected, now that they are grown.

Life in the commune, however, was not idyllic. The commune, like any community, had its tensions and conflicts. Whereas everyone was seemingly equal, there was a clear social hierarchy ("The Farm was never egalitarian. It was always a vertical hierarchy even though we pretended that it wasn't" – Gordon). Gaskin and his inner circle were at the top, "and then came the four marriages, and the band and then... the Book Publishing Company, the bank lady, and the lawyer... I was married to a midwife, that helped" (Andrew). Single people were at the bottom, carrying out the worst jobs ("We had somebody at the gate 24/7, and usually single men would do the night shifts" – Roger). They were also treated "like slaves because couples could say 'well, I can't clean up because I have to get my kids to bed' and the single people were like, 'that's exactly it, it's your kids that made all the mess in the kitchen, why should we clean after them'" (Cindy's spouse).

To keep the "good vibes" and promote spiritual growth, members were encouraged to express objections to each other's behavior, and meetings to "sort it out" were held at any time that people felt it was necessary. Rebecca explained:

> Has anybody told you that one of the earlier concepts we had on The Farm was "mental nudity"? Everybody was supposed to be totally transparent with everything they thought and felt, and we were letting other people know, and we're supposed to be telepathic. So, we are supposed to pick up on it. It was kind of a general hippie thing, but it was more specific and intense on The Farm.

Whereas "sort sessions" were often helpful, they irritated some commune members: "We were all amateur psychologists working on each other's minds... more than half of the time this was just nonsense and a waste of time" (Harold).

Lastly, the *ethics of opposition* to establishment culture were reflected in nearly all aspects of the commune's values and daily life. The Farm posed a self-sustaining rural, agrarian alternative to the mainstream capitalist economy. Money was forbidden and was not needed, and if cash was required for a need unmet by the community, one applied for funds and received the exact amount required from the "bank ladies." Similarly, vehicles were parceled out: All cars or trucks were obtained at the Motor Pool and signed out for a specific time and use.

"Love" was the rationale for almost every commune decision. It guided policies regarding matters such as sex and marriage and the "open gate" policy that allowed anyone who was interested to join the commune. Love also motivated the community's conscious efforts, which last to this day, to form friendly relationships with the neighboring communities in rural Tennessee and its outreach activities in and outside the U.S. Love also meant love of nature and the natural – as reflected in the commune's efforts to use alternative energy and promote recycling – and nonviolence, as exemplified in the commune's opposition to abortion and its strictly vegan diet, which stemmed from spiritual respect for the environment and animal life. However, it should be noted that whereas many commune members were enthusiastic vegans ("So we kept thinking about coming here just to be with like-minded people, vegans; we were vegans" – Cindy), others perceived veganism as a price they were willing to pay ("I became a vegan overnight, no problem, never miss meat, never had any since" – Elizabeth).

Overall, it may be said that one can place a tick next to all mandatory hippie characteristics. Although The Farm in its commune days was not at the far end of the sex, drugs, and rock-n-roll triad, it respected and practiced all three and formed a lifestyle based on strong community values, spirituality, environmentalism, and anticonsumerism. Despite a work ethic resembling the Judeo-Christian ethics, Farm members found ways to involve play in work and leisure. While being somewhat "serious hippies," they definitely posed an alternative to mainstream society. Therefore, to an extent, they embodied the "visionary" type of hippie.

### THE CHANGEOVER (1983)

Although The Farm is considered the largest and most successful hippie commune, it clearly failed in establishing an adequately functioning management structure. The commune regarded itself as a "family monastery" with Gaskin as its abbot. Insisting that he was only a spiritual teacher, Gaskin was undoubtedly The Farm's leader ("He used to say, 'I'm a teacher, not a leader.' But that wasn't true" – Paul). Although he formed a "tribal council," whose role was to manage all Farm affairs, council members were appointed by him or by other council members and were typically yes-people, who followed his rulings, as Sam summarized it: "He had the final say."

This unprofessional centralistic governance system led to two destructive outcomes, the first being an acute economic crisis. For several years things went well, but Gaskin's open-gate policy brought to the commune more people than it could support, and his speaking tours, as well as Plenty and other generous projects, gave away money and labor that the commune needed to maintain itself ("The Farm had made so many bad decisions, that it became kind of a little moniker of 'oh, that's a bad idea, here, here is too much money for it'" – Jerry). In addition, the commune did not carry health insurance, so any disease or injury that could not be handled at The Farm's clinic and required hospitalization caused huge bills. Moreover, a national agricultural recession in the late 1970s and early 1980s affected The Farm just as it did other parts of the U.S., and the oil crisis along with the high interest rates at the end of the 1970s led to a sharp decline in the construction industry, which by then had become the primary source of the commune's income.

The second outcome of the centralistic management was unrest among commune members. Individuals who were not part of Gaskin's inner circle started to realize that the commune was not as equality-based as it aspired to be and that Gaskin, despite his incredible charisma, was far from being a saint: "It became evident that he was simply a man – a good man, but one who had ego issues that were the obvious result of too much power" (Stevenson[9]). Gradually, many members lost faith in Gaskin's spiritual authority, judgment, and ability to lead the community. Acknowledging his kindness, good intentions, and irreplaceable role in establishing the community, they started to see his weaknesses: "There was a discrepancy between what he taught and what he lived" (Jane). "We were supposed to question authority except you couldn't question his" (Charles). "There were some other aspects that I don't think were being lived out in Gaskin's household... some things were going on there that we said we wouldn't do" (Cliff). "He was not an enlightened spiritual teacher; he did not have control over his anger" (Andrew). "He was using his spiritual authority to have total control about the secular decisions on The Farm... he was just so full of himself, and he wasn't honest, and he was a womanizer" (Laura). "He was a world-class bullshitter" (Paul).

The level of initial admiration for Gaskin among community members varied. Some of the members, especially those who came later in the 1970s, did not even consider him their spiritual teacher. Cliff, for example, said, "I never really got to know Stephen very well. I don't know if he ever knew my name... A lot of people on The Farm were very serious students of spiritual teachers, not just Stephen. I never was his student." Similarly, Gordon recalled, "I was the worst student and I kind of thought of myself as a black sheep on The Farm." For the majority, however, Gaskin was a significant teacher and even a father figure to an extent. Sobering up from the idealization of his character was thus very painful for them. Simultaneously, however, it seemed to be a natural side effect of those young people's maturing process, as Anna described it: "People were getting disgusted with Stephen. People were growing and flexing their muscles, and it [his authority] was just too tight." In addition, members started to get tired of the hardship and wanted more space and better conditions for their children. Having no "older generation" on The Farm, they were also deprived of the wisdom and practical know-how that such a generation would have provided and had no grandparents to fall back on for financial help or watch over their children while they worked.

In 1980, The Farm chose its first elected officials, the Council of Elders, a group with over thirty members that was supposed to sort out spiritual and cultural matters but had no actual authority, and as quickly as it was formed, it faded away. However, during its short lifetime, the Council of Elders formed a Constitutional Committee that examined the community's legal framework as an "institution," as defined by the Inland Revenue Service. The committee revised the foundation's rules and bylaws and redrew its structure into a more formal system. This process led to electing a Board of Directors that was fully authorized to take whatever steps were needed to save the community from financial collapse.

The various hardships continued and prompted many people to leave. Some wanted to continue with their careers, reside closer to their parents, or live in a different climate. Even those who wholeheartedly supported the commune ideology and genuinely appreciated the love and fraternity culture were experiencing burnout. Many could not deal anymore (or did not want their children to deal) with the demands and personal sacrifices necessary to live in primitive, tribal conditions.

Study participants' reports on the quality of life at the commune were quite dreadful. They described poor infrastructure ("We didn't have any paved roads back then, so there was a lot of dust and a lot of pollens in the air" – James), lousy nutrition ("We always ate, but sometimes it was nothing but soybeans and wheat germ and whatever the hell else and not enough fruit and vegetables" – Cliff), ongoing health challenges ("We had some communicable diseases, you know, from our international projects that we brought back here" – Sam), and not enough resources to support their children's development ("Had four kids, wanted to give the kids more opportunities and exposure to the stuff that wasn't available here. The opportunities were out there and not here... I kind of joke about just having sticks and stones to play with" – Ben). In addition, they felt they were "too old" to live in such poverty.

> I was turning 30, truthfully, and I got tired of living in these big households and really having not much. You know, you had to get on the list for shoes for your kids, and because you had no money, you didn't have any control. And I was sick of not having electricity, not having a refrigerator, things that living in the big households required, and I just looked at myself, and I'm like 30 and I'm like, what do I have going on here? (Sarah)
>
> At that time, there were starting to be cracks. We were moving from our 20s into our 30s, and the idea of outhouses and dusty roads and having to go work off The Farm on a Saturday to get money so we could maybe buy shoes for the kids or get holiday presents, it was getting a little old for some of us. The living conditions were improving, but people were still getting sick. (Roger)

Gradually, the population decreased from almost 1,500 in 1980 to about 800 by 1983, leading to an even more restrained income. By 1983, The Farm had accumulated an enormous debt, which could lead to its bankruptcy given the interest rates at that time. After months of discussions and solution seeking, the Board of Directors concluded that if The Farm was to survive, it had to decollectivize and abandon the dream of a cashless communal existence. In a meeting held in September 1983, the Board announced that the community would no longer pay members' living expenses and that each member would have to be self-supporting. In addition, members would have to pay dues to cover the debt and ongoing operating costs (e.g., roads, water, electricity). This act, known as the "Changeover," transformed The Farm from a commune to a cooperative community (Figure 3.4).

**3.4** Part of a mural describing The Farm's commune era, which decorates the living room of a couple that participated in the study.

## FROM COLLECTIVE TO COOPERATIVE (1983–PRESENT)

The changeover was a radical and painful game changer for many community members. After much discussion, however, it was widely supported. The Farm's communal nature was preserved to some extent as the land and other assets of the community were still held in common (as they are to this day). Yet, each family was now on its own and had to support itself. The transition was easier for some members than for others. The members who already worked outside the commune could keep doing that ("Those who worked in construction were fortunate because they had work" – Cindy). The same applied to those who operated independent businesses such as Nicholas, who in 1981 started a media business, so "when everything changed, I had a business going already, and so we were in a better position than many people."

However, members whose jobs were based in the community (e.g., clinic personnel, midwives, school teachers, storekeepers, soy dairy operators) were potentially jobless. One solution, which provided jobs and income to some community members, was turning The Farm's services (the midwifery center, clinic, motor pool, soy dairy, construction crew, and store) into private businesses. Another solution, which also helped to cover part of the debt, was selling shares of community-owned businesses to individual members and investors. The Ice Bean business of Farm Foods, for example, was sold to some departing members, part of Solar Electronics (currently SE International) was sold to several of its workers, and part of the BPC was sold to an external investor.

Yet, many had to figure out how to get a real job and make a living in a depressed rural economy. A popular trend, especially among women, was going back to school. Many of them enrolled in a two-year nursing program at Columbia State, the regional community college, and then worked as registered nurses in nearby clinics and hospitals. Other members found jobs in local towns (twenty individuals, for example, worked at a local mobile home factory) or opened their own businesses. Daniel, for example, opened a tie-die business and Henry started a construction company.

Despite all possible solutions, however, the majority could not find a good source of income in the area, and about two-thirds of the remaining Farm members left shortly after the changeover and moved elsewhere. Others, who were away at that time, could not come back. Albert, who was in California, said, "I never left The Farm. I just moved my office and stopped sending money to The Farm." Similarly, Evelyn, who was in Memphis, explained, "We were a satellite. I actually never really left The Farm. The Farm just kind of fell apart, and we were off doing the thing we were doing, and then we just kept going." Bill, who was in Washington, DC, recalled, "I couldn't come back because there was no house for me to live in. So, that left all of us just like, okay, now what? I was starting from scratch at the age of 30 or something." Those who stayed at The Farm managed to pay off its total debt of 1.2 million dollars in a little over three years, securing the land for remaining members, for those who had to leave, and for future generations.

On the individual level, for both the remaining members and those who left or stayed away, the changeover not only involved a financial challenge. It also caused significant emotional distress and a sense of loss. Carolyn, for example, described "lots and lots of issues and hard feelings, lots of wounding," Laura confessed "I was in grief for a year after leaving," and Rebecca, who left The Farm because her spouse insisted on doing so, said: "I loved The Farm. I would not have moved normally. I was a true believer. It took me many years to deprogram myself... I really loved being on The Farm and never wanted to leave. I had a serious life-time commitment to it, and I felt really sad that I had to leave."

After investing their "best years" (as well as a considerable fortune in some cases) in building an ideal community or helping those less fortu-nate, members had to start over – a state that was frustrating and stress-ful. In addition, "the ending, as some saw it, of the initial Farm project felt to many Farm members like one big divorce" (Traugot[10]). For many couples who left The Farm, the changeover also involved real marital difficulties ending in many divorces. Sam stated, "After we left, it [mar-riage] didn't work so well. We didn't have the support of our friends, and, you know, we drifted apart." Similarly, Paul shared, "We just went in different directions. We had come together within the context of The Farm society, and when we got out of that context, we had less of a core to hold onto." Anna, too, said, "He [spouse] and I split up not long after we left The Farm... The thing that kept us together wasn't there any-more, so we ended up splitting up like a whole lot of people did."

Parallel to these hardships came several blessings, of which a dom-inant one was a profound change in gender roles. With many women acquiring higher education and having their children grow older and more independent, the job scene at The Farm equalized ("I went to nursing school, and my life changed dramatically. It worked out because when the kids came home from school, he [spouse] was nearby. He still worked at the dairy factory" – Sarah). Other community members appre-ciated the downsized population ("I did feel better after the changeo-ver. It gave you more freedom to take on responsibility if you wanted to because so many of those people left" – Cindy) and the greater inde-pendence and sense of choice, as Tim described:

> It was great. Suddenly, we had better food. We bought a refrigerator, you know, we could start buying things. All of a sudden, we had our own home again. No more communal. It was good because, by that point, we were get-ting tired of the communal. We were ready for more freedom. When you have your own money, you can make your own choices. You don't have to ask somebody. You don't have to ask our committee, "oh, can I do this?" You just do it. If the old Farm had stayed, there would not be anyone in here.

At the community level, the changeover not only involved the alteration of economic arrangements and considerable downsizing, it also led to radical reform in governance. Although Gaskin and his family remained community members until Gaskin's passing in 2014, he no longer had any authority. Instead, the Board of Directors became an elected body managing the community's finances and assets and supervising the implementation of the annual budget. Decisions on topics such as the annual budget or new projects are now made based on democratic voting after holding community meetings and discussions. Critical decisions, such as changing a bylaw, granting, or revoking someone's membership require two-thirds of the votes. The Farm also has an elected Membership Committee, whose role is to handle visitors and potential members,[11] as well as several volunteer committees dedicated to specific matters, such as the Land-Use Committee, which oversees the management of forests and fields and addresses issues such as the removal of invasive species; the Finance Committee, whose main roles are to collect membership dues and administer the community's development fund; and the more recently established Community Conflict Resolution Team that handles problems between members.

Since the late 1980s, the population has stabilized on a little over 200 residents. Although some families left over the years, quite a few former residents moved back after spending several years in mainstream America. Brian, who moved back after eight years, said, "We would have a reunion [the annual Ragweed Day] every year, and we came back some years, and we started thinking, 'boy, really it's nice to be back here' when we were here, and we thought if there was any way we can get back here." Similarly, Bill, who stayed in Washington, DC for ten years, recalled, "I came back for Ragweed, and I was like, 'Oh my god. Why am I anywhere else? This is where I belong.'"

Interestingly, since 2010, the number of applications submitted every year to the Membership Committee has been constantly growing. Some of the new members were born on The Farm but had left it with their parents or went to college and now want their children to have the same experience they had growing up there. Furthermore, the recent trend of intentional communities in the U.S. brought to The Farm complete newcomers who choose to join what they perceive as a sustainable and even flourishing intentional community rather than building a new one. In addition, quite a few former residents reached retirement age and decided to move back to The Farm, which they continued to consider their home despite the many years they had lived away from it. Ben, for example, moved back after living in Florida for thirty years:

> And, you know, getting to be retirement age, kids are all grown and on their own and self-sufficient. So, I looked around, wondering, "what do I want to do in this next chapter?" And having deep roots here, I still want to make a difference in the world. I'm not one for protesting in the streets, but I feel that small sustainable communities are an important option for people to participate in, if that's what they like to do, and not have to be in a city setting.

Jane, too, moved back to The Farm after residing in California for twenty-eight years. She explained: "I retired and I had a nice sum of money and I thought, 'Okay, now, what am I going to do?' I remembered what it felt like here. It's just a spiritual family feeling, and I missed that." Currently, Jane serves on the Membership Committee. When I visited her one morning, her entire kitchen and dining area were covered with piles of papers she had organized for the next committee meeting. Overwhelmed by the interest in The Farm but also by the amount of work these applications required, she looked at me with a desperate face and said, "Can you believe it?"

Current community members vary in economic status. Some, especially those who spent years outside the community, are relatively well off and even have multiple homes. Others live close to the official U.S. poverty line. Nonetheless, The Farm today has an overall appearance of modest prosperity. There are quite a few successful businesses and a bunch of children, teenagers, and young adults. In a conversation I had with some of the younger members near the campfire held while I was visiting, all agreed that they feel fortunate to live in that place and be part of such a unique community. These members relate to the commune years as almost marginal in the community's history ("only 12 years out of 50"). Acknowledging the past adventures, achievements, and failures, they mainly see the future of the place and the many ways in which it can still develop.

Spread throughout the U.S., especially in California, many of the former residents have stayed connected. They formed enclaves of "Farmies" who live close to each other, get together quite often, and sometimes even work together. Many of them keep in touch with The Farm in Tennessee through Facebook groups and interpersonal communication, receive The Farm's newsletter, and attend the annual Ragweed reunion gatherings. Similar to the people I met in Tennessee, most of the former residents interviewed for this study expressed pride in The Farm: "We did an amazing thing together. We built a town from the ground up. We build the world's largest hippie commune. We started Plenty. We did a lot" (Andrew). They never regretted the years they spent there and felt that this experience shaped who they were. Rebecca, for example, said, "All the time on The Farm really shaped my life for better, for worse. I wouldn't say that I have regrets." Similarly, Stephanie commented, "I'm so grateful. I don't know who I'd be without The Farm, without that time, without that tribe." All former residents reported feeling blessed to have both the good memories and the lifetime friendships they have gained thanks to this experience.

# CHAPTER 4

# Once a Hippie, Always a Hippie

A TED TALK FROM 2018 titled *Out to change the world – Living the hippie dream* opens with the speaker standing on a dark, empty stage and stating: "Well, there is no hiding the fact that I'm a baby boomer." He then turns on the screen behind him, which shows two photos of a young hippie couple, and continues: "But as you might guess from these pictures of my wedding day, I'm also a hippie." Comparing the sixty-something man on the stage with the young, long-haired version of himself on the screen, the audience laughs, and the speaker continues: "Not a former hippie, but a twenty first-century hippie, and so it gives me a certain way of looking at the world." In this opening and throughout his talk about The Farm community in Tennessee, Douglas Stevenson (member since 1973) stresses that although time has passed, community members still view themselves as hippies and live their lives according to the hippie ideals. Other media content about The Farm I consumed before visiting suggested the same continuity in members' self-perception. The content, however, did not indicate *how* members settled the alleged contradiction between aging and hippiedom.

As exemplified in the famous hippie saying "Never trust anybody over 30," being a hippie originally meant being young, and thus getting older should have inevitably negated one's hippiedom. Moreover, just like others in their age group, aging hippies cope with various physical (e.g., health decline, notable alterations in appearance) and social changes (e.g., retirement, spousal loss) associated with older age, which signify the transition from the accepted group of "young" to the less desirable group of "old."[1] These changes may pose numerous challenges to their young/hippie identity, trigger re-evaluation of their social status, and make them susceptible to identity degradation.[2]

The fact that members of The Farm still consider themselves hippies suggests that they engage in some sort of identity work – a process of bridging between internal self-identity (i.e., people's notion of who and what they are) and external social identity shaped by cultural, discursive, or institutional ideas of who and what they could or should be.[3] The literature on identity work in later life describes a variety of mechanisms individuals apply to deal with their move to the out-group of older adults, ranging from "accommodation" to "resistance."[4] Some scholars also suggested the concept of "ageless self," according to which older adults tend to see and present themselves as the continuation of their younger identities.[5] Others discussed the "mask of aging" perspective that sees the older adult as a youth trapped in an aging body.[6] Both concepts may be supported by the many studies demonstrating that older adults typically report that they feel younger than their chronological age – a feeling related to better psychological, cognitive, and physical wellbeing, and even longevity.[7] Identity work in later life was also described in terms of lifestyle choices, reflected in how people spend their time and money.[8] A consumer-led lifestyle enables choice and agency, including the use of various masquerades that allow a matured inner identity to evoke a more youthful façade to ensure continued social inclusion.[9]

Aging hippies make a fascinating case for a study on identity work in later life because by preserving their hippie identity, they also maintain a young version of themselves. This chapter explores to what extent older hippies define themselves as "old," their self-perceptions as "hippies," and the identity work mechanisms that they apply to settle the tension between these two constructs. By comparing people who reside at The Farm with those who left it, this chapter also examines the role of the place of residence in identity preservation.

## "ONCE A HIPPIE": SELF-PERCEPTION AS A HIPPIE IN THE PAST

Discussing their lives as young adults before The Farm, most study participants explicitly presented themselves as hippies. Such presentations were spontaneous and occurred incidentally when describing a particular period or a specific situation. Joe, for example, shared that before moving to The Farm, he went to school for a year, "and other than that, I did the hippie thing at Haight-Ashbury... wandering around Golden Gate Park, playing the flutes, smoking a lot of pot and various other drugs, and working as a bicycle messenger. We were just getting by." In a similar incidental manner, Paul mentioned that he was a hippie when he described the day he got himself exempted from serving in Vietnam:

> I went in to talk to the shrink, and he's like a high-up guy in the army, and I'm sitting there, and, you know, I'm wearing my Big Sur outfit: white pants, white top, sandals, my hair is down to here [lower back]. I was a real hippie. It wasn't a costume. That was how I really dressed. I'm sitting there in front of this army guy, and he's reading this letter [from a friend's father who was a psychiatrist], and he goes, "Is this all true?" Because basically, the letter said that I was part of a religious group that uses psychedelic drugs. Yeah, it was true, and he goes, "Why don't you want to go in the army?" I just said, "I can't kill."

Several study participants did not state that they were hippies, but their stories clearly implied that they were part of the counterculture. In such cases, I asked the participants directly if they considered themselves hippies before coming to The Farm. Some simply answered "Yeah," but others had some reservations regarding the use of the word "hippie." One type of reservation, typically mentioned by the older study participants, was that they considered themselves "beatniks that embraced a lot of the hippie culture" (Harold), whereas another type of reservation resulted from the negative stigma associated with this term.

Brian, who expressed both types of reservations, told me about his life after graduating from college:

> I'd been taking psychedelics, and I'd been reading Timothy Leary, Krishnamurti, and Alan Watts... It wasn't really working out for me at [place of work]. I was just so distracted by my studies of the mind and spirituality and psychedelics that I couldn't concentrate on becoming an engineer. So, I decided to take Timothy Leary's advice and turned on and dropped out.

Three elements in this brief quote imply that Brian was a hippie: his experiments with psychedelics, the books he had been reading, and his decision to drop out. Indeed, when I asked him if he considered himself a hippie, he immediately said, "Yeah, I felt like I was a hippie." Soon after that, however, he expressed his reservations about the term:

> Oh no, we preferred to call ourselves beatniks. I'm a little older than some of the people here. I was in my early 30s when I got here... I did consider myself a hippie, but not necessarily always identified as one because there was somewhat of a negative connotation of hippies: not very serious, just want to take drugs and listen to rock-n-roll and free love and that kind of thing. We weren't necessarily into that, but we were hippies, and I wasn't ashamed to be called a hippie.

The negative connotation of hippies was mentioned by many interviewees, including those who felt comfortable with this term. Reflecting on the days after the Summer of Love in San Francisco, when "hard drugs had moved into Haight-Ashbury, and it just turned into a dangerous grungy scene" (Anna), participants described how the "media made this a big deal" (Dennis), leading to the demonization of the hippies. Feeling uncomfortable with the change in the public discourse, they distanced themselves from the negative portrayals of the hippies by distinguishing between "good hippies" and "bad hippies." Explaining that bad hippies are "guys that look like my brothers, but they're not nice guys" (Ben), participants provided pretty detailed descriptions of both (see summary in Figure 4.1).

Echoing the "heads and freaks" typology,[10] the distinction between good and bad hippies was not applied when discussing the old days only. In addition, some study participants expressed harsh criticism on the various "offspring" of the hippie movement, describing them in manners resembling the "midnight" and "plastic" hippie typology.[11] Harold, for example, criticized people attending Burning Man events for "playing hippie" for a week:

> It is an attempt to emulate something that is related to the hippie experience. That's probably honest – and people are really trying to do something, but at the same time, I feel that it's like, you know, dentists and doctors who buy Harley-Davidson motorcycles or drive very large pickup trucks. They imitate rednecks because they think it's cool, but it's not. If you're going to do something challenging, do something that is really challenging.

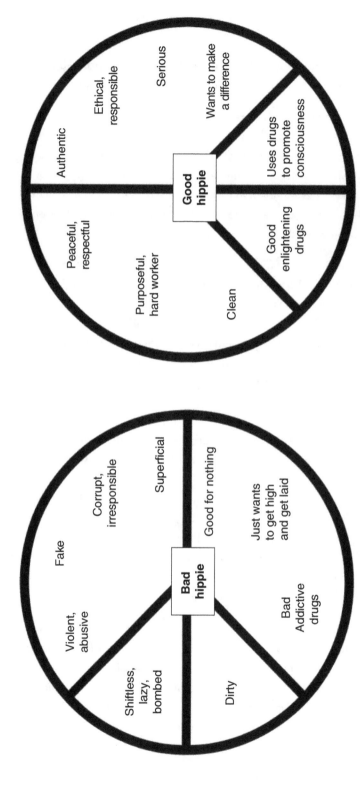

4.1 The "bad hippie" versus the "good hippie," according to the study participants.

Distinguishing good hippies from bad hippies and original hippies from their superficial imitations may be considered identity work done throughout the interviewees' lives. Moreover, it seems that Farm members also differentiated themselves from other good hippies. Ben, for example, said that "part of the reason for getting out of San Francisco back in 1970 was to get away from that culture... We didn't blend in, and we didn't want to blend in. We thought we had a message, a worthy message that needed to be heard." Joan, too, commented, "We were different, a different type of hippie than a lot of hippies outside of the community," and Bill clarified that "The Farm was never laid back. This was a working community, and we had to survive, and we weren't dependent on anyone else or welfare or anything else. We took our hippiness [sic.] quite seriously." Similarly, Rebecca noted, "The Farm was white-collar hippies, white-collar working hippies," and someone I met at The Farm even went as far as describing Farm members as "high-class hippies."

## THE THREE LEVELS OF HIPPIEDOM

To better understand what study participants meant by referring to themselves as hippies, I asked them to define this term for me. Their responses provided very rich and complex descriptions of what being a hippie means to them. Generally, these descriptions suggested three levels of hippiedom: essence, behavior, and look.

THE HIPPIE ESSENCE According to the participants, the hippie essence is a rather complex construct composed of multiple components. Figure 4.2 presents a word cloud based on the frequency of the keywords used by the participants in their descriptions of the hippie essence. As seen in the figure, the hippie essence's central and most dominant component is "love." Nicholas explained that "Love is not just romantic love, but love of humanity, love of nature, not just people but the universe, love as a vibration," and Jane expanded:

> The basis of the hippie is love. Of course, in those days, it was free love, which I was never into. But it was just about love, love, love. Love with the policemen, love your neighbor, just make everything about love. And

**4.2** Word cloud based on the frequency of the keywords used by study participants in their definitions of the hippie essence. (Generated by the online software "Word it out" – https://worditout.com)

that's really what I think a hippie is. It is about not restricting the love to anyone and spreading love instead of division, hate, and separation. It's like opening up that love for everyone regardless, unconditional love. Hippies have unconditional love and unconditional forgiveness... When you open yourself up to love, that means love for the trees, that means love for the animals, that means love for people, that means love for yourself. I mean, that expands your universe quite a bit more than our former generation would ever admit or allow.

This description captures the deep meaning of love as the highest hippie ideal, which is the source of most other components of the hippie essence, such as environmentalism, which results from the love of nature, and authenticity as a manifestation of loving and accepting oneself.

Closely linked to the love component is "peace" and its related elements, *antiwar* and *nonviolence*. Going back to the origins of the hippie movement in the 1960s, study participants explained that their opposition to the war in Vietnam applies to all wars. Cliff said that "the hippies continued to oppose various military adventures over the years," Karen mentioned, "We were peaceniks, you know," and Chris stated that "the problems of the world could be decided better without using armaments." Participants stressed, however, that peace means more than avoiding war and physical violence: Peace stands for nonviolence in all human interactions ("It means not creating more problems, not creating conflict, using non-violence in your words, in your internal vibration, how you treat people" – Nicholas), and it is the ideal outcome of love, as Evelyn explained: "Peace is what we're supposed to be working toward that can only happen once we have love."

Whereas peace and love encapsulate the alternative to mainstream America in the 1960s and beyond, a separate cluster of the hippie essence components – as described by study participants – represents the "opposition" to the mainstream and its establishment. Departing from the disapproval of war, the *antimainstream* component ranges in intensity from "not participating wholly in the culture of the United States" (Cindy) to feeling "completely estranged from the culture of the United States and the politics and the economic system" (Cliff).

Closely related elements are *antimaterialism* and *questioning authority*. As a hippie, one is "anti-capitalist... that does not care about the material plane" (Karen), and is not "into consumerism" (Rebecca). Instead, one is more interested in "exploring things that matter more than materialistic things" (Ben). Hippies "reject the middle-class trajectory" (Joe), do not "buy into a nine to five" (Karen), or "turn into squares and join the rat race" (Gordon). They believe that "we should all more or less have the same level of income, and wealth should be more evenly, fairly distributed. Rich people are selfish. Rich people are arrogant. Rich people take more than they need. Rich people are messing up the world, the earth" (Roger).

Historically, doubting authority stemmed from the loss of faith in Washington officials during the Vietnam War, as Sam explained: "I didn't have great faith in our government because of not only the war but other things as well, and I didn't want to follow the philosophies. I wanted a change in our country, philosophically as well as physically." The doubt developed, however, into a tendency to question all types of authority, as Charles explained:

> Questioning authority means that I'm not going to go along just because you're a democrat or a republican, or Christian or Jew. That doesn't matter. It's beyond that. Whose authority is it? Left or right, Christian, Jew, Buddhist, all that kind of stuff, who is to say what's right? To me, the hummingbird that's flying by, that's the authority at the moment without being silly about it.

Both the opposition to the mainstream and the hippie alternative of love and peace are related to the "hippie qualities" of being more liberal (and even radical at times), open-minded, and able to think outside the box. James explained:

> It's more of a state of mind, a way of looking at the world with an open mind and an open heart, trying to listen more carefully, to see more deeply, feel more deeply, and trying to be more human and less of a product of a culture that's materialistic in its outlook and the way it deals with life from a materialistic standpoint. It's a person who has a spiritual understanding of life and tries to live according to those understandings.

As demonstrated by this quote, the outcome of the hippie qualities is a *different worldview*, which has a strong *spiritual* dimension. Focusing on the word "hippie," several people explained that it comes from being "hip," and hip means being "in the know" (Nicholas), knowing that "we're all one thing, that you and I are not different from each other" (Bill), and "understanding the natural laws and how they interact with reality versus man-made laws" (Ben). Gordon added that hippiedom is "kind of a large mindset having been around the block in a big way, in a big social way, in a big spiritual way. More so than most of society."

Acknowledging that being a hippie also means having fun, celebrating, and partying (e.g., "The hippie part is the fun part. Go with the flow, that sort of thing" – Daniel), study participants stressed that it is mainly about spiritually induced *understandings*, *ideals*, and *values* often described as "consciousness." Although this term was frequently used, I was not able to get anyone's precise definition of it:

GALIT: How does one become a hippie?

ELIZABETH: All you have to do is have the consciousness.

GALIT: Can you define "consciousness" for me?

ELIZABETH: No.

GALIT: Do you have to smoke to get consciousness?

ELIZABETH: It's the consciousness whether you smoke or not.

GALIT: Okay.

ELIZABETH: But the grass promotes the consciousness.

GALIT: Okay, what kind of consciousness?

ELIZABETH: You haven't figured it out by now?

GALIT: I think I have, but I still want to hear your takeoff.

ELIZABETH: No. Some things cannot be put into little word boxes.

GALIT: Okay.

ELIZABETH: You have to understand it from a broader sense and your intuition.

Involving political, social, and spiritual understandings, the consciousness does not remain philosophical only but rather directs the hippie's lifestyle. Participants explained that being a hippie means being "spiritual ahead of the day-to-day" (Albert) and practicing "spirituality as a part of your lifestyle" (Sandra). Harold even compared being a hippie

77

with being Buddha: He argued that by putting into practice the hippie values of love, appreciation, and respect, "you're paying attention to someone else besides yourself." As a result, "you're greeting all situations in a compassionate way, in a non-judgmental way, a helpful way... when you're doing that, you are – you're a hippie, you're a Buddha."

Being more spiritual in daily life, therefore, means aiming to be a "better person" – nice, kind, respectful, caring, compassionate, and forgiving people who do their best to help others. The ambition to be a better person is the basis for connecting with others and forming a "community" where "you could do something positive as an alternative to what we didn't like" (Cliff). All components of the hippie essence together serve the ultimate goal of spreading love and by so doing "changing the world."

THE HIPPIE BEHAVIOR The hippie behavior is the external expression of the hippie essence and has three major components: "practicing the hippie ethics," "promoting hippie ideals," and "spreading love." In their definitions of the hippies, most study participants described the hippie ethics of dope, sex, rock, community, and opposition[12] as lived practices. They explained, however, that practicing hippie ethics does not only mean doing certain things (e.g., "living in a commune, smoking grass, taking psychedelics, listening to rock music, creating a certain kind of poster art" – Dennis). It also involves refraining from certain practices, such as "getting a nine-to-five job" (Charles) or "driving a Lexus rather than a Prius or a total electric car" (Karen). Stressing that both do and don't practices originated in ideology (e.g., "It was about the attitude of peace and love, and the free love and the partying were an expression of that" – Andrew), participants described them as factors leading to a nonconventional lifestyle, as Roger explained: "A hippie is a person that is not conventional and has a certain style that is different than what's conventional, who lives a freer type of life with fewer conventions and standards to follow."

Whereas practicing hippie ethics revolves around personal choices, "promoting hippie ideals" is a behavioral component directed at affecting others. Often, this component was described as hard work. Nicholas, for example, defined hippies as "people who work really hard for something they really believe in," and Daniel mentioned that "some people think hippies are like lazy or something, but everybody I know works really hard. The hippies really did a lot to save America." According to some study participants, the "promoting" component reflects the most notable difference between the beatniks and the hippies. Ben explained:

> The beatniks were "turn on, tune in, and drop out" society before the next decade, before the '60s. So, their thing was more passive... Then came the culture happening and the Vietnam War, and it got a little more crazy, political fascinations and civil rights and stuff, not like the '50s. So, then you're getting into these more active situations that are affecting everybody, and that's when the young people started growing their hair out and standing up and protesting and actively emphasizing love and peace and harmony.

Interestingly, only a few respondents made a similar distinction between the hippies and the New Left. Joe noted that "all the politicals were in Berkeley, and all the hippies were in San Francisco." Similarly, Evelyn described some of her friends as "radical politicos, some kind of violent stuff that really offended me," and Rebecca commented: "I was never an activist. There's a difference between hippies and activists. While we didn't disagree with protesting or anything like that, we were trying to be more 'you can solve everything if each individual is enlightened or whatever.'" Typically describing themselves as "always sort of politically left of the left" (Carolyn) and sharing various stories about involvement in the antiwar protests and marches of the 1960s, the majority of the founding members of The Farm seemed to come from the "hybrid" stream of the counterculture. Hence, they appeared to be both hippies and New Leftists rather than "purists."

Participants' definitions, however, stressed that the hippie activism is not necessarily political and that, eventually, all behavioral hippie components stem from the aspiration to be more spiritual in their daily lives and become better people who "spread the love" for humanity and nature in any way possible. Having numerous manifestations, spreading love is basically about a "kind of the 10 commandments, you know, just being a good person, a caring person" (Sarah). Accordingly, it involves "honor, tell the truth, be fair and consistent" (Sam) and "treating each other with respect and treating each other in a loving way" (Brian). Daniel explained, "My conception of hippie is somebody who basically tries to integrate, take bad vibes and turn them into good vibes; somebody who really wants to help," and Debbie added: "The thing about the hippies is that they are more accepting of other people and have no prejudices against whatever gender you are or whatever race you are. Hippies are usually not being so individually oriented about your own needs, but, you know, looking out for other people and helping them out." To be able to help others, people must first love themselves ("I had to learn how to love myself to be able to love other people" – Daniel) and have the consciousness that makes one realize that "similar to my fingers, all coming from the hand, we're all the same, coming from the same spiritual basis" (Bill).

THE HIPPIE LOOK Although how people dress or do their hair may be considered behavior, the hippie look stood out as a distinct and vital construct of being a hippie. Analyzing the numerous references study participants made regarding the hippie look suggested that it served, first and foremost, as an "external expression" of the opposition to the mainstream. Referring to the three main dimensions of the hippie look – hair, clothing, and accessories – Table 4.1 summarizes the portrayals of the differences between the mainstream and the hippie look.

As an external expression, the hippie look not only manifests the opposition to the mainstream. It also reflects the deepest hippie values of loving and accepting oneself, others, and nature. Joan shared that "when we first came here, you weren't supposed to cut your hair, you weren't supposed to wear any makeup, you weren't supposed to wear jewelry because you were supposed to be your natural self." Julia described blue jeans and T-shirts as both personally liberating ("You didn't have to care who had their best outfit on, or whatever clothes were hip for the day") and as a factor that helped to promote "social class-wise" equality. Dennis mentioned that "as vegetarians, we opposed wearing leather," and Harold added that Farm members, who were predominantly white, grew their hair long as a form of support for Afro-Americans:

**Table 4.1** The mainstream versus the hippie look.

|  |  | The mainstream | The hippie alternative |
|---|---|---|---|
| Hair | Men | Short haircuts | Long hair |
|  |  | Shaved faces | Beards and mustaches |
|  | Women | Hairdos | Long natural hair |
|  |  | Shaved armpits and legs | Body hair |
|  | Gray hair | Beautiful for men, a must-dye for women | Natural and thus beautiful for everyone |
| Clothing |  | Formal | Casual |
|  |  | Dull | Colorful |
|  |  | Uncomfortable | Comfortable |
| Accessories |  | Makeup | – |
|  |  | Jewelry (women) | Beads (everyone) |
|  |  | Bras | – |
|  |  | Leather items | – |
|  |  | Shoes | Nonleather shoes, sandals, and walking barefoot |

Someone who's black lives that way 24 hours a day, seven days a week their entire lives... So, Stephen said, "Well, you know the hippies are growing their hair long." He was trying to get us to feel what it feels like to be black because these people are different, and people will look and frown on you. They're going to make the same kinds of judgments about you, you know, or similar... Not all hippies maybe thought that way, but that's the way we viewed it as a community.

Such explanations may clarify why study participants sometimes described the hippie look as a "spiritual practice" that they were adamant about keeping even if it required significant sacrifices. For example, Chris shared that before serving as the commune's "barefoot dentist," he "got into dental school, but the experience was horrible because they didn't want my hair." Although he "tried to tell them it was my spiritual and religious belief, they didn't want to hear it," eventually leading to his dropping out of school. Similarly, Gordon, who was in jail with Stephen Gaskin after being charged for producing marijuana, shared that they were assigned to do yard work, a job that required wearing leather shoes. Because wearing leather was against his principles, he refused to do so, and "when it came down to 'we're going to start extending your sentences because of the refusal to wear shoes,' it was a pretty heavy time."

Knowing that he could "get out in eight and a half months or if I say 'screw you,' I can get out in 11 and a half months," he chose the latter option and told the prison management that he "wasn't going to put on the damn shoes."

It should be noted that the hippie look also signifies "belonging to the hippie movement," as Nicholas explained: "That would be just an outward way of identifying someone or a common thread that you might see." Accordingly, becoming a hippie required, among other things, adopting the hippie look. Bill, for example, shared his experiences soon after arriving in San Francisco:

> At first, it was a bit of a shock. I saw these people with hair down the middle of their backs and, you know, people that had radical lifestyles relative to what I was used to. At first, I was thinking, well, you know, this is too crazy for me. I was never quite that radical. But sure enough, it didn't take me long before I just quit cutting my hair and got involved in that whole scene.

As many Americans adopted the hippie look like a fashion rather than the manifestation of hippie ideology, the hippie look lost its significance as a sign of belonging. James explained: "I see long-haired men in town frequently. They're not all hippies by any means; some of them are redneck characters. There might even be some Trump supporters and some blatant racists, you know, that look that way."

## THE "OLDER" IDENTITY

Before visiting The Farm, I told a friend about my study, and she wondered whether aging hippies perceive themselves as old at all. If I am to answer her question briefly, I would say, "Sure, they do. Still, the extent to which they identify with their age and perceive it as part of who they are depends on the number and strength of age-related cues they experience and how they interpret such cues." Based on the literature on identity in later life, I believe that this answer probably applies to most older individuals, hippies and nonhippies alike.

Study participants varied in the extent and manner in which they related to their age and the fact that they were getting older. Some of them completely ignored the topic, or at most mentioned even before the interview began that they were "not good subjects for a study on aging." Others seemed preoccupied and troubled by their advanced age and the changes accompanying it. The majority, however, was somewhere in the middle: They neither denied their age, nor perceived it as a problem, at least not at the moment. Accordingly, they did not feel they should hide it. Joe explained:

> You know, there's a cult, the stay-young cult in America. I've kind of rejected that. There's this kind of stereotype – older Miami Jewish guys who wear athletic clothes. They are like 70 or 80 that try to look 50. I kind of take a little bit of a different attitude towards age. Now, I don't know if that holds true with all the hippies, but some of it probably does. I'm not trying to prove I'm young. I'm never afraid to tell anybody my age.

Study participants talked about age as a condition they have to accept and regarded being "older" as part of who they are (or becoming). Interestingly, they used the relative term "older" to describe themselves much more frequently than they did the definitive word "old." This tendency may indicate some identity work in itself: Rather than embracing an "old" identity, participants accepted being older than others or than themselves in the past.

Typically, chronological age was mentioned as a piece of purely objective information (e.g., "I'll be turning 70 next month, and in the United States that's when you get your full amount of social security" – Rebecca). Sometimes, however, it was discussed as a catalyst for considering the rest of the time one still has either in terms of autonomy versus frailty (e.g., "Living alone and getting older and something happening to me and I'm here by myself. That would worry me" – Jane) or in terms of time left for fulfilling personal goals (e.g., "Okay, I am 69 and I have been feeling for a while: 'Whatever it is you think you are going to do – when do you think you are going to do it if it's not now?'" – Cliff).

Chronological age did not seem to play an important role in how participants perceived themselves. Carolyn and Chris, for example, were both seventy-five years old and in good health at the time of the interviews. Yet, while she frequently referred to herself as "oldie" and commented that she was "more physically challenged... a little bit more dependent on others" and "just ready to rest," he declared, "Most people who look at me, they go, 'You don't look 75' and I go, 'I don't feel 75.' I don't know what I feel, but I don't feel that number." Surprisingly, visual aspects of aging (e.g., gray hair, wrinkles) were hardly mentioned, although some referred to their look compared to others at their age or said – like Chris – that people think they do not look their age. Instead, what seemed to affect self-perception most was the number and strength of age-related cues, including "physical," "cognitive," "psychological," and "social" ones.

Physical cues involved chronic health conditions, physical constraints, lower energy levels, and a general sense of reduced competence. Many study participants reported feeling healthy and fit, but this did not mean that they did not feel the impact of age on their bodies. The effect could be reflected in a minor way (e.g., "My hands are weak and they don't do what they used to do" – Karen), but ranged to the extent of facing significant mobility limitations or health issues (e.g., cancer, cardiovascular diseases). In addition, many said that they no longer have the same level of energy they used to have as younger people. For example, Tim, who looks forty-five to fifty years old, described himself in our email exchange as "still working construction every day and in pretty good shape." Yet, when we met, he shared that "I used to come home from work and go work in my garden or do a project around the house, but now I'm tired. We're getting older. The big change is that we're slowing down."

Cognitive cues were mentioned far less often than physical cues and mainly referred to somewhat reduced memory and verbal abilities (e.g., "I don't have the memory that I used to have. I used to be able to remember and... now I have to kind of think of the word, what was that word?" – Bill). In contrast, psychological cues of aging were described quite often. The latter predominantly involved having less motivation (e.g., "We're too old to demonstrate. I did my share of rock-throwing and getting arrested, and lighting fires" – Albert), which was often intertwined with attributing less importance to things that mattered in the past. Carolyn, for example, shared that she spends "more time in solitude, going in, you know," because "social connections are not so important to me anymore."

The age-related social cues described by study participants were diverse and mainly included the aging of family and friends ("We get together with a group of friends and that's much like a retirement community" – Bill), the maturing of children and grandchildren ("That's, whoa, that means, 'If they are that old then I'm…'" – Dennis), changes in the workplace, and retirement. Several people said that they retired when they felt like an irrelevant minority at work. Jane, for example, retired because "I was older and everyone else was younger, and the technology was getting a little more complicated," and Sarah retired because "they [management] sent us down through the emergency room and that was really hard because everything is different down there and it is staffed by young people. I was 60 years old, and it made me very nervous." People who were interviewed after the onset of the COVID-19 pandemic also mentioned it as a social cue in itself: "They [media] said, 'don't go out if you're 60 years old,' and he [spouse] goes, 'are we old?,' and I said, 'well, they're saying we're old'" (Julie).

Of the various cues, the physical ones seemed to impact participants' identity the most. It was mainly the people who had been dealing with significant health issues that frequently presented themselves as "older." How the various cues were interpreted, however, also made a difference. Some people regarded specific cues as signifying the transition to the out-group of older adults. Sam, for example, shared that "from years upon years of heavy construction and activity and sports," he had had both knee and hip replacements. Being unable to walk very well, he has to use a cane, and he cannot work as hard as he used to. Accordingly, he defines himself as an "over-the-hill hippie."

Others, however, chose to ignore age-related cues as much as possible, and several people even embraced some of these cues. Carolyn described her reduced interest in social connections as liberating because she no longer has to "convince myself and everybody else I was okay." Joe, who is an enthused dancer, shared that he feels very comfortable being an older man in a group of young salsa dancers:

> They call me "abuelo salsero," which is like grandfather and Salsa dancer. And yeah, I like it. There are two or three people my age in the whole community of 500 to a thousand people, but they're nice to me. They

kind of appreciate the fact that I'm older, and I don't mind. I can dance as well as most of them, you know, and because I run the dances, they all know me.

Joe mentioned that before turning to salsa, he did contra dancing, where attendees "were more people with my background, a lot of old hippies," but he liked the salsa group better. Hence, unlike the people who retired when they became the older minority, he seems to like being different. It should be noted, however, that such positive views of age-related cues were relatively rare. They also only referred to psychological and social cues and not when discussing physical constraints.

## "ALWAYS A HIPPIE": SELF-PERCEPTION AS A HIPPIE AT THE PRESENT

Although study participants considered themselves "older" people, the majority still viewed themselves as hippies. This self-perception was sometimes reflected in spontaneous descriptions of the present (e.g., "As a hippie I am...," "I live the hippie dream"), but it mostly came up in response to my direct question. When I asked Elizabeth, for example, if she still considered herself a hippie, she replied, "I do, of course," Henry answered, "Never left," Sandra reacted, "I do. Yeah... I'm still a flower child, and now I grew up," and Karen said, "Yes, I call myself hippie all the time; I would tell my students I'm a hippie, you know."

Although I expected that the people who live at The Farm would identify themselves as hippies more than those who had left it decades ago, differences between the groups were hardly noticeable. In fact, the individuals who no longer live at The Farm described themselves as hippies more frequently and more assertively than the lifelong residents. This difference may suggest that the place of residence has a minimal role in hippie identity preservation. Still, it may also indicate that just by living at The Farm, members identify themselves as hippies, as Cindy explained: "Just being here, just living here, it's like so out of the mainstream, and when people find out, like when I was working for the state, and people would find out where I live, they'd be like, 'oh,' and they'd have a million questions and so you do feel like you're different, just living here." Additional probing led to identifying two types of identity work applied to settle the alleged contradiction between being old and being a hippie: "Age does not change the essence" and "hippiedom as a continuum."

AGE DOES NOT CHANGE THE ESSENCE Written by Sylvia Tepper, an essay titled "Through the eyes of a hippie flower child" exemplifies the identity work applied by many of the interviewees:

> The dictionary says a hippie flower child is a young person who rejects conventional society and advocates love, peace, and simple, idealistic values. Obviously, I'm not that young person anymore, but my flower child values and ideals have remained the same since I was very, very young. And what I am seeing on our planet right now is a welcome and stirring sight for these old, starry, psychedelically enhanced eyes... Now, as seniors, we're softening. Our passions for our hippie flower children ideals are still strong. Oh yes. We're still living them every day... And we watch the young people of today in this movement [Black Lives Matter]. They are carrying the torches for peace, love, human rights, fairness, and universal kindness now. We are leading the way with flowers in our arms. We are voting and campaigning for the peacemakers still. We are donating to their causes. We are wearing their colors and speaking their truths. We are praying for them and meditating for them, and chanting for them. Om Shanti Shanti Om.

Describing a transition to the backstage of social protest in which older hippies are supporters rather than the ones who "carry the torches," Tepper distinguishes between the external levels of hippiedom (look and behavior) and the internal level (essence). She emphasizes that while the first may tone down with age and even change ("wearing *their* colors and speaking *their* truths"), the latter is not affected by getting older. The "values and ideals," she stresses, "remain the same," and the "passions" for them "are still strong."

Attributing greater importance to the hippie essence while de-emphasizing the centrality of look and behavior was common among study participants. Although many of them preserved some aspects of the hippie lifestyle and look, their answers to my question "Can one be

THE AGING OF AQUARIUS

over 60 and a hippie?" – which were always positive – tended to focus on internal elements. Cliff said, "I don't think that age matters. I think it's the frame of mind." Nicholas explained, "We're still hippies; we're just not so blatant about it," and Karen clarified, "You can still be a hippie without long hair. It's not a look; it's a state of mind." Even Brian, who was probably more reluctant to describe himself as a hippie than anyone else, stated, "We were flower children. And now, we're elderly people, and we still have some hippie ideals. I think it's a matter of ideals and beliefs... Yeah, I think I'm still a hippie at heart. Yeah. Aging hippie."

Stressing that hippiedom is "a lifestyle and a system of beliefs and one of the beliefs is 'it doesn't matter how old you are'" (Daniel), some participants suggested that values may mature or become refined with time (e.g., "I guess I still have the same ideals, but I define them somewhat differently" – Rebecca). Still, there was an overall consensus that people cannot "un-hippie" themselves. Bill, for example, said, "I don't think you can shed your hippie skin," and explained that even though he is currently "more focused on the medical problems that I have to deal with... I still try to live my life in a giving way." Similarly, Ben stated:

> I'd rather be a hippie than anything else, you know. If I had a choice between A, B, C, and D, I don't know what else – probably a hippie, I guess. I don't think about it much anymore. I assume I am how I am. I definitely got hippie roots, so I'll always be a hippie. I guess, if I started thinking about it... Probably once a hippie, always a hippie. Once you have certain realizations of fairness, I don't know if you can go back. It'd be hard to go back. You take it with you, and you turn it on, off. For me, I think it's a 24/7 bank kind of. But I try to be just who I am and not altered and always try to be a little better.

HIPPIEDOM AS A CONTINUUM In addition to distinguishing between "good hippies" and "bad hippies," study participants described the good hippies as a heterogeneous group comprised of people of varying degrees of hippiedom. Using different terminology, they portrayed a continuum of hippiedom ranging from "almost straight" to "very hippie" (Cindy), from "quieter" to "wild" (Roger), from "closet hippie" to "very outwardly hippie" (Nicholas), from "light" to "hardcore granolas who are stuck in the '60s" (Dennis), from people who are "more in line with science" to people with "cuckoo beliefs, like hocus pocus I'm going to heal you from across the river" (Shirley), or from "clean, conservative hippies that wear underwear" to "unchained woo-woos who are not in touch with reality and are just out there dancing" (Jane).

Such continuums of hippiedom were often described as multidimensional. Referring to both external and internal components of the hippie identity, the dimensions included elements of look, behavior (e.g., dope, sex), and essence (e.g., spirituality, environmentalism). One could be high on one dimension and low on another. Jane, for example, said that she was "high" on the spiritual dimension, "in the middle" on the back-to-nature and dope dimensions, "low" on free love, and "never" on dirtiness ("Never, never. My house is never dirty, even when there were 50 people in it"). Similarly, Cindy described herself as someone who was "closer to the straight" in terms of drugs, sex, and rock-n-roll, but high on "being fair to Earth, and people, and animals" as well as on hippie "appearance."

Perceiving hippiedom as a multidimensional continuum may support the preservation of the hippie identity in later life by allowing people to move closer to the lower end of some or all dimensions without making them nonhippies. Such transitions were generally described as convenience-driven compromises rather than a significant idealist transformation. Comparing himself to his brother, who remained a "real" hippie, Bill explained that he became less hippie as he aged because "I've got a dog. We go on vacations. We live in a nice house. I'm not as selfless as my brother is." Similarly, Rebecca stated, "I have many compromises with the modern world. I drive a car. I fly in airplanes. I do tourism in places. Like most people, I have many contradictions in my own life." Stephanie added that transitions on the hippie continuum could be temporary and context-dependent: "Maybe at this moment, I'm hippie-ish. But at that moment, I can be a professional speaker in front of 300 people giving understandable scientific data."

The elasticity of the hippie identity, which allows one to move up and down on the continuums of its various dimensions, may be well exemplified by Andrew's testimonial. As a teenager, he was a "Goldwater supporter, a Republican." Yet, by the time he graduated from college in

1968, he had become a "Maoist Hindu," who "had taken enough psyche-delics to know that I hadn't learned anything at Stanford." However, he felt he "was more of a radical politician than a hippie" because he had "moved to the left-wing, and had been tear-gassed and beaten during the anti-war demonstrations." In the following three years, among other things, he worked for the Whole Earth Catalog (a counterculture maga-zine and product catalog), studied Hinduism, did yoga and meditation, and smoked dope. Still, he did not consider himself a hippie: "I felt more preppy than hippie... I didn't feel like I was a real hippie because I hadn't taken enough acid. I hadn't made enough love. I was not a good specimen of a hippie."

Andrew was among the founding members of The Farm and lived there until the early 1980s. By then, he already considered himself "a confirmed hippie" because "my perception of what a hippie meant changed. It wasn't about the partying; it was about the viewpoint." His self-perception has remained steady to this day, even though moving to mainstream America required some adjustments, of which the most symbolic was cutting his hair and shaving his beard. After retiring from work, while traveling in Thailand on a sailboat, he felt he could switch back to the high end of the hippie continuum: "I decided, I don't need to cut my hair anymore. I can go back to being a hippie." This decision suggests that getting older does not necessarily mean toning hippiedom down. On the contrary, it may allow the intensification of specific hippie dimensions.

It should be noted that whereas most responses to my question "Do you still consider yourself a hippie?" were definite, several were accom-panied by some hesitation. Hesitancy resulted from the aforementioned negative stigma (e.g., "Yeah, but I wouldn't call myself that because it puts a label on me" – Shirley) or from perceiving hippiedom as only one part of the identity (e.g., "I just feel a little more cosmic than having one label of who I am. I wouldn't say I'm throwing that out, but it's just one part" – Carolyn). In addition, eight participants said "no," explaining that they no longer perceive themselves as hippies because they do not look like hippies anymore, maintain a hippie lifestyle, or use any labels. Further probing, however, revealed that most of them still identify with and strongly believe in the hippie ideals.

Only two participants completely rejected any consideration of themselves as hippies. Roger explained that as he aged, he had become more conservative, and "a friend of mine even said that we are becoming more Republican." He shared that he was considering moving back to The Farm, but he was not sure about it because "I am not a hippie anymore, so I don't know if I would fit in. I don't know how well I would fit in." Tim, too, insisted that he was no longer a hippie: "I like to tell my friends, 'I'm not really a hippie, I just like being around them.' When I tell someone that, they just laugh at me. They say, 'Now, you're a hippie.' In their minds, it's like a joke."

## SUMMARY: LOVE HAS NO AGE

According to the findings presented in this chapter, the hippie identity is a broad and elastic construct comprising internal and external elements that may vary in degree and importance. At the center of that identity stands the hippie essence – a complex set of values and ideals that stem from the highest ideal of "love." This ideal, which may be regarded as an umbrella concept, is also the rationale behind the external elements of the hippie identity, defined here as behavior and look. Because love, as an ideal, is not challenged by the changes associated with age, the hippie identity is pretty resilient to age-related physical and social strains. Accordingly, as long as people believe in love, peace, nonviolence, and the like, they can be both "old" and "hippie" without sensing a significant contradiction between the two identity constructs. Nevertheless, it seems that cultural, discursive, and institutional notions of old age and hippiedom lead aging hippies to apply various identity work strategies to preserve their internal self-identity.

As a whole, study participants tend to view and present themselves as hippies. This clear continuation of their younger identities supports the notion of ageless self,[13] but it does not negate the emergence of new identity components in later life. In response to various physical, cognitive, psychological, and social cues, study participants also perceive themselves as older people. This perception may be regarded as *identity accommodation*,[14] representing a normal and healthy process. Some even embrace older age and reshape their older identity by focusing on its positive aspects – identity work described as *social creativity*.[15] For these individuals, the transition to the out-group of "old" enables a continuation of being in an out-group – a positively perceived condition previously caused by belonging to the counterculture. Such individuals, however, were rare. The majority accepted being older rather than old by applying a relativist approach to advanced age.

The visual aspects of aging, typically described as particularly problematic,[16] did not seem to trouble study participants and were hardly mentioned. This somewhat surprising finding may be explained by the hippie ideal of love that includes loving the body in its most natural form, including the aged one. Moreover, the fact that most interviewees were not trying to disguise signs of age by means that might evoke a more youthful façade (e.g., wearing makeup, dyeing hair) may be considered a manifestation of the hippie value of opposition to the mainstream – in this case, the antiaging culture characterizing Western societies. This silent yet visible opposition both preserves the hippie identity and signifies *resistance*[17] to the box provided for older people by cultural messages supporting age denial. Rejecting the antiaging culture preserves the hippie identity also by being consistent with the hippie ideal of anti-consumerism. Hence, when it comes to lifestyle choices, identity work in later life may be described not only in terms of how people spend their time and money but also by the goods and services they choose *not* to consume.

However, the interviewees described several lifestyle modifications that were not entirely in line with the hippie ideals. Interviewees felt somewhat uncomfortable about the lifestyle changes, whether they resulted from free choice or objective constraints (e.g., deteriorated health, less energy). To resolve the dissonance, they applied two strategies of identity work. The first is attributing more importance to the hippie essence while de-emphasizing the significance of behavior and look, and the second is turning hippiedom from a dichotomous construct (hippie – nonhippie) to a multidimensional continuum allowing changes in the degree of hippiedom. Both strategies may be described as *identity balance*[18] as they enable incorporating age-relevant experiences while maintaining a consistent view of the self. Both are also built on identity work conducted earlier in life, distinguishing between good and bad hippies to cope with the hippies' negative perceptions and media portrayals in the late 1960s and early 1970s.

The effect of the various identity work strategies on participants' perceived age was unclear. My impression was that many of them looked younger than their chronological age. Some even mentioned they felt younger than their age and offered no indications of a sense of youth trapped in an aging body. Yet, the transition to the out-group of "old" and fear of such change did not seem to be the main catalyst for their reported identity work. Rather than refusing or denying age by trying to remain in the in-group of the "young," they focus their identity work on staying in what may be described – depending on the point of view – as the in-group or the out-group of the hippies. By so doing, they preserved a significantly more critical component of their self-identity.

# CHAPTER 5

# Still Changing the World

A S EXEMPLIFIED IN "ALL YOU NEED IS LOVE," the canonic Beatles song, the music of the 1960s counterculture reflected the centrality of love to the hippie essence and the notion that spreading love can change the world. Moreover, music was regarded as an important means of promoting the idea that love is not merely an emotion. Love, according to the hippie movement, is a force – a source of strength and energy that can be transformed into action. As the Beatles specified, it enables anything one may wish to do, sing, say, make, and even save.

This idea that love can change the world may sound naïve to a twenty-first-century cynical mind, but is it baseless? The answer lies in the interpretation of the term "world." If you think of the world in global terms, it may be hard to imagine how a single person can change things such as ongoing wars or environmental catastrophes. However, if you believe that "we are all one" or simply trust that any small change matters, then by being at peace with your neighbor or recycling empty cans, you can make the world a somewhat better place. Moreover, if "Everybody get together, try to love one another," as the Youngbloods and later Jefferson Airplane suggested, then "You can make the mountains ring or make the angels cry."

The hippies truly believed that by getting together, opposing the mainstream and its establishment, and posing an alternative lifestyle and culture they could create a new, superior society. More than fifty years after the Summer of Love, however, they still wake up every morning to a world driven by capitalist forces, that harms the environment and allows conflict, violence, hate, inequality, racism, misogyny, and many other social ailments to exist. In today's reality, they may be disappointed with the extent to which they have changed the world and be significantly worried about the world they are going to leave behind.

Caring for the next generations is central to "generativity" – an idea introduced by Erik Erikson[1] as the seventh of eight stage-related purposes of development unfolding over one's lifespan. Generativity is defined as the concern to guarantee the wellbeing of future generations and, ultimately, to leave a lasting legacy.[2] It can be expressed in various activities, manifested in private and public spheres, and be reflected in contrasting ways: Efforts to create social change, for example, are clearly generative but so are attempts to protect certain traditions or resources.

Although some studies demonstrated generativity in younger cohorts, the peak seems to be in later life.[3] Generativity may persist as a developmental task into the latest period of the life course where, according to Erikson, one's legacy becomes part of the life review process. Associated with positive, healthy adult development and enhanced wellbeing,[4] generativity is not inevitable in the course of aging. There is considerable evidence that its various expressions are socially constructed,[5] historically situated,[6] and vary as a function of personal background and resources available.[7]

Witnessing the persistence and even aggravation of some of the world's problems may have reasonably made aging hippies feel that their generative efforts as part of the 1960s counterculture were fruitless, and that they failed in posing an alternative to the mainstream and in making the world a better place. Accordingly, their belief in the power of love may have decreased, and their motivation for and involvement in generative activities may have diminished. Yet, if they regard even slight changes as success, they may be as motivated to change the world as they were in their youth, if not more. Distinguishing between the hippies as a collective, The Farm as a distinct community, and the individual level, this chapter examines aging hippies' evaluations of their past achievements and current generative actions and attempts to leave for future generations a somewhat better world than the one they received from their predecessors.

## THE HIPPIES CHANGED THE WORLD

When I asked Dennis if he thought that the hippies had changed the world to some extent, he said: "Peter Coyote, a gentleman who lived in

San Francisco during the '60s… who is a very good writer, wrote a statement that kind of answered your question." While browsing his smartphone, he clarified that "I kind of adopted what he says, okay?" and once he found the article,[8] he read the following paragraph aloud:

> If you look at all the political agendas of the 1960s, they basically failed. We didn't end capitalism, we didn't end imperialism, we didn't end racism. Yeah, the war ended. But if you look at the cultural agendas, they all worked. There's no place in the United States you can go today where you can't find organic food, alternative medical practices, alternative spiritual practices, women's issues and groups, environmental issues and groups. All those things got injected into the culture on a very deep level. My feeling is, and my hope is, that those things will eventually change the politics.

Beautifully phrased by Coyote, this quote reflects a rather consensual approach expressed by all interviewees according to which the hippies' impact on the world was (1) limited, (2) more cultural than political, but (3) profound and long-lasting.

Two explanations were offered for the limited impact of the hippie movement, the first being that human nature is hard to change. Evelyn stated, "We did think that by now it [hippie mindset] would flourish… who knew there were all these haters and you know, I mean, it's crazy, it's horrible." Similarly, Albert explained that "We couldn't quite get it all done. We affected the world, but we couldn't save it. There are too many Trumps." Joe added that "It's still McDonald's and Walmart – and people still are all trying to get rich… they think it's fine to make a hundred dollars an hour while other people make seven dollars an hour, that's still the ethos that we live in." The second explanation for the limited impact was that the hippies were only part of several counterculture movements that tried to change the world in the 1960s and beyond. Accordingly, failures could not be attributed to the hippies alone, nor could successes (e.g., "That wasn't all just the hippies" – Henry, "The hippies can't co-opt Martin Luther King. I think the combination of the hippies and the Civil Rights Movement made a huge difference in the way the world looks at culture" – Andrew).

Differentiating between the "pure" hippies and the New Left seemed to ease the acceptance of the relatively few changes achieved in the political realm. As Andrew put it: "The hippies tended not to be political because the political people, like SDA [Students for Direct Action], were more oriented towards a violent revolution – and the hippies were strictly non-violent and continue to be." This claim implies that because the hippies were not actively involved in changing the politics, they did not fail. Nevertheless, many study participants voiced significant frustration with the political situation in the U.S. and other countries and expressed sincere worries about the future. Nicholas, for example, stated: "I'm worried about the world that my grandchildren will inherit, and I would say the racist fascist that has been elected to the White House and has emboldened this country is worrisome. If he [Trump] gets elected for another term, which is up for grabs, I call it Hitler Lite, Hitler 2.0."

Some participants, however, tried to be more optimistic by claiming that "the hippies have balanced it [the right wing] out and kept it from going really, really nasty and really, really weird" (Daniel). They also argued that certain phenomena we witness today (e.g., "Bernie Sanders is running for President" – Nicholas, "Alexandria Ocasio-Cortez making the speeches that she makes" – Andrew) would not have happened if there had not been a hippie revolution. Quite a few reported being currently involved in online political debates and blogging, several mentioned donating to politicians they believed in or participating in political meetings, and a few even described being members and campaigning for political organizations.

Such activities, however, did not tend to involve individual initiatives, not even among those who were political during the heyday of the counterculture. A possible explanation for this somewhat surprising finding is that they became a bit skeptical about political activism. Sarah, for example, shared that in the last primaries, she "did phone calls for our local reps [sic.] and went to a couple of their meetings," but found it "very discouraging." She noted, "Well, I'm a little more cynical. I think that going out with signs and standing on the road doesn't make much of a difference." Similarly, Stephanie said, "I don't march in groups and carry signs. I'm glad people are doing it, but I don't know how to change things anymore. It may be part of the aging process... I do not have the energy I did, and I do not have the motivation I did."

Politics aside, all study participants agreed that the hippies had a vast and long-lasting impact on American values. Elizabeth stated, "We have been contributing this whole generation of people that were back-to-the-landers and flower children, and all of that has shaped some of the more liberal values that are happening around here." Declaring that "we really did break a lot of the chains that were constraining people's thought," Andrew also provided an example: "The idea of 'do your own thing as long as it doesn't bother someone else' was not prevalent in the '50s and the early '60s, and it's much more prevalent now."

Current awareness of environmental issues and social justice was particularly viewed as a direct outcome of hippie values. Claiming that "lots of people are now saying: 'Hey, the hippies were right about taking care of nature'" (Gordon), participants explained that "the idea of being custodians of the planet is very deeply rooted in the hippie culture" (Andrew), and that "Greenpeace came out as a hippie" (Carolyn), "Earth Day was invented by the hippies" (Brian), and "the whole environmental movement came out of the hippie movement" (Nicholas). Similarly, they argued that many of the current social protests are rooted in the hippie ideology: "The Me-Too movement came from the women's liberation which came from the hippie movement" (Nicholas), and "if you look at the Black Lives Matter Movement, you'll agree that it feels very familiar" (Andrew).

The hippie values were also described as a force that led to dramatic changes in American culture. Domains most often mentioned were nutrition ("Things like natural foods, organic foods, became so popular" – James), fashion ("Now it doesn't matter so much what you're wearing. You can go all kinds of places that used to be, you could only go there if you were dressed up" – Joan), music ("The explosion of music is just so embedded in the culture... today everyone's got music on their phone" – Nicholas), drugs ("The national view of marijuana use has really changed because of the hippies... and now it's actually being legalized" – Cindy), and sex ("It was free sex, you know, 'Hi! how are you? Let's fuck.' It was an era, and yes, we changed things" – Stephanie). In addition, it was argued that by opening the door to new spiritual practices, such as meditation and yoga, and making them more acceptable ("It's okay to do yoga and be a Christian" – Julia), the hippies initiated the whole New Age movement. Gordon, for example, commented: "People didn't know what the word 'karma' meant in the United States until the hippies came, and now it's a common thing. Everybody knows it and things about it and goes even beyond it and stuff."

Stressing that any small change matters ("Anybody that's a peaceful person and trying not to destroy the planet is helping out" – Ben), study participants claimed that the changes in American culture were dramatic and intense to the extent that hippiedom became the mainstream ("A lot of the stuff that we lived has now become mainstream" – Joan). Some of them even described global impact ("It was worldwide in the developed nations and the Western world, yeah" – Brian; "It was a consciousness that was happening everywhere. It wasn't just here" – Lillian; "The non-violence and anti-war, that has really spread" – Cindy). Overall, the changes brought by the hippie movement were described as having roots in the 1960s and lasting to this day, and as initiated in the U.S. but reaching the entire world. Chris summarized:

> There are hippies everywhere! There are people who do not necessarily call themselves hippies, but they believe in peace, and they're good folks. There are millions of us! I see people that come in here [The Farm] to visit, and I go, "The revolution is alive and well." Young kids. And I don't think it's just here or just in America. I think that those seeds were sown through a lot of different avenues.

Several interviewees criticized the mainstreaming of hippiedom. James, for example, said: "Wherever the hippies congregate and focus their attention, the capitalists go – 'oh there's a market,' and they go for it, whether it's housing or food or music, even clothing and styles. A lot of it was initiated by these kinds of folks, hippie folks." The majority, however, expressed great satisfaction with the hippies' impact on the world. They felt that even though it was limited, it was significant: "Evolution is very slow and may not be completed in our lifetime, but we can affirm that 'yeah, we did make a difference in the world,' and it feels so great" (Carolyn).

## THE FARM CHANGED THE WORLD

In their discussions of how the hippies changed the world, study participants often switched to talking about The Farm. Bill, for example, explained how the hippies were the first to draw attention to climate change. Quickly, however, he turned to describing how The Farm was a pioneer in sustainable living and how even in its early days, "everything had been used multiple times until it just had no value and no usefulness." Arguing that "The hippies changed the world, yes, and we were a part of that" (Sandra), interviewees described The Farm as a model: "We were a major example of how it can be done. There were hundreds of communes in the 70s that came and went, and The Farm just kept getting bigger, and everyone in the counterculture knew who we were" (Albert). Practicing most hippie ethics, The Farm was presented as an ideology that turned into reality, as Dennis put it: "Here we are 50 years later, and people can actually live in this community, work, make a living, build a house, have kids, go to a school. That was our ideal coming here originally, and some of that actually came to fruition."

Despite the considerable overlap between the hippies and The Farm, three impacts on the U.S. and the world were credited specifically to The Farm, as follows.

THE FARM CHANGED THE WAY PEOPLE EAT Two businesses operating at The Farm since the commune period have had a considerable impact on the eating habits of individuals in the U.S. and elsewhere. The first, Farm Foods, is known as a key catalyst for the popularization of soy-based foods (Figure 5.1). Soy foods are rich in essential amino acids and protein and may replace meat and dairy products. In addition to their nutritional value, they are friendlier to the environment (and animals) and relatively cheap. In the early 1970s, however, they were mainly consumed by people of East Asian origin. In a recent online interview,[9] Robert Tepper – one of the founders of Farm Foods and the "last soldier standing" – explained that "an acre of land can produce one pound of beef and 10 pounds of soy foods... and thus we felt that our mission, and we were mission-based, was to contribute dramatically to the world hunger problem by educating what you can do with soy foods."

Farm Foods started as a small dairy aiming to produce soy milk and tofu for the commune. According to Tepper, it turned into a big business thanks to "super-smart technicians and great equipment" and a marketing strategy that combined establishing additional production

**5.1** Farm Foods: A key catalyst for the popularization of soy-based foods in the U.S.

centers, operating vegetarian restaurants and catering services, applying direct sales to health-food stores, and even having a national distribution system at some point. The company produced soy-based milk, yogurt, Ice-Bean (the first nondairy ice cream product to be commercially produced in the U.S.), and the like, as well as tempeh (a product made from fermented soybeans) and texturized vegetable protein. Yet, its most prominent and long-lasting contribution to the American diet was firm-pressed tofu. Tepper explained that before Farm Foods, one could only get the traditional soft tofu, but thanks to longer pressing, "our tofu was chewier and little more what a Caucasian palate prefers." Following this development, sales started to grow, and although Farm Foods products are now sold in Tennessee and Georgia only, the growth in tofu consumption continues. As Tepper said: "Growth is still happening… today, you go to Safeway, and you find three–four brands, let alone health food stores. The vegetarian movement is strong, and it is still soy-based."

Farm Foods' marketing efforts were supported by educational pamphlets and vegetarian cookbooks published by BPC. Dedicated to publishing books that aligned with The Farm's core beliefs, many of the books that BPC issued over the years promoted a plant-based diet. In 1978 it published *The Farm vegetarian cookbook* by Louise Hagler, the first fully vegetarian cookbook ever published in the U.S. This book was followed by titles such as *Tofu cookery* and *Tempeh cookery*, and to this day, plant-based cookbooks make up a primary category in the company's catalog.

When I visited BPC, I saw numerous cookbooks and nutrition titles, starting from basic guides for vegetarians and vegans, continuing with books that focus on specific methods (e.g., raw food, juice fasting), dishes (e.g., salads, healthy desserts) or ingredients (e.g., chia seeds, cranberries), and ending with nutritional guides for certain age groups (e.g., children, seniors) and for people coping with specific health conditions (e.g., allergies, diabetes, cancer). Some of these books were written by community members.

After interviewing Debbie and Tim, I stayed over for dinner and had one of the best meals I have had in my life. If I had not been a vegetarian already, I would probably have considered turning into one after that night. Unable to stop praising Debbie's cooking (and eating it!) I asked her where she had found the recipes. She replied that she had invented all of them and then noted that she had published several health-food cookbooks with BPC. Later, when we talked about her plans for the future, she said that she was considering giving health-food cooking workshops. Changing the way people eat, therefore, seems not only a shared mission but also a personal one.

THE FARM CHANGED THE WAY WOMEN GIVE BIRTH Much of the medical practice at The Farm during the commune days centered around the midwives, who perceived birth giving as a sacrament and developed a longitudinal program that (1) prepares the family for the birth with close attention to fetus and mother for a while, (2) supports natural and meaningful birth giving, and (3) monitors the newborn and mentors the family for a period following the birth. With the backup of a medical doctor, either living on the property or in a nearby town, most childbirths ended well. Moreover, the program had impressive statistics of only 1.8 percent caesarean rate, and it became a significant catalyst of midwife-attended births, in general, and home births, in particular. The program also paved the way for practices that seem routine today, like letting the fathers be present at labor and having skin-to-skin touch between the mother and the baby immediately after birth. Ina May Gaskin's book, *Spiritual midwifery*, sold over 500,000 copies, and The Farm Midwifery Center acts to this day as a place of pilgrimage for people from around the world who go there to deliver their babies and for midwives, nurses, and doctors interested in learning about the center's approach to childbirth.

Many study participants mentioned that The Farm's midwives delivered their children, and some of the women shared beautiful, touching stories about their birth-giving experiences. Cara Gillette, who worked as a midwife, also sent me a couple of written stories demonstrating the spirituality involved in supporting labor. One of them, for example, described a thirty-two-year-old woman who was in labor for the second time after giving up her first baby, who was born when she was eighteen, for adoption:

> The baby's heartbeat started decelerating during contractions, a sign of fetal distress... I called the backup doctor, who said, "You don't have time to get her here. She needs to have the baby." ... I went as deeply as I could in my mind, asking for help, and what came out was what I said to her, "We need to talk about that baby that you gave up for adoption." That was nothing I had thought about, it just came out. She started weeping and said, "I didn't love that baby. I gave him away." I went back into this "other" place within myself and responded, "You did love that baby. You gave him to people who could love him and take care of him." She had the baby within minutes.

Not all births went smoothly, and some of them ended well by sheer luck. Actually, Gillette's first child, who was born during The Caravan, stopped breathing soon after the birth, "but Stephen Gaskin, who had been a medic in Korea came in, did mouth-to-mouth and saved her life." Reflecting on the birth of her twins, Rebecca commented that having them "delivered by the midwives at home was definitely a mistake." The Farm did not have ultrasound equipment yet, so nobody knew that she was having twins. In addition, when she went into premature labor, "my water broke, and they kept me in bed for a week which is something that shouldn't be done because of the possibility of infection." Fortunately, her daughters were born healthy.

The Farm's impact on birth giving was not only through the midwifery center. Some members who left the Farm became midwives too, or advocated natural birth. Charlotte, for example, was among the commune members who wanted to become midwives but were not let into the midwifery team. After leaving The Farm, she went to nursing school, became a certified midwife, and opened a clinic that "served the underserved – multi-ethnic, multi-generational population of women from all around the world." She also became an activist who advocated legalizing lay midwifery via her work for an association of midwives. Suzanne Hope Suarez, another former resident, who had recently moved back to The Farm, wrote a most influential article published in the *Yale Journal of Law and Feminism*. Based on extensive research, the paper[10] argued:

> Lawmakers can afford to ignore neither the risks involved in hospital birth nor the research and statistics validating the safety and importance of the midwifery profession... If public policy is to improve the health of mothers and children, it must allow the profession of midwifery to develop fully, independently, and in its rightful place – the home.

Years later, in 2009, Stacey Marie Kerr, another former resident, wrote a book titled *Homebirth in the hospital: Integrating natural childbirth with modern medicine*. Realizing that many young people who are about to become parents would not consider homebirth, Kerr suggests that the personalized and empowering experience of home birth can also occur in a hospital setting and guides readers on making their hospital birth emotionally satisfying.

THE FARM GAVE "PLENTY" TO THE WORLD Since its establishment in 1974, Plenty International – The Farm's first not-for-profit organization – has been involved in numerous national and international projects aiming to "protect and share the world's abundance and knowledge for the benefit of all."[11] Based on a philosophy that claims that the best way to strengthen a community is to help it help itself, the organization "supports economic self-sufficiency, cultural integrity and environmental responsibility in partnership with community groups and organizations in Central

**5.2** A grain bin next to Plenty's office: Plenty is committed to promoting the wellbeing of native communities.

America, the U.S., the Caribbean, and Africa" (Figure 5.2).[12] Relying on donations and hundreds of volunteers, Plenty encourages local control and responsibility by helping communities promote their resources and economy. It also advances residents' health via nutritional and medical programs, provides young people with educational opportunities, and, when needed, assists in disaster relief and recovery efforts.

The projects in Guatemala and the South Bronx, which took place during the commune era, seem to be the model for many programs Plenty developed over the following decades. In 1978, it formed a six-year project in Lesotho, South Africa, where volunteers carried out projects in tree planting, potable water and sanitation, soy agriculture and food processing, solar energy, and primary healthcare. In 1982, it helped open a free clinic in Washington, DC for Central American refugees in collaboration with the Central American Refugee Center. This clinic became the largest full-time bilingual free clinic for refugees in the country. In 1983, Plenty joined a group of international environmentalists to seed alternative energy and food projects throughout the Caribbean, and in 1986, it started an agricultural development project in South Dakota and a project with indigenous peoples residing in southern Belize. From 1987, it collaborated with MBA programs at Wharton, MIT, and Stanford University, which sent their students to volunteer in Plenty projects in Dominica, Belize, and South Dakota.

Throughout the 1990s, Plenty continued its work in Guatemala, Belize, Dominica, and South Dakota. In 1997 it formed Plenty Belize – a registered Belizean nongovernmental organization that works to this day with other local groups to support projects in agriculture, health, nutrition, solar energy, women's development, micro-enterprise, and education. In 2005, Plenty was among the first citizens' aid organizations to respond to the Hurricane Katrina disaster in New Orleans. Within days it sent relief supplies, followed by teams of volunteers, including medical personnel, builders, and other emergency responders, who took part in emergency relief activities along the Gulf Coast over the next three years. Similar relief projects were held after the earthquake in Haiti (2010), the super typhoon that struck the Philippines (2013), the earthquake in Nepal (2015), and Hurricane Maria in Puerto Rico (2017).

Many study participants had been involved in Plenty projects in the past. Quite a few – residents and former residents alike – continue to be involved in its actions to this day via volunteering, donations, and serving on its board. Stressing that "Plenty is a huge part of The Farm" (Elizabeth) and does "great work" (Sam) and "amazing things" (Tim), they explained that Plenty is a direct outcome of The Farm's ideology according to which "we're all the same... and Plenty embodies that kind of sensibility of living your life in a giving way" (Bill). Paul, who took part in the Bronx project and helped to establish a Plenty office in Washington, DC, testified:

> I was very proud to be part of that. I think Plenty is a noble organization that has a really good sense of what its scale is. It doesn't try to do more than its capability. And also because of Peter [Peter Schweitzer, the executive director of Plenty]. I mean, Peter basically lives like a peasant. So, it must have the lowest overhead of any non-profit anywhere. And I believe in that mission still.

Plenty was the first recipient of the Right Livelihood Prize, annually awarded in Stockholm, Sweden. Many of its past projects still affect the lives of individuals around the globe, and it continues to leave a mark on the world through its ongoing and new projects. However, one of its greatest challenges nowadays is attracting younger people who could lead it in the future. When I asked Peter Schweitzer about it, he said:

> It's either going to be picked up or it's not. The Farm really needs to be doing this kind of thing. Otherwise, it just becomes another place to live in. If you really want to do it, you can do it. It doesn't matter what you have been trained to do. You can learn it, but you have to be committed to doing it, and if you just want to make a lot of money, this is the wrong place to be... It would be okay if Plenty didn't continue, but I don't think the Farm would survive without doing something beyond The Farm. There needs to be an opportunity to do something for the world.

## INDIVIDUAL INITIATIVES CHANGED THE WORLD

The wish to change the world was often described as a motivation to join The Farm, and for some, it was also a motivation to leave it. Even after the commune days were over, many study participants – residents and former residents alike – found a way to make a living in jobs and businesses that aligned with The Farm's ideals and promoted goals in which they wholeheartedly believed. Charles, for example, worked in a homeless shelter, Cindy worked for a State Department of Environment and Conservation, and Laura dedicated her entire post-Farm career to consulting and teaching in low-income housing programs across the U.S. Many interviewees also reported being very active in their communities. Rebecca, for example, volunteered for the American Association for Retired Persons ("We do people's taxes for free, mostly older people, but really anybody... this was my 11th year"), and Joe was very involved in supporting refugees: He had several refugees live with him, and he still runs a Facebook group for the refugee community in his area.

Changing the world was a recurrent theme in most interviewees' life stories. Unfortunately, the scope of this book does not allow me to elaborate on each of these stories, but a brief review of one of them – Stephanie's story – may exemplify this point. When she talked about her decision to join The Farm in 1971, Stephanie mentioned that "We were going to save the world, and that's all I wanted to do." During the commune days, she did various jobs, including working at BPC, taking care of the horses, assisting the midwives, and working as a teacher at The Farm's school. Having an academic degree in education, she tried to make the pedagogical curricula more structured, but the school staff did not accept her ideas. In response, she formed "an alternative school in the alternative community." Together with her spouse, who did the construction work, and with a woman from Guatemala who had a Master's degree in education, they turned an abandoned trailer into a Montessori School. This alternative school had forty pupils, and "it was a huge success from the children's point of view... it changed every kid's life to do school one year that way on The Farm." Unfortunately, the parents did not like it that she was setting boundaries for the children, and then "politics stepped in," and the school was closed after one year only.

Deeply disappointed, Stephanie had a moment of epiphany:

> I was sweeping the floor in our house and thinking, "This is not changing the world. I'm getting old. Working this hard, I have to chop wood to take a hot shower. That was good when I was 25. Now I'm 30, and if I keep doing this, I don't see how I'm really going to make a difference like I intended to and just going to get old here, and – no, I got to do more. I have more than this to give. I have to do more... And with the reasons we started The Farm still integral to my being go out and do more... You get one time around on the planet, as far as we know. I don't want to waste it." It's like that song from Hamilton: "I'm not going to waste my shot. This is my shot."

Determined to use her shot, Stephanie left The Farm with her family, went back to school, and graduated with an MD degree. She practiced clinical medicine until 2004, "when the environment changed to where I could no longer practice in a personal way, where you deliver the baby and help grandma die and you know everybody in between and they know you." Retiring from work, however, was an impossible transition for her because she could not be "like a cat who lies around with no guilt, not feeling a need to save the world to have the right to breathe

the air in this world. I feel the need to be doing whatever I can to save the world. I'm not too good at chilling." She thus became a journalist and wrote a column on health topics for a newspaper for six years, and "that satisfied my need to make a difference for that period." Then, she quit and started to work as a medical director-educator for a company that produces medical cannabis, and "now I have a name in that field as well."

Reflecting on her life, Stephanie noted, "I call myself a deep dabbler. I mean, I've been a teacher, I've been a doctor. These are not light-weight things, you know. I've been a journalist, I've been a writer, I'm a lecturer, and then I have my fun life, my non-professional life." Even her "fun life" includes some activities aiming to change the world. Among other things, she recently started riding a Harley-Davidson motorcycle and formed a group of "older badass biker chicks" who take road trips together. In addition to being pure fun, this activity is a statement that serves a social purpose:

> I'm an older white woman in the United States. I am invisible. As we get older, I think we need to be seen even more because we have so much to say. So, I get on my Harley, and I feel powerful again. I feel valid again. Not male powerful like fuck you all, not that. Just I'm powerful. I am who I am. I'm more expressing myself on that Harley than I am in my Lexus. I look at it as I'm seen, and I have my power back... it counteracts some of what I've lost by getting older in our society.

Although Stephanie's story may seem extraordinary, it is only one example of many stories I have heard about lives lived with an intention to change the world. In addition, just like Stephanie, who exhibited several individual initiatives (i.e., the alternative school, the bikers' group), many interviewees shared stories of independent initiatives aiming to make the world a better place. The extent of individual initiatives that study participants exhibited and continue to demonstrate today is one of the most striking findings of this study. As The Farm in its early days was led by a most charismatic leader, one could expect community members to be followers rather than proactive social leaders. This assumption, however, could not be less true, as the number and variety of members' independent initiatives are genuinely outstanding.

Despite their significant number and diversity, most individual initiatives could be classified according to the following five categories.

PROMOTING PEACE After the September 11 events, a group of former residents of The Farm living in California was horrified by the violent American response to violence. One of them, Michael O'Gorman, whose daughter was outside the World Trade Center before its collapse, "called a bunch of us together and said, 'What do we think of this and what can we do?'" (Lillian). The group decided to form a nonprofit organization that would promote pacifist beliefs through direct action. Then, in collaboration with The Farm in Tennessee, they established PeaceRoots Alliance and started campaigning for peace.

The first project was a national billboard campaign under the slogan "Wake up America and vote for a change." Following that campaign, O'Gorman was contacted by young veterans reporting not surviving very well, economically and psychologically. Realizing that many of these veterans had their roots in rural America and having great faith in the healing power of farming, the group founded "Farms Not Arms" – a project aimed at creating jobs on farms for returning veterans. Quickly, however, it "started getting feedback from some of the veterans, who were told, 'Oh, you should not be involved with these hippies because that makes you look anti-military'" (Lillian). Putting the cause first, O'Gorman started a separate nonprofit – the Farmer Veteran Coalition, which to this day sponsors and encourages both employment and self-employment of veterans in agriculture. This could entail full-time or part-time employment, or a critical supplement to disability-related income, so that they may earn for themselves a meaningful and financially sustainable place in the agricultural community. Lillian shared, "In that way, he [O'Gorman] could get grants from the government and stuff, and we were – 'okay, that's great.' He went on his thing, and we remained friends."

PeaceRoots Alliance activity today is relatively low key and centers on "throwing a party every year and giving some money away trying to push peace" (Andrew). Most of the 200–300 people who attend the annual fundraising event are former residents of The Farm who live in California. Some of the money raised supports international initiatives.

The latest was the Fukushima Response campaign aiming to raise awareness of the emerging crisis at the nuclear power plants in Japan. Most
funds, however, are donated to Plenty projects.

PROTECTING THE ENVIRONMENT Several study participants
reported initiatives aiming to protect the environment. Brian, for
example, created a Facebook group of 350 members, to whom he posts
information about health and the environment that he finds via Google
alerts and the like. This activity somewhat continues his past employment
as a research writer who authored books on health for BPC. A similar
continuity was reported by Joan, who during the 1970s was a Greenpeace
activist and currently runs a successful company:

> We were flushed with cash, and I thought, "We have enough; we should
> do something else for the community." So, we set up a community sustain-
> ability grant program, and different groups got together with different
> ideas that they wanted to be funded. We had to evaluate all of the grant
> applications and decide which ones we would pass out grants to, and then
> we funded those. So that was a lot of fun.

Yet, what seems to be the spearhead of The Farm's environmental
efforts is the Swan Conservation Trust – a nonprofit land trust organization established in 1992 to preserve, protect, and restore native
hardwood forests on the Western Highland Rim of Tennessee. Henry
and Cindy, who were among the founders of the trust and serve on
its board to this day, explained that a big timber company that came
to Tennessee in the 1970s bought up to 50 percent of some counties.
As long as they did not cut the trees, things went well, but in the early
1990s, they started harvesting the woods near The Farm: "We could
hear them cutting, and then you go out there, and you could see the
devastation... it was awful" (Cindy). To protect their environment
and its many natural treasures, they decided to "organize a land trust
so that people can donate money and we use it to buy land and save
it" (Henry).

Since 1992, the Swan Conservation Trust has bought about 1,500
acres in the headwaters of Big Swan Creek near The Farm, which is
home to rare plants and a wide variety of birds and wildlife habitats, as

well as several adjunct conservation easements. When I visited The Farm and attended the trust's board meeting, the main topic discussed was the purchase of an additional 138 acres. The trust also organizes volunteer workdays to accomplish tasks such as invasive plant removals and trail improvements, conducts outings for the general public, runs educational activities for children and adults, and collaborates with other organizations on regional ecological projects.

Trying to explain what made him and others invest so much effort and so many years of their lives in the Swan Conservation Trust, Henry said:

> I came here to live in the community, but there are two kinds of communities – the community of people and the community of everything else. They're both my communities. If you love something enough, you learn to communicate with it. Land preservation is so rewarding; it makes you feel like you're really doing the right thing. You can feel Cindy's passion for it... You know, sometimes when I'm driving around the city, I think, those creeks are coming along where birds are free since we're committing up here. We've done that. We've done that. We've done that.

Many study participants shared that they donate money to the Swan Conservation Trust and participate in its activities. Some also served on its board, and Ben, who is currently on the board, even has a related initiative: marking the boundaries of the property "for the public to realize and respect that it's owned and appreciated by a group of people." Using a motorized four-wheeler and GPS machine programmed with the coordinates for the property, he spends many hours outdoors putting paint on the trees every hundred feet (Figure 5.3). Ben is also considering starting a new construction business with "a group of the second geners [sic] that will do alternative building with hempcrete." He explained that he decided to move back to The Farm seven years ago, after leaving it in 1983, because he wanted "to help out the planet, and part of that is having a lifestyle that doesn't have a strong negative impact, and living here is a light footprint on the planet." Via the new business, he will be able to "pass something on... because along with natural building, there's a lot of traditional carpentry that's all still involved. I can learn new stuff and pass on the old stuff, and everybody wins."

**5.3** The author, while touring the Big Swan Headwaters Preserve. On the tree behind her are Ben's marking of the property's boundaries.

**CARING FOR CHILDREN** Working for the wellbeing of future generations is typically expressed in parenting and grandparenting.[13] Most study participants shared that they are pretty involved in their children and grandchildren's lives and described many forms by which they provide them with instrumental and emotional support. For example, when I interviewed Carolyn, she had just returned from visiting her son and his family, who live abroad. She said that she spent an entire month there trying to help issue a passport for her grandson. Simultaneously, she spent hours on the phone with her spouse's daughter, who was going through a rough divorce. Carolyn shared that even though they are not affluent, she and her spouse give their children "some money here and there to help them out when they get in a tight spot... grease their wheels, I call it." She also added, "I tend to get too involved in the children's lives."

Naturally, the level of involvement was higher among those who were already retired, who lived close to their children, and whose grandchildren were young. Elizabeth, for example, said that she "half-raised" her grandchildren, and Sarah testified that when her grandchildren were little, "they were here all the time." Roger, who lives in California and had considered moving back to The Farm, admitted that he decided to stay in California because such a transition would have taken him away from his six-year-old granddaughter whom he visits regularly. Even those who live far from their children and grandchildren described frequent contact via phone and digital communication and extended visits, especially during summer breaks and holidays. Many mentioned that their relationships with their grandchildren are a primary source of satisfaction in their lives. Harold explained:

> There's nothing like a grandchild. Hanging out with my grandkids is one of the most amazing things I've ever experienced in my life. I don't have to raise these kids, but I should be respectful and wise. I can't just encourage them to do stupid things. But they just – sit there, if you treat them properly. You really give them the love they deserve and teach them to be respectful of adults. They will reward you 100 times over with love and want to just hug you, climb all over you and stuff when they're young.

For some study participants, however, caring for children did not only include their families. Quite a few volunteered for actions aiming to support children, and three individuals – Mary Ellen Bowen, Judith Meeker, and Tomas Heikkala – even initiated such actions. Mary Ellen Bowen is the person behind Kids to the Country (KTC), one of Plenty's flagships (Figure 5.4). She joined The Farm in 1976 because she "wanted to get them [her three children] out of Chicago" and worked as a teacher in the commune's school. After the changeover, she and two others started managing the school ("because we didn't want our kids not to have school"), and in 1986, in collaboration with Plenty, she established KTC. This program allows urban kids at risk the opportunity to take a one-week break from their troubled lives and experience nature. Operated at The Farm every July and August, the program offers children aged six to eleven from nearby cities, primarily Nashville, an intense schedule of physical activities (e.g., horse riding, biking, and swimming), educational activities (e.g., science classes, arts and crafts) and socializing. For many of these urban children, "who might otherwise be deprived of an

**5.4** Participants of "Kids to the Country" at the swimming hole. (Photo from the program's Facebook page.)

opportunity to run through a field alive with butterflies, or gaze up at an unobstructed night sky adorned with twinkling stars" (KTC's brochure), this week includes many first-time experiences, from learning how to swim to eating fresh fruits ("Some of them have said, 'this is the first time I've ever had fresh fruit.' These kids are poor kids" – Bowen).

At the age of seventy-six, Bowen is still the director of KTC. She is responsible for every aspect of the program, starting with fundraising and planning, continuing with training the counselors and supervising them, and ending with bookkeeping. She explained that every summer, the program has four or five cycles and that more than 5,000 children have participated in KTC since it began. Each cycle has forty to fifty children, of whom fifteen to twenty are from homeless shelters, refugee centers, and low-income neighborhoods in the city. The rest are children from The Farm, and "that's part of the beauty of it! How often does this white community get to see a lot of black kids? It's a win-win." In a later email correspondence, she shared that during the summer of 2020, when it was impossible to bring the children from the city to the country due to the COVID-19 pandemic, KTC "decided to bring a little country to the city." They put together gift bags with books, a plant to nurture, an art and nature activities workbook, colored pencils, some fresh fruits, and a couple of protein bars and distributed them to urban children at risk.

A second prominent children-oriented initiative is More than Warmth – an educational project aiming to foster understanding, knowledge, and compassion among children of various cultures. This project was initiated following the September 11 events by Judith Meeker, a former resident of The Farm. Meeker, who worked as a teacher in the poorest neighborhoods in Nashville, had her fourth-grade students draw pictures on fabric and make "a quilt from their heart, non-political, non-religious and non-violent" to send to the children of Afghanistan. The project seemed to be rather transformative. One of the children, for example, started with the idea of drawing the American flag and writing, "We are all Americans." After discussing this idea in class, he "ended up doing a picture of kids of all different colors holding hands and wrote, 'We are all one.' It was really beautiful."

Inspired by what had happened to her students, Meeker founded a nonprofit organization that operates to this day in many schools around Tennessee. She stressed that collaborative quilt making is an educational activity ("It has an art component. It has a social justice component. It has a social studies component. It has a geography component"), but also described how the quilts provoked joy and hope among those who received them. Over the years, quilts and accompanying letters from the children were sent to conflict, poverty, slavery, and disaster zones in fifty-five countries. This nonprofit is greatly supported by Farm people from Tennessee and elsewhere, who donate money and volunteer for the project. Meeker said that "a lot of that made me want to come back here [The Farm], and so we're building a house here again."

The last and most recent children-related initiative is Karen's Soy Nutrition Program (KSNP) at the Guatemala City waste dumpsite. This program started after "a group of women in Guatemala City contacted Plenty to see if it could help them create a food supplementation project for the benefit of the children of the dump." Tomas Heikkala became involved in this program to commemorate his spouse, Karen, who died of cancer in 2009. Two years earlier, after watching a documentary about the place, Tomas and Karen visited Guatemala City and went on a tour of the dump. In an article for *Plenty Bulletin* (35/1, Summer 2019), Heikkala wrote:

> The dump was huge, over 40 acres and 300 ft. deep, the biggest in Central America. Thousands of men, women, and children scramble over the piles of rubbish and garbage spilling out of the continuous stream of large trucks entering the grounds. It smelled awful. There were hundreds of vultures diving in to get their share. It was a shocking sight and one that caused a remarkable response in my heart... I wished I could do something to make a difference in the lives of these struggling folks.

Karen was on Plenty's board of directors for many years and even served as its president. Before her passing, she expressed a wish to help the children at the Guatemala dump. In 2010, Heikkala and Plenty started KSNP, which aims to promote the nutrition of malnourished children, improve parents' understanding and ability to address family nutrition needs, and expand employment opportunities. In collaboration with a local organization, they rented a building outside the dumpsite entrance, purchased equipment, and trained local women to produce soy milk. As a result, twice a week, about 300 children and some of the older adults living nearby receive soymilk and cookies fortified with essential vitamins and minerals. The local organization also uses the same building to carry out monthly soy food processing and general nutrition education activities for families who live in the dump area.

**ADVOCATING DOPE USE FOR HEALTH** In its early days, The Farm advocated dope use for spiritual purposes. After Gaskin and others were charged for growing marijuana, they even took the case to the U.S. Supreme Court. The appeal – later published as *The grass case* – was denied, and they were sent to jail, but it drew a lot of media attention and may have contributed to the much later legalization of cannabis use in some states. While many study participants mentioned this milestone in The Farm's history, three also shared that they currently advocate dope use for health.

The first, Jeffrey Hergenrather, made it his life goal. Hergenrather was among the regular attendees of Gaskin's Monday night classes in

San Francisco. When he told Gaskin that he was going to study medicine, "Stephen said, 'Awesome, go to medical school, keep your compassion and your hair, and then come to The Farm,' and I said, 'Well, I'll catch up with you later.'" Indeed, Hergenrather completed his studies and residency, and then he and his family joined The Farm, where he served as a general practitioner. After the changeover, they left for California, where he continued to practice conventional medicine. However, in 1996 he decided to "get out of the E.R. and practice cannabis medicine." Since 1999, that has been his main occupation.

Hergenrather's interest in the healing power of cannabis was sparked when he practiced medicine at The Farm and learned from his patients how cannabis helped various conditions. He also reported that about two-thirds of the women who gave birth on The Farm used cannabis during their pregnancies, "and I saw the wonders of it being so valuable for labor and delivery." In his clinic, Hergenrather consults people about cannabis use for various health conditions:

> People will come to me and say, "Well, you know, I'm 60 or 70-years-old, and I've never smoked pot, and I want to use it for my dementia or my cancer or my..." whatever their condition is. And so, I will sit down with them and explain how it works, what it's doing in their body, and how they should get started, and what they should look for. So, I lead them into a way to use cannabis as a medicine, so it's just not so random when they go to a dispensary or want to grow plants in their yard, they would have some idea of what they're trying to do.

Hergenrather shared that after the consultation, he also calls his patients to follow up on their conditions and make adjustments if needed. Stressing that "cannabis really acts on the natural system in our body and it is really harmless to use it," he explained that "because I was a general practitioner, I'm serving a population from birth until hospice care through any age group, any disease. I'm comfortable with talking about it in any disease."

Hergenrather is also involved in scientific research on the medical use of cannabis (e.g., for Crohn's Disease and Attention Deficit Hyperactivity Disorder), publishes scientific articles based on his studies, and participates in scientific and medical conferences around the world "to share my knowledge and learn what is going on in the basic science."

He also serves as President of the Society of Cannabis Clinicians, "and if you were to go to the website of cannabisclinicians.org, you would see that we offer a lot of free information for the public."

For Stephanie, advocating cannabis use for health is a relatively new activity to which she only dedicates part of her time. As mentioned earlier, she currently works as a medical director-educator for a licensed cannabis dispensary. Applying her knowledge as a medical doctor and fulfilling her passion for science, her work involves consulting, giving talks, and writing about the many health benefits of cannabis use. When we talked, she mentioned that she was "just working on an educational program on the use of cannabis in neuromuscular disorders." She clarified, "my mission is to educate people about whether they need it or not and, if they do, how to use it safely."

Unlike Hergenrather and Stephanie, who advocate cannabis use, Anna is interested in the healing power of psychedelics with an emphasis on mental health:

> The indigenous folks had their ways... and then came the second wave
> with the hippies and psychedelics, and now there's this big upswell going
> on. The research is opening up: Johns Hopkins, the Cleveland Clinic,
> UCSF, and reputable clinics, including the military, are studying the
> healing properties of psilocybin, MDMA, and ketamine. There are clinics
> in San Francisco that use it for depression... and the Multidisciplinary
> Association for Psychedelic Studies are in their level three FDA trial now
> for PTSD. The research is being legalized, and it was kind of steaming for
> a bunch of years. It's just a super exciting time, you know?

In 2005 (at the age of fifty-five), Anna completed a Master's degree in Counseling Psychology and became a licensed therapist who runs a private practice. Having had a very positive experience with "sacred medicine" that helped her cope with a series of personal losses, she recently started participating in the Multidisciplinary Association for Psychedelic Studies' three-year training program for therapists. She noted, "I'm definitely heading deeper into the use of a plant medicine to augment therapy in the appropriate, you know, set and setting," but clarified that she will "not offer it until I'm very well trained and have plenty of experience and then we'll see."

TELLING THE FARM'S STORY When I interviewed Jane, she mentioned that she volunteers at The Farm's Welcome Center by giving people tours and added, "I have lots of stories to tell them about all the different things that happened on this land." She graciously offered to give me a tour, and, indeed, one freezing morning two days later, we met at her house again and hit the road with her electric golf cart (the most popular vehicle around The Farm). Although I was well dressed, she covered me with blankets, and when she realized that her audience was already quite familiar with The Farm and its history, she made some adjustments in the tour and told me many anecdotes I had not heard before.

Like Jane, all study participants were pretty excited about telling the story of The Farm and appreciated my interest. In an email exchange around Thanksgiving 2020, for example, Anna wrote me (with a cc to all study participants): "It is so moving to have someone – you! – express such valuing of our life stories." Yet, several interviewees seemed more committed than others to documenting the story of The Farm. Brian, for example, shared with me a link to a website that he set up, where one can find many photos, videos, and stories from The Farm's commune period. When I visited him at the book company, he also showed me many boxes holding thousands of photos and videos that he planned to review and scan.

Daniel and Bill, who are members of the community's archive committee, explained that "we have lots and lots of videos, but those are all on tapes, and that's going to deteriorate. So, we've got to digitalize it, and it takes a lot of time and just sitting there and watching and transferring it" (Daniel). They also mentioned numerous audiotapes that Bill had been recording for many years, starting with the Monday night classes in San Francisco and during the entire commune period. When I asked his spouse, Sarah, how come she did not know him before they met and became a couple in 1993, she said: "On the old Farm we'd never cross paths because we never lived together, and when I went to meditation and things like that he was always back in the bushes, recording."

In addition to the archive project, Daniel is writing "the first little history of The Farm... that I'm trying to put together as a book." Dedicating some time to it almost every day, he found that "the story is different from what I experienced because there are so many different people, and they have different experiences." Bill is also conducting a series of video-recorded interviews with the founding members of The Farm. Feeling that he is running out of time he is currently focusing on the oldest and most frail members. Both he and Daniel are also planning to turn an old Farm building into a counterculture museum, and are looking for ways to fund this project. In addition, Bill will soon collaborate with a film producer on a documentary about The Farm. He explained his motivation for having the story told:

> We didn't come here to disappear into the fabric. We felt that we had something positive to contribute to the larger society, even if it was just a matter of saying "Look, there's another way" or "Here's how you can learn to get along." That seems to be lacking in the culture; there's so much conflict. We've been here almost 50 years, and we've learned something about getting along... I think it's useful for the greater society to see the model and see that it is possible. It may give some encouragement to try to do something similar.

Driven by a similar motivation, Douglas Stevenson – often called "Mr. Farm" by the community members – took the unofficial role of being the community's spokesman: "I put myself out there, and I have been doing it long enough that most people accept that I do that, and I have got a track record of being pretty good at it, and so they don't object to me doing it." He published two books about The Farm and set up and runs the community's official website. He also edits and authors most of the content posted in the community's newsletter sent monthly to about 5,000 people and manages the "Friends of The Farm" Facebook group, which has more than 6,000 members. In addition, he organizes the "Farm Experience Weekend" – an event offered several times a year in which attendees learn about The Farm's history and philosophy, tour the place, meet the residents, and participate in various workshops. He also lectures in a variety of forums and gives interviews to the media whenever an interest arises.

Stevenson became involved in these activities in 1990, when USA TODAY "came and wanted to do a story, and nobody wanted to do it with them... so I contacted them and basically produced the story. I set them up with people to interview, and it was very large – several articles." Since then, he has volunteered to talk to anybody interested in writing about The Farm. Stevenson explained that he was "sympathetic" to the reporters for several reasons. First, he was a journalist in the past so he could understand the challenges that they faced. Second, after the changeover, "there wasn't that much interest, and some of the interest that was coming was 'Oh, look, The Farm failed, it's a ghost town.' We don't need that." Third, he realized that the reporters "were mostly closet hippies who could not write editorials, but they could find us and use us as the vehicle for them to say what they believed in." When he said that, I thought it could apply to me just as it did to those closeted journalists.

## SUMMARY: A MULTILAYERED GENERATIVITY

There is no doubt that the hippies' unusual involvement in generative actions at a young age was an inherent part of the 1960s counterculture. This study highlights their *continued* involvement in such actions and sincere desire to make the world a better place. Moreover, it supports existing models of generativity[14] and even develops them by suggesting that generativity may be multilayered (see Figure 5.5).

The first layer is the individual level, where people are involved in various generative activities both in the private sphere (e.g., by caring for their grandchildren or writing a book) and in public domains. Next is the community layer, in this case, The Farm and its three unique contributions to the world (i.e., soy-based foods, natural birth giving, and Plenty International). All residents and former residents were very proud of these contributions regardless of their involvement in them. Hence, being associated with a collaborative action may result in a most meaningful generativity script. Lastly, there is the generational level: The study suggests that if there is an ideological affinity between individuals and their cohort, then the generational impacts on the world may be woven into the personal narrative and create a great sense of accomplishment and satisfaction.

Two factors seemed to act as threads that rendered the three layers synergetic, the first being a sense of mutual efforts. Study participants

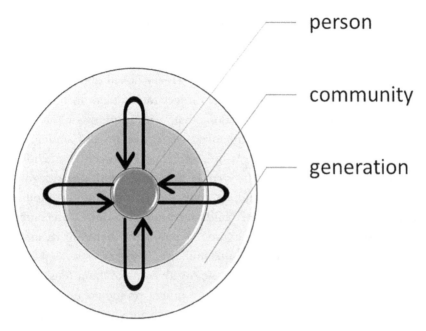

person

community

generation

**5.5** Multilayered generativity.

used the first-person plural ("we," "us," "our") when they talked about The Farm's impacts on the world because they felt that they had contributed in one way or another to The Farm's actions in the past. In addition, many described lifelong involvement in The Farm's efforts by means such as advocating its ideals or volunteering and donating to Plenty's projects. Consequently, they interwove the community's contributions into their personal narratives. The lifelong and returning residents also felt that they had changed the world by setting an example for "how it can be done."

Interestingly, interviewees also used the first-person plural when they discussed the hippies in general. Seeing The Farm as the ultimate realization of the hippie ideals, they hardly differentiated between the hippie movement and the community. They felt some ownership and responsibility for both the achievements and the failures of their generation. Moreover, they used "we" even when they talked about individual initiatives. This finding may be explained by the fact that they spent most of their formative years as young adults in a commune and became accustomed to thinking about themselves in collective terms. Yet, it may also be associated with their tendency to recruit community members – residents and former residents – for their individual initiatives. This tendency may clarify, for example, why Henry talked about the Swan Conservation Trust as a community project rather than an individual one and said three times, "We've done that," with emphasis on the "we."

The second factor, which enhanced synergy within and among the three layers of generativity, was the connection between the actions. Some of the individual initiatives could fit in more than one category. More than Warmth, for example, could be classified as "promoting peace" just as it is "caring for children," and the Swan Conservation Trust also had a "caring for children" component thanks to its many educational activities. Many of the initiatives also corresponded with The Farm's main contributions to the world: Some of them (e.g., KTC, KSNP) were executed by Plenty, while others promoted nonviolence (PeaceRoots Alliance, More than Warmth), healthy nutrition (KSNP), and environment preservation (Swan Conservation Trust). In addition, all generative actions were associated with at least one of the core hippie ideals. The similar ideological basis led to a sense of coherence and somewhat blurred boundaries between the three generativity layers.

Although generativity is typically more prominent in later life,[15] it seems to reflect continuity between early adulthood and older age in the case of aging hippies. Whereas some selectivity was reported, especially when it came to political involvement, the reason for reduction did not seem to be age or age-related constraints but weaker faith in such actions and a certain degree of cynicism. There were also some indications for change in essence, especially in the transition from advocating dope use for spiritual purposes to encouraging its use for health. This initiative, however, may be considered an extension of The Farm's efforts to promote healthy lifestyles. Overall, most respondents were still pretty much out there trying to change the world, as Sylvia Tepper summarized in her essay:

> But there's still this sense that we're out to make the world a better place.
> We haven't lost that, and I know I feel that, I know he [spouse] feels that.
> I know that people in the prayer circle feel that. The people that we're

friends with still on The Farm feel that still. We're still in the effort, no matter what we do, the way we live our lives, to make the world a better place.

Both continuity and generativity are associated with wellbeing in later life. Continuity Theory[16] posits that continuity is a primary adaptive strategy for dealing with changes related to normal aging. It argues that individuals maintain internal continuity of psychological and social patterns adopted during their life course by preserving existing activity patterns. Generativity has aspects of both communion (i.e., sharing oneself with others, giving up of self for greater purposes) and agency. The latter is reflected in the sense of self-expression and self-development as well as in a feeling of having a lasting legacy,[17] which leads to enhanced wellbeing in later life.[18] By maintaining a high level of involvement in generative actions, the people interviewed for this study demonstrated a combination of continuity and generativity. This combination preserved and deepened their personal, communal, and generational narratives and resulted in the sense of accomplishment and great meaning in life.

# CHAPTER 6

# Sex, Drugs, and Rock-n-Roll?

**D**OPE, SEX, AND ROCK were among the central tenets of the hippie ideology.[1] Yet, they were not only ideological principles. They were also practices celebrated by the millions who participated in or sympathized with the counterculture in its blossoming period. Free love, the use of recreational and psychedelic drugs, and rock music were a part of their lifestyle and a way of expressing their vision of the world, mainstream society, and life. These activities also allowed for self-exploration and provided a context for connecting with others. Assuming that they were freely chosen and enjoyable, these activities may also be considered *leisure*, and all three may be regarded as part of the hippie ethics of play.

Defining leisure may seem easy, but scholars often refer to different phenomena while using the same terminology. The most common concepts associated with leisure are time, activity, and experience. When defining leisure as time, writers refer to it as distinctive by being relatively free from obligations and offering a high level of choice. Labeling leisure as an activity relates to what people *do* in their free time, and describing it as an experience relates to a state of mind or mental condition, usually associated with pleasure.[2]

The issue of leisure in later life has been studied extensively for several decades. By applying various methods and measures, studies have provided considerable evidence demonstrating that involvement in leisure activities has a significant impact on older adults' physical, psychological, social, and spiritual wellbeing.[3] Furthermore, some longitudinal studies found leisure to be a central factor explaining successful coping with later-life transitions, such as retirement and spousal loss.[4]

Despite the many benefits of leisure, participation tends to decline with advancing age.[5] This tendency may be explained by the numerous constraints to leisure participation that older adults face, including health-related, psychological (e.g., lower motivation, low self-efficacy), cultural-environmental (e.g., social isolation), and technical constraints (e.g., availability of activities, transportation). In addition, although studies demonstrate that adopting new leisure activities in old age may promote wellbeing by creating an opportunity for broadening and deepening a sense of meaning in life,[6] people are less interested in exploring new leisure pursuits as they age and tend to prefer familiar activities.[7]

Considering the hippie ethics of play, one may assume that aging hippies would have a most active and diverse leisure repertoire. Predicting what activities are included in that repertoire, however, is a more challenging task. Similar to other seniors, older hippies may exhibit continuity in their leisure activities, just as they do in their efforts to make the world a better place (see Chapter 5). Hence, they may still celebrate sex, drugs, and rock-n-roll, at least to some extent. It is just as possible, however, that they explore new ways to enjoy leisure.

This chapter aims to provide a glimpse into aging hippies' leisure style. Specifically, it explores their involvement in activities associated with dope, sex, and rock. Still, it also examines other activities in search of commonalities among the individuals interviewed for the present study. Although generative and spiritual activities may also be considered leisure, they are typically more purposeful than something done for its own sake (i.e., in anticipation of satisfaction with the activity itself). They may also involve a great sense of commitment, and some of them may even be perceived as obligatory. Consequently, they are discussed in separate chapters.

## FROM SEXUAL LIBERATION TO LIBERATION FROM SEX

Of all the topics examined in this study, sex was the least discussed and the most ambiguous. Unlike many in the hippie movement, The Farm in its commune era did not support free love and regarded sex as having a profound relational and spiritual meaning. This approach may explain why merely half of the study participants talked about sex in general, and even fewer discussed sex in their lives at present. Accordingly, the insights presented here cannot be generalized to the entire group of individuals interviewed for this study, nor can they be applied to aging hippies as a whole.

Freely chosen sexual activity performed for its own sake can be understood as leisure.[8] Still, it is an activity that may be practiced in various ways and for many reasons.[9] The study participants' reports suggested that the way they perceived and practiced sex considerably changed across their lives. Although each person had their path, the various experiences shared a somewhat similar course: In their youth and early adulthood, most interviewees exercised free love, but upon joining The Farm, they restricted their sexual activity. Then, after the commune days were over, they could experience more authentic sexuality less influenced by generational trends or community laws. This authenticity lasted into their later years and allowed for experimentation with new forms of sex, exploration of different kinds of relationships, and some level of reduced centrality of sex.

Before joining The Farm, many study participants enjoyed the sexual liberation enabled by the contraceptive pill and endorsed by the hippie movement. Dennis, for example, noted, "I was into sex, drugs, and rock-n-roll, but I also had morals about my sexual behavior." Ben's partner explained, "It [the hippie era] was after birth control and before HIV, and so it was just part of that culture that things got lucky." Upon joining the community, however, members dramatically changed their perceptions and attitudes toward sex. They turned it from casual leisure to a most significant component of life that was viewed as a holy sacrament involving great intention and commitment.

This change was typically voluntary and considered part of one's spiritual development. Agreeing that abortion violates their ideology of nonviolence and that the use of the contraceptive pill goes against the body's nature, members accepted and even supported The Farm's conservative approach according to which "you just cannot get intimate with somebody else unless you are willing to marry them" (Paul). Acknowledging that this approach eventually led to many divorces because the couples hardly knew each other due to brief dating periods and "weren't necessarily a good fit," Nicholas explained:

The Farm wasn't as liberal as one would expect of a commune of hippies. We were definitely going in the other direction. I think it did us good because nothing will make you crazier than the turmoil of relationships, and the more you complicate them, the crazier or ungrounded you can become. As we kept that to a minimum, it allowed us to be a much more stable community.

Most commune members believed that "going in the other direction" was a constructive policy for the community and individuals alike. Joe, for example, said: "We were about as conservative as the pope. We didn't do birth control; we didn't believe in having sex before marriage. So, all of that kind of looseness of the Haight-Ashbury got tossed out, which for me was good because I felt like it taught me the moral discipline to be who I am now."

The extent to which the strict conservatism resulted in a more stable community and more peaceful commune members is questionable. It seems that the commune's approach to sex caused numerous problems and tensions. Many of these problems may be attributed to the contradictions associated with the formal policy. Certain contradictions were inherent to the policy because some of its elements – the "four-marriage" in particular – were clearly unorthodox. This specific format was also problematic in itself. It may have been "an incredible learning experience," as Harold said, but it also involved unbearable hardships. Charles, for example, testified: "I was constantly jealous. The other guy and Lillian seemed to have a better relationship than I did. It was hard." Lillian added that after the four-marriage fell apart, "it complicated the rest of our lives for everybody" because she had children from the two men she was married to, and for the children, both men and both women were their parents.

Most inconsistencies, however, were between the declared policy and the daily reality. For example, some of the study participants who were married during the commune era reported having affairs or secretly experimenting with partner swapping. Those who were single described quite a bit of underground sexual activity. Bill explained: "Everybody was young and flower of youth, and as much as it was not accepted, that didn't stop it from happening. The human nature was in existence and thriving in ways that we weren't able to suppress totally."

Single people who adhered to the formal policy admitted that it was challenging and involved tensions with other members and even with Gaskin. Paul, for example, confessed, "I was not ready for the celibate life." He shared that at some point, he became attracted to a married woman. Though Paul "never did anything about it," Gaskin got mad at him "and threw me out of the band I was in, and yelled at me in front of a bunch of people... just because he felt like I was going to screw around with women I shouldn't be." What added to the tension was that Gaskin himself, as some people implied, did not fully practice what he preached. Actually, according to some of the women, he took advantage of his leadership position. Stephanie, for example, noted: "Stephen did come on to me at one point, and I rejected him. I sometimes wonder if my poor social status at The Farm had something to do with it; if you had to be intimate with Stephen to be in the hierarchy."

Although The Farm was supposedly open to gays, same-gender sex was very uncommon and perceived as unnatural. Laura argued that "the Farm never really dealt with homosexuality. It didn't even acknowledge that anybody might be gay." Rebecca added, "We considered homosexuality to be a psychological problem... it wasn't the natural way to be; men should be with women." She even blamed The Farm for being "very backward... stuck in the '60s up until the '80s and didn't catch up with a lot of things." The outcome was that people attracted to the same gender often concealed their sexual orientation and married a person of the opposite sex, hurting themselves, their partners, and their children.

An even more disturbing accusation was made by Evelyn, who claimed that the commune's attempts to help the unprivileged often sacrificed the wellbeing of its members, women and children especially. Among other things, she talked about two people who molested Farm children. One of them was a teenager from the Bronx project brought to the commune, and the other was a "guy that they were helping out, who had been injured." Although such incidents ended with the expulsion of the offenders, Evelyn argued that "they're still hiding this, and I think it's so unfair because only by talking about the trauma they [the victims] can heal."

The consequences of all the commune era's phenomena were devastating: People found themselves in unhealthy marriages just because of unintentional pregnancies, many single and married members alike were forced to lie and conceal their sexual activity, gay people could not realize their sexual orientation, and sexually abused people did not receive proper therapy. In addition, this turmoil caused tensions among members, loss of faith in the community's leader, and life lived in contrast to the ideology of being true in all doings.

There is no wonder, therefore, that when the commune era was over, many members experienced liberation – either from unsuccessful marriages or from the need to conceal who they were and what they did. Such liberation, however, often came at a painful price. People who divorced because of fundamental incompatibility or after finding out that their spouses were unfaithful to them described a lot of misery. Bill, for example, revealed: "When I found out that my second wife has a boyfriend too, I said, 'Why does this keep happening. I'm out of here.' Well, we had a kid. That tore me apart to lose access to my daughter. We were very close, but I just couldn't stay there." Laura shared that after leaving The Farm, she "felt more and more disconnected" from her spouse. At some point, she told him, "I know our marriage is dead, and I want to know why," and "he finally admitted he was gay... it was like an atom bomb went off in my life." Laura described a most distressing divorce that caused years of misery to her, her spouse, and their children.

Naturally, the children were profoundly affected by the divorces. Nadine Mondo, who created a documentary film about The Farm (*American commune*, 2013), was one of many children who grew up in the commune and experienced their parents' divorce after the changeover. The more personal parts of the film draw a clear line between the commune's conservative policy regarding sex and the hasty marriage of her parents, who hardly knew each other when they got married and then "lived together for 13 years without love." The marriage ended with an excruciating divorce, following which Mondo and her sister moved to New York with their mother, whereas her brother and father moved to Florida. All family members were interviewed for the film, and their testimonials suggested that this wound never completely healed. In one of the most touching moments, Mondo wipes a tear and tells her mother: "Our family had so much turmoil since you guys divorced, so many years."

What seems to be clear is that from the 1980s to this day, some of the people who participated in this study felt liberated to live a significantly more authentic life as far as their sexuality was concerned. Many of those who divorced found better and more sustainable relationships. Others had a series of short relationships or experimented with various associations, including relations with individuals of different age groups and people of the same gender. Stephanie, for example, said that she tried same-gender sex, and "that was fun, but I'm wired to be heterosexual." In contrast, Rebecca, who was always bisexual, is in a long-lasting relationship with another past member of The Farm who is transman ("He went as a woman with the male partner, but they were not really together, and they did get separated").

Lastly, some people testified that as they got older, they experienced some liberation from the centrality of sex in their lives – a centrality that was both an outcome of young age and a result of the socio-cultural construction of sex during the 1960s. For example, Jane, who moved back to The Farm after many years in California, said that she knew that it would be hard for her to find a new partner after moving because she "already knew everyone on The Farm." Yet, she found out that nonsexual relationships with men may be quite satisfying: "I have two or three male friends who I talk to every day and who call me and have over for dinner and stuff, and that's really not a sexual thing at all. It's just friendship." Similarly, Chris said that one of the most pleasant things about living at The Farm nowadays is the nonsexual friendships between the older men and women: "Nobody is hitting on each other. We're just friends. You can love people but not have to get physical. We can just appreciate each other for the lovely people we can be." Chris added that some decline in sexual desire is what enabled this blessing:

> Men are like – we're led around by our genitals for the most part until we're like 50 or 60. If you don't get laid every day, your genitals are driving you around. I'm being really honest with you. Even when I was married, I was still crazy. And now it's a lot better. I learned that I could look at a beautiful woman and think she's like a beautiful flower. Don't smell, don't touch, but you can appreciate the flower for what it is.

After four marriages, Chris had a girlfriend who lived far away. As they did not often see each other, this relationship was primarily platonic. Yet, it lasted for quite a long time. Andrew, who experienced a rough divorce from his second wife, told me he was no longer interested in any romantic involvement and preferred focusing on spiritual growth. When I insisted that he might still find good love, he said he would not rule it out but would not actively seek it. Someone else, who confessed that he had not had sex for many years, explained that this celibacy was intentional because he was in love with a woman who only recently divorced and is waiting for her to be ready for a new relationship. Thus he, Chris, Jane, and others seem to place relationship above sex – a priority that signifies a noteworthy transition in their perception of sex since the days before joining The Farm when they – as Ben phrased it – "allowed love to flow freely."

### A PUFF A DAY KEEPS THE DOCTOR AWAY

Unlike sex, dope was a topic often and extensively discussed by study participants, though there was a notable difference among them: Whereas former residents freely talked about it, the people who live at The Farm were hesitant. Ben, for example, noted, "I usually don't talk about it," Henry was surprised, "Have people been talking about psychedelics?" and Jane even went as far as unplugging her Amazon Echo (Alexa) device when the topic came up. The caution was explained by the fact that cannabis use is still illegal in Tennessee. In addition, some of the men shared stories about being arrested and even spending some time in jail for possessing, growing, or selling drugs. These incidents occurred decades ago (before establishing The Farm or during the commune period) and were often described with a smile. Yet, they seemed to leave an unpleasant mark driving study participants to be careful not only in their use of dope but also in talking about it.

The Farm, in its commune days, considered itself a "dope church" – a hippie imitation of the Native American Church that had the historical tradition of drug use for ritual purposes and thus was authorized to use peyote (cactus) as a psychedelic substance. Some of the hippie dope churches consisted of young people who just wanted to get high. The

Farm, however, was among the "serious" communities that truly admired the Native Americans and viewed dope as a means of spiritual discovery and growth. Like other hippies, the community differentiated between "good" substances that gave vision and clarity and "bad," addictive, harmful drugs that "you couldn't go back from" (Dennis), including nicotine and alcohol. However, unlike most hippies, it also differentiated between "natural" drugs (e.g., cannabis, hallucinogenic mushrooms, and cacti such as peyote and San Pedro) and "synthetic" drugs, LSD predominantly. Similar to the contraceptive pill, synthetic drugs on The Farm were banned as "bad" drugs.

Most commune members had used LSD among other drugs before joining The Farm, and some described pretty intensive use ("I did LSD a couple of hundred times back in the 60s" – Gordon, "I took a hundred dozen trips" – Elizabeth). Many also shared quite powerful experiences using it, but their experiences somewhat resembled those resulting from using natural psychedelics. Carolyn, for example, said that she once "had a little half a tab of acid" (i.e., LSD), following which she "started hearing these angelic voices" and saw a vision of "a seed of consciousness that had come all the way to the west and had taken root and blossomed wherever it was, but then had to be carried back to the rest of the world… and I just felt I need to be part of this." A somewhat similar story was shared by Andrew, who during a mescaline (cactus) trip "saw the clouds make a change and there's this huge light coming out of the cloud and God is talking to me." Likewise, Cliff and Chris shared similar stories: Whereas the former said that while being high, he "became 100% telepathic with a dog," the latter said, "I sat with a cow for hours, and I realized that cow's my cousin. That's how I became a vegan."

The somewhat similar hallucinogenic experiences caused by various psychedelics may explain why the banning of synthetic drugs on The Farm did not result in as dramatic an impact as the one caused by the sex-related rules. Commune members could still use natural drugs, and they did so quite intensively. In addition, they believed that giving up on synthetic drugs was a reasonable step when aiming at a healthy lifestyle, as Gordon explained: "I was already heading towards organics, and I didn't want to put chemicals in my body, so the stronger psychedelics – LSD particularly – I let go of that."

The use of cannabis during the commune era was described as a daily practice, though some members used it less frequently than others ("I loved smoking dope, but I hadn't gotten into it quite as heavily as some of these people had" – Andrew). The use of peyote and mushrooms was less common due to their limited availability and stronger impact. When possible, however, commune members used them as part of their spiritual practice. Evelyn shared that on her first visit to The Farm, she was impressed by how cheerful everyone was until she realized "that it was a mushroom Sunday, so the entire community had taken mushrooms."

Trying to clarify what was spiritual about drug use in general and psychedelics in particular, participants often used the vague term "consciousness" (e.g., "My consciousness loosened up and expanded" – Paul). They explained that dope yielded "heightened awareness spiritual experiences" (Roger), "opened up a window into a world that I didn't know existed and I never understood" (Bill), and made them feel "more and more smart so to speak" (Jane). Some interviewees, who were a bit surprised by my questions, advised that I try psychedelics to understand their spiritual aspect and reassured me that nothing bad might happen. Such advice, for example, came up when I interviewed Henry:

HENRY: Have you ever taken a psychedelic?

GALIT: No. I haven't.

HENRY: No?

GALIT: No. I am not against it; I am just a chicken. I'm afraid of losing control, I think.

HENRY: You'll do fine.

GALIT: I'm also afraid of what I may find.

HENRY: No, you know your mind. You're who you are. It's not that you need it... but it shows you that there are multiple solutions to every problem.

In a similar conversation, Nicholas stated, "I consider psychedelics to be my primary teacher," and advised me, "Try mushrooms. It's fairly safe." Harold, who stated that he wants to "go back to psychedelics," recommended that I "start with micro-dosing."

The spiritual dimension of dope was often intertwined with a social aspect. Explaining that "it was a way for us to be together" (Charles), participants testified that dope "gives you a sense of the oneness of everything and the connectedness of everything" (Brian). It thus "changes your consciousness, you get telepathic, and you get compassionate and you know when you connect with someone that they're there, that they're present and have some openness of mind" (Julia). The openness created by using dope with others led some interviewees to deep socio-psychological understandings. Rebecca, for example, said, "I felt like I was learning more about people through taking psychedelics and getting insights," and Stephanie commented, "psychedelics was like 'Interpersonal Relationships 101' for me." This openness also created a sense of community with other commune members, as Andrew commented: "The receptivity that you get from psychedelics opens you up and leads you to having a really strong interaction with others. If you do that for 10 or 12 years, which we did on The Farm together, you get to know each other really well, and you get to really love each other." Bill added that such a sense of community was prevalent among the hippies in general because "there were so many other people going through that same process that even if we didn't know each other, we could recognize the similarities in our life experience. We were on a journey together in a sense."

As far as dope is concerned, the journey somewhat changed with age. The most notable change was decreased use of psychedelics. For some study participants, this change came early, during the 1970s, with the primary reason for reduction being the need to function at work and home. Ben, for example, said that he restricted "psychedelic activity and drug activity" to the weekends. Defining himself as a "weekend warrior," he explained that "having a job keeps you a certain amount on the straight and narrow and functioning." Stephanie shared that she stopped using psychedelics when her children were very young. After having "a great trip" with her spouse and a couple of friends, she slept for three days and realized, "No, I don't want to do this anymore. I don't have time to waste myself like this for days."

About two-thirds of the study participants said that they currently do not use psychedelics at all or that they have not done so in a very long time. Whereas some talked about a loss of interest ("I said, 'Okay, I get it. I don't need it anymore'" – Jane, "There are some things you grow out of" – Albert), the majority explained that it is "too intense, too exhausting" (Sandra), and that "life is trippy enough right now without that" (Stephanie). Interestingly, having bad trips was not mentioned as a reason to quit using, although many reported that they had had them. Those who still use psychedelics described low frequency ("Sometimes once or twice a year, sometimes every few years" – Nicholas), and everyone seemed to agree that psychedelics have a long-lasting effect that may last a lifetime ("It [psychedelics] changes you forever. There's no going back. Once you see this stuff, there's no way to un-see it or forget about it" – Cliff).

In contrast to psychedelics, cannabis use remained pretty stable during the participants' life course. Work and parenting responsibilities had relatively little effect on cannabis use, though users had to teach their children to be confidential: "We just told the kids it was not to be spoken of, because mom and dad could go to jail" (Karen). Perceiving cannabis as a positive substance that is much healthier and safer than nicotine and alcohol, some participants let their children use cannabis at a pretty young age. Chris admitted, "My boys never asked me, 'Dad, can we have some pot?' They never said, 'Can we smoke?' They just did it as if it was ice cream in the freezer. But I have always lovingly thought that they were too young, 13, 14." Two people even have children that make a living from growing cannabis in California, where it is legal, and only one participant reported having an offspring with drug issues ("My oldest daughter got badly into hard drugs. About six years ago, she moved in with her mom and was finally able to quit. She's been clean since then" – Gordon).

Several participants said that they use cannabis today at a lower frequency than they did in the past, and a few even quit using it altogether. The majority, however, reported daily or almost daily use. The main change was not reflected much in the frequency of use, but rather in the *purpose* of use: Whereas in the past the purpose was predominantly "spiritual" and "social," the main reasons for current use were "social" and "instrumental," and the use of cannabis for spiritual practice was hardly discussed.

The cause for the reduced association between cannabis use and spirituality is not clear. A possible explanation, which will be further discussed in Chapter 7, is that people's interest in spirituality or spiritual path had changed. Another explanation may stem from the aforementioned long-lasting effect of past experiences. If the expansion of consciousness remains after use, it is probable that it has a limit and that at some point, more use does not yield new spiritual insights. It is also likely, however, that people found new means to expand their minds, as Jane said: "Realizing that there's more to life and looking at things differently... well, Bob Dylan did that for me. Later on, pot did it for me. But right now, I can see it just looking out the window or sitting on my back porch."

Using cannabis as a social practice was mainly mentioned by the people who use it occasionally. Debbie, for example, stated that "Sometimes I get high, I can feel like smoking when I'm with others but not on my own initiative. If a friend comes over, okay, I'll always smoke with him." Similarly, Cindy said, "My husband still uses it pretty frequently, and so sometimes we smoke together, but I don't do it a lot; it's very moderate." Dennis shared that when he visited a friend who "smokes grass because he has Parkinson's disease," they "smoked a joint together because I felt like it was a way I could commune with him, I could make a connection." Ben also noted, "Definitely got to be with friends to smoke. I guess it's part of my hippie roots."

The most notable change in the purpose of cannabis use was its use for "instrumental" reasons, including *medical use* and *mood management* (Figure 6.1). Because such reasons were mainly described by former residents of The Farm who live in California – where cannabis use is legal – there is undoubtedly a contextual explanation for this change. When use is not limited, people may be more creative and have more diverse practices. Yet, the instrumental use also seems age-related because the purpose was often coping with later life challenges. The *medical use* was associated with declining health and was typically discussed concerning specific health conditions. Gordon, for example, suffers pain from an injury that occurred when he was seventeen years old: "I've got a vertebra that kind of sticks out a little bit, nothing too serious, but it qualified me for medical cannabis." Harold, too, uses cannabis every day because of a neuropathy condition that he has. He explained:

Friends of The Farm Tennessee

VICE.COM
Cannabis Is Officially a Medicine, Following Historic UN Vote

Friends of The Farm Tennessee

NPR.ORG
Rigorous Study Backs A Psychedelic Treatment For Major Depression

Friends of The Farm Tennessee

FORBES.COM
New 'Cannabis For Dementia' Podcast Launches
A new podcast explores professional and personal experiences usin...

Friends of The Farm Tennessee

CALGARYHERALD.COM
Cannabis shows promise blocking coronavirus infection: Alberta researcher

6.1 Messages posted on the Facebook group "Friends of The Farm Tennessee" in 2020. The online discussion definitely reflects the more instrumental approach to dope.

It helps me. I have a prescription for medical marijuana, it gives me a little discount, and I use it at night to sleep because my feet can become very – it's a pain unlike anything I've ever felt before. It's just for the pain because there's no cure for what I have, but I think it [cannabis] might be improving my condition because now I can actually ride my bike.

The use of cannabis for *mood management* had two opposing functions: relaxing and energizing. Explaining that "cannabis is very helpful, especially if this is about aging, it is an ally of the aging body and mind" (Sandra), most frequent users described the relaxing effect. Stephanie, for example, testified:

I try to think before I use it. It's not a habit... and I don't need much, but I sure like having some around in case that I need it. I might be having a really hard day, like every-corner-is-a-sharp-corner today – one of those days. I might take a toke in the middle of the day to shift that, but it's very – it's mostly conscious use.

The relaxing effect was also mentioned as contributing to one's quality of sleep. Henry, who had a strong smell of marijuana when we first met, said: "I mainly do it for sleeping more, but I never do it at work or anything." Yet, the calming effect seems to depend on the person and the context. Paul, for example, quit using drugs because "I don't do well smoking pot. I get very paranoid, you know, it relaxes some people, but it makes me very erratic and anxious." James, in contrast, said, "I don't mind tripping a little bit now because it usually ends up being a positive experience." Yet, when he was coping with anxiety following his spouse's passing, he needed "pharmaceuticals" because "cannabis wasn't effective enough, and often it turns the spotlight in and tells you, 'watch what you have to deal with inside.'"

The energizing function of cannabis was less frequently mentioned, but some people, like Nicholas, explained that it all "depends on whether you're using indica or sativa."[10] He added that he preferred sativa because it is "more of a fast meditation... and I like to do it before I go out in the garden or use it before I clean the house. I get everything I see. I am like, 'okay, I got to do that, now I got to do this, now I got to do that.'" Brian, too, said that he "smoked grass every day for 50 years now, and that's one of the constants, and I enjoy it." However, that did not seem to be enough to keep him energized. After being diagnosed with a mild form of leukemia three years ago, Brian has to take an oral chemotherapy medication every day. Although this medicine usually has many side effects, the only one Brian is suffering from is fatigue: "And so, I find that I don't have the energy to do some of the things I used to be able to do, and the inclination, and the inspiration. A lot of that has gone away." As his daily use of cannabis does not seem to help, Brian is planning to go back to psychedelics:

> I haven't taken any psychedelics in 25 years, but I'm looking for some inspiration and a way to break through some of this lack of energy and get into a new mindset. So, I'm going to be taking some psilocybin, mushrooms, magic mushrooms. I've been reading a book by Michael Pollan, *How to change yourself*, and I got inspired to get into it again.

In a follow-up email exchange nine months later, he reported: "COVID-19 caused me to delay my decision to take a mushroom trip. Perhaps someday soon it will happen, and I will get the reboot I'm looking for."

Overall, while acknowledging the limitations of cannabis use in certain conditions, study participants described it as a formula for aging well. Elizabeth said that when she sees nonhippie seniors, "they all look older than me even though I'm sure I'm older than them because smoking grass keeps you more contemporary." Karen, too, said that pot is the key to youthful appearance and even admitted putting it on her face every day, but she mainly advocated its health benefits: "I really do think it's good for you. It's anti-inflammatory, it's neuroprotective, it obviously opens your mind and helps you to be more an accepting person." To support her arguments, she added that when she "visits a new doctor for this or that," they usually want to know her list of medications. When they find out that she does not take any medicines, "they are amazed, 'you're 70-years-old, and you don't take any medicines?' We are all held hostage by the pharmaceutical industry. It's worldwide, and it's horrible. But I say, a puff a day keeps the doctor away."

## MUSIC IS A LIFELONG BLESSING

Playing and listening to music is a widespread leisure activity and one of the oldest documented in human history. Therefore, the hippie movement was not revolutionary in its love for music but rather in the importance it attributed to it; as Nicholas put it: "Everyone loves music. It's a human trait more than just the hippie trait, but the hippies acknowledged that and brought it forward to a new place, to where it's more embedded in the culture." Similarly, Sandra noted, "We called rock-n-roll our spiritual music. That was our church music."

Of the sex, drugs, and rock-n-roll triad, the latter seems significantly less influenced by time or aging processes. Music appeared to be of great importance in the study participants' lives from a very young age to this day, and it was described in very favorable terms such as "gift" and "blessing." Some interviewees shared pretty enviable stories about their experiences as teens and young adults at the big hippie "be-ins" and festivals (e.g., Woodstock, Monterey). Those who grew up in the San Francisco Bay Area also described frequent attendance at the music scene around there ("I went to the Avalon quite often in high school" – Gordon; "When I was 14 years old, I went to a Rolling Stones concert. I just completely obsessed about rock-n-roll after that, and that was also fueled by the times... this is when the two rock ballrooms [Fillmore and Avalon] got going" – Paul). In addition to spending a lot of time listening to music and attending concerts, many played an instrument, were part of amateur bands, and even created original music. Based on participants' reports, the counterculturalists did not only view the famous musicians as their role models; many of them also wanted to *become* such models.

The large number of musicians among the founders of The Farm and the rock ethics of the hippies may explain the centrality of music in the commune period. People were listening to music all the time, many members who could play or sing were part of a band, and live music was the main program in all social gatherings and events. In addition, "over the years, maybe eight or 10 different bands or individuals have gotten their music recorded" (James). The official Farm Band that accompanied Gaskin on his speaking tours was even defined as the "new wave of music" by a representative of a record label from Nashville. The band signed a contract with him and recorded its first and sole album "that has since been seen on eBay for over 100 dollars... probably just because it's rare" (Bill).

The centrality of music in The Farm community has lasted to this day. People still listen to music quite often, attend concerts at The Farm (and elsewhere when possible), play music on their own and with others, and

SEX, DRUGS, AND ROCK-N-ROLL?

even perform on various occasions. The same applies to those who no longer live at The Farm. In contrast to sex and dope, there were not many signs of reduced frequency, interest, or excitement about music. Moreover, some of the study participants reported greater involvement in music as a leisure activity to the extent that it may be regarded as "serious leisure," namely, an activity characterized by considerable commitment, effort, and perseverance, and associated with many enduring psychological rewards.[11]

Three factors seemed to catalyze more involvement in music: having more time, other people, and technology. "Having more time" was typically associated with retirement. Sam, for example, moved back to The Farm after the company he was working for was sold ("I could look for a new management job but I was 61 and could retire and move to The Farm"). The first thing he did after moving back was to form a rock-n-roll band with a group of "some younger people and some older people":

> We play the music of the Grateful Dead. We are a quintessential garage band. We practice here and there, and we perform about three times a year. We play at the New Year's Eve party, and we play at Ragweed [annual reunion], and we play at parties sometimes. I formed the band because Grateful Dead is common music around here, especially for the old-timers. I've been listening to that music since the old days, and that's my favorite band.

On the other side of the country, Sylvia Tepper had a similar post-retirement initiative. Music was always part of her life. She took piano lessons from the age of five and had her first band when she was seventeen. Later, she dropped out of college to sing in a rock band, and then, at The Farm, she was part of several bands, including the official Farm Band. After moving to California, she "picked piano up again so that I could accompany myself and sing." She continued to "do occasional concerts here and there, just singing and playing the piano." Today, as a retiree, Sylvia is "a bandmate of other Farm alumni in a rock band called The Farm Band" (Figure 6.2). In addition, she formed a choir:

> It's a wonderful small women's choir, maybe 16 to 20 people, and most of them are Farm women. We call ourselves Best Witches. And we do all kinds of music from chanting in the Sanskrit stuff to oldies, to songs with

143

**6.2** The Farm Band performing at the annual fundraising event of PeaceRoots Alliance.

meaning. Our big hit last year was a blues tune called *Put a woman in charge.* You can find it on YouTube.

Unlike Sylvia, Cliff did not touch his bass guitar for many years. He explained, "I was in bands in high school, after college, on The Farm, but as soon as I left The Farm, I was on my own... So I let it slide, and then my guitar got stolen, and in 20 years, I haven't replaced it." He plans, however, to pick it up again when he has time. In his case, that does not mean retirement, but after "a couple of knee replacements" that will require a long recovery period. He declared, "When I do that [the surgery], that's when I'll learn my bass again. I absolutely want to play music; that's part of the plan."

A second trigger for renewed or extended involvement in music was "other people." In Cliff's case, it is not only the time he will have during recovery but also a friend who inspires him to go back to playing music: "I consider him to be the best songwriter of life, he is out there, he is awesome, he is my friend for 20 years now, and I would love to play with him one day even if it's two songs." For Bill, it was "someone who came in [to his recording studio] and recorded about six months ago, and something in that recording session inspired me to pick the guitar up." Like others, Bill had a long history of music playing, including being in the official Farm Band during the commune period and writing its music. Later, however, he quit performing as he "was afraid on stage, and I didn't like being so nervous even among my friends." After the recording session with that person, he realized, "Hey, this is fun. And in a way, it's like a security blanket. There's certain peacefulness that I find in playing music still." Since then, he plays quite a bit in his basement. During the COVID-19 pandemic, he even wrote me, "I am happy to just 'shut up and play my guitar' I have been playing more music than I have in probably 40 years!"

Other people leading to more involvement with music could be a random encounter like Bill's client, a friend like Cliff's mate, or other community members, as in the case of James who joined The Farm's drumming circle after moving back to Tennessee: "That usually happens on Saturday nights, and I'm one of the leader drummers because I have more experience than some people do, but often I'm a follower, somebody will set up a rhythm and the others just play with them." During my visit at The Farm, I attended a session of the drumming circle, and indeed James was there along with some other older community members that blended nicely with the group of mainly young drummers.

Family members, too, were mentioned as a reason for more music playing. Gordon, for example, told me that he and his current partner play together: "She's a keyboarder, she's got a Fender Rhodes [piano], and I've got an upright stand-up bass. So, we play old Beatles songs and things like that together." In addition, because his partner recently "hooked up with local hula dancers," he got together with some of the women's spouses, and they became "a band for our dancers." Elizabeth, a piano player and a composer who studied in a most prestigious school of music, shared that "one of the most significant things" in her life is that her entire family plays music: "We have a band, we played for every Ragweed. We just had a big gig in November. And everyone is so good that sometimes we don't even practice; we just talk back and forth via email about what songs we will play." Brian, whose oldest son is a musician, said, "Both he and I are in a little group together, and so we play music. We play for our friends and family. We played at the concerts here on The Farm over the years. We might do it once a week, get together and play music."

The third factor that seemed to enhance involvement in music was "technology." This was relevant for music players and audiences alike. Some of the players use online platforms such as YouTube and Soundcloud to share their music with others. Ben, who only started playing bass guitar "a few years ago because there weren't many bass players around The Farm," said that he was self-taught, but "just a few weeks ago I got a book and a CD and I'm finally trying to learn the proper way." He has also thought about taking bass lessons online because he is "well into utilizing technology."

Information and communication technologies opened new possibilities for music audiences, too. Nicholas mentioned that "everyone's got music on their phone and before that, it was the Sony Walkmans and Discmans and iPods, that all came from the hippie movement." Dennis discussed the internet as a goldmine for music lovers:

> Music motivated me earlier in my life, but in the '60s, there was nowhere to go. You could listen to music, but you didn't know who the people were or the songwriters were and everything else. As I've gotten old, the internet happened, and now, if you want to know about Chicago Blues, you could spend years just studying it on the internet. I like that. Music has always been a part of my life, even though I've never been a musician.

James, who is currently in charge of The Farm's radio station, acknowledged the benefits of technology, too: He can create playlists ahead of time as he "figured out how to cut and paste pieces and put them together." He added that the radio only broadcasts music nowadays: "Fairly positive stuff. Nice, nice, nice music in my ear… and there are people here that listen to it. I'm listening too. I like the variety that it plays a lot."

Some people mentioned getting to know and like various genres of music such as "Americana, bluegrass, folk, just rap, whatever" (Nicholas), "World music" (James, Anna), "Reggae music and Afro-pop" (Gordon). Andrew, who took piano lessons and sang in the Glee club in elementary school, reported renewed interest in classical music: "I've been singing in classical music choruses since 1995, first in San Francisco and now where I live I sing with the county's Bach Choir and am on their board." The majority, however, still like rock-n-roll best.

The only thing that seemed to somewhat decrease with time was the effect of music on people's aspirations. In their descriptions of their youth, many said that music had shaped who they were. Charlotte talked about Joan Baez as her model and noted that her music "redeemed" her, and Chris described The Beatles as his inspiration: "The Beatles made really strong statements about being a good person. Those are my values." Others spoke about how music affected their life course: Sam mentioned that "the music was a scene, you know, and that led me into the hippie days," and Bill said, "Music was what really drove me into that whole [hippie] movement." Bill added that his life-altering decision to move to San Francisco was taken after he "saw a magazine that had a picture of the Grateful Dead and it looked fun and interesting," and Jane shared that it was Bob Dylan who brought her to The Farm: "I would sit in my room and listen to the words over and over and over again every night... And then, I thought, he left the Iron Range and went to New York, so maybe I can too. He inspired me to think differently." Only one person, however, referred to music as an inspiration today. When asked about his plans for the future, Gordon answered:

> I'm going to continue to work on trying to be a better person. I'm really into this streaming music from Africa... and there is one tune that I really like listening to, it's called *Be a better boyfriend*. It's all about that, becoming a better boyfriend. I want to continue working on that to be a better boyfriend for my partner and just continue to try and struggle to try to be a better person.

Apparently, at the age of seventy and over, music is not so much about who you want to become. More commonly, it is a kind reminder of who you were, are, and can still be.

## DIVERSE LEISURE REPERTOIRES

Probing interviewees' involvement in other leisure activities revealed rather diverse leisure repertoires. Involvement depended on interests, health, financial situation, and work status, as individuals who are already retired have more free time. Still, the analysis identified two commonalities among study participants: Social and physical activities seemed to be the most dominant activity types, and two specific activities – taking long walks and gardening – were common to most participants. In addition, several people reported involvement in various forms of serious leisure, to which they dedicated considerable time and efforts and which were central to their identity. Typically, such individuals were less involved in generative and spiritual activities, though these activities could also be regarded as serious leisure.

Leisure activities may be classified according to many dimensions, including formality (formal or informal), interactivity (solitary or social), skills activated (e.g., social, intellectual, creative, physical), location (domestic/out-of-home, indoors/outdoors), content (highbrow or lowbrow), level of commitment, and freedom of choice. Despite the significant variance among study participants, they all reported being highly involved in social leisure, or, as Bill put it, they were all "hardcore 'socialists,' so to speak." Their social leisure included activities that involve interaction with others (e.g., playing games, dancing) or focus on the interaction itself (e.g., having dinner, potluck, or a party with family and friends). Both Farm residents and former residents enjoyed the two types of activities, but there were notable differences among them. First, thanks to their physical proximity, Farm residents reported significantly more unplanned encounters (e.g., "I stopped by their house to return a book and ended up staying for 40 minutes" – Tim). Second, whereas Farm residents typically associated with other community members, former residents usually had wider social circles, as Anna explained:

> We [former residents] have a really strong little community here. This has been an ongoing kind of community of eight families that we were managing for 25 years. And then, because of my previous and current careers, and because of the schools and my kids growing up here, we have a lot of friends just because we've lived here for so long.

Physical activities were also prevalent among study participants, with the most frequently mentioned activities being aerobics (e.g., walking, hiking, biking, swimming) and mat exercises (e.g., yoga, Pilates, stretches). In addition, several interviewees mentioned exercising at a gym or playing ball games (e.g., tennis, basketball). Several also shared that they dance regularly, with the type of dance being very diverse: from square and contra dance through swing, tango, flamenco, and Latin dance to Sufi and ecstatic dance. These activities were described as having numerous physical, social, and mental benefits. However, whereas ball games and dancing were perceived as hobbies, the rest were described as instrumental activities mainly aimed at health-related outcomes. For some, the aim was general health maintenance (e.g., "keep in shape" – Debbie, "self-care" – James, "a longevity program" – Sandra, "you have to, you're getting older and you can't – otherwise your body is going to fall apart" – Harold). For others, the aim was associated with a specific health condition (e.g., back pain, osteoporosis, high blood pressure) that they were trying to manage or prevent deteriorating. Cindy, a cancer survivor, even said: "I don't know if it's just superstitious, but I feel that because I exercise so much, I'm strong and healthy, and that's why I didn't get a recurrence of cancer."

Of the various leisure activities, two were mentioned by most study participants and were usually done daily or almost daily. The first, walking, combined physical and social leisure elements, as many people reported that they take long walks with their partners, friends, and even walking groups. Others, like Jane, mentioned that even when they walk by themselves, they "always manage to see people along the way." In addition, because the walks were typically taken in nature (e.g., parks, forests, around a lake), they were described as "peaceful and meditative" (Charles), "fulfilling, inspirational and kind of uplifting" (Brian). Sarah explained: "I love walking. That's my favorite thing to do. We walk in the woods, and we just get out and have that beautiful view, and, you know, I just love being outside."

Gardening seemed to provide similar physical, social, and emotional benefits. Quite a few described it as an activity that they do with their partner, and those who have a plot in the community garden also reported interacting with others. Being outside, breathing the fresh air, touching the ground, and following the growth process also seemed to have a therapeutic value, as Sarah explained: "If I'm upset about something, I just go out and get involved with the dirt, you know, planting seeds or weeding or whatever needs to be done and I just forget about it." Others even described gardening as a spiritual practice. Gordon explained that it makes him feel at one with nature ("Nature is us. We don't love it, we are it. We were made for it"), and Evelyn stated, "We have a fabulous garden, and the garden is our synagogue, our sanctuary. It's just amazing." Nicholas, who organizes "Organic Gardening Intensive" workshops, added, "I call it [time at the garden] the sanest time of the day because you just can either be meditating or processing or think about processing and just be very present in the here and now with you and the plants."

It should be noted that gardening also has an instrumental purpose as most gardeners reported growing some or most of their food. The variety of fruits and vegetables they produce is quite extensive, leading to great satisfaction with their gardens supporting their nutrition and health (e.g., "I have had lettuce, arugula, collards, and kale all winter, so I always have fresh food or fresh greens" – Jane). Many also mentioned that their gardens provide more than they can consume. Accordingly, they are "constantly canning and freezing" (Karen), "force food on people, you cannot leave without a bag of plums" (Evelyn), and even "sell vegetables at the local store or the market day" (Cindy).

Gardening seems to be an interest shared by the entire Farm community. Related articles are frequently published in the monthly newsletter, and numerous posts, photos, and discussions of various aspects of gardening fill the "Friends of The Farm Tennessee" Facebook group. For some interviewees, however, gardening seems to be more than an interest but rather a form of serious leisure. Joe, for example, said, "Gardening pretty much fills up my life," and Lillian described gardening as "the main source of satisfaction and happiness" in her life. Daniel was portrayed by his spouse as someone who "really got the green thumb, and he loves it. He's just so involved in it. And he'll just come in and go, 'Look at this cabbage.' Just like you know, droll. It's his life."

Charlotte, who together with her partner nurtures "four acres of a permaculture paradise," also explained that for her, gardening is a family tradition: "My parents had gardens. They had a map of their rose garden. My mother grew tomatoes and cucumbers, and when I was somewhere between four and six, I had a little succulent garden... and now I

**6.3** Charlotte's garden. Taking long walks and gardening were common to most study participants.

have a greenhouse, and my granddaughters planted them with me. So, they've just started blooming" (Figure 6.3). In addition to gardening per se, Charlotte described a host of related activities, from sitting quietly in the gardens and feeling "like my closest spiritual connection is nature" to hosting friends for "blackberry-picking potluck parties." She also attends lectures, associates with "other farmers," and even sells "bouquets and flowers for weddings." Trying to explain the significance of the garden to her identity, she mentioned a friend that "toured the gardens and told me, 'your heart and soul are in the garden,' and that really moved me. I felt like I was being seen."

Another activity that could be described as serious leisure in some cases was cooking. Quite a few mentioned that they love cooking and spend a lot of time preparing to cook (e.g., shopping, looking for recipes) and "playing" in the kitchen. Charlotte defined herself as "a kitchen

artist" who has "fun experimenting with vegan mayonnaise or vegan sun-
flower cream or vegan cashew cheesecakes" and sometimes does "some
catering for workshops." Shirley shared that she is "a really good cook,"
who is "certified in a whole-foods, plant-based diet," and that one of her
plans for the future is to offer educational programs for people who
want to learn "about how to eat food that's healthy for your body." As
most study participants were still vegan or vegetarian, most amateur
chefs focused on healthy food. Often, they were also enthused gardeners who grew the food they were cooking. Interestingly, many of them
were men who declared that they "cook quite a bit" (Albert), "cook a lot"
(Cliff), "do all the cooking" (Harold), or act as "the primary cook these
days" (Nicholas). Whereas for these men cooking was usually a relatively
new hobby, some women reported decreased interest. Cindy clarified
this switch in gender roles:

> I'm not as much into cooking as he [spouse] is at this point. I did so
> much cooking when my children were growing up, and he was gone. I was
> cook, cook, cook, cook. Especially after we started living alone, we used to
> share it. But anyway, he enjoys cooking, and I didn't realize how much he
> enjoyed it until he retired.

Lastly, while playing music was the most common art among study
participants, quite a few reported being engaged in other art forms to
the extent that may be considered serious leisure. Some said they were
absorbed in theater (acting, directing) or writing (plays, prose, poems,
haikus), but visual arts and photography specifically were the most popular. Several interviewees described themselves as photographers, and
most of them shared that they mainly take photos in nature. Cliff, for
example, stated that he considers himself a "fine art landscape photogra-
pher." He explained:

> I'm actually trying to develop a style of photography that I call Photographic
> Impressionism. I'm also really into documentary photography of interest-
> ing rural buildings, but what I really am is a naturalist... I have series of
> photographs of trees and flowers. And the last three or four years, a friend
> of mine introduced me to the world of fungus and mushrooms, and now
> I'm photographing them.

Cliff does not only take photographs of fungus and mushrooms, as he added, "I grow them, gather them, and cook them. It is very satisfying. So intact." In this manner, he combines three passions: gardening, cooking, and art. A similar pattern of "interwoven passions" was demonstrated by people who combine hiking and photography as well by Sandra, who defined herself as "a flower freak, a flower child that is totally into flowers." She shared, "I have a wonderful garden of flowers and vegetables... I take many pictures of flowers every year, and I make a calendar of my 12 favorite pictures of flowers. They are like portraits with one for each month." She and Albert, her spouse, print about 150 calendars every year and give them to family, friends, and Albert's clients. By so doing, Sandra expresses her love for art, nature, and the people in her life.

## SUMMARY: MODIFICATIONS IN INVOLVEMENT AND MEANINGFUL PLAY

Although play is typically associated with children's leisure, the hippie movement stressed its power and significance for all human beings in all age groups. Acknowledging the instrumental value of play as a means for meaning making, the hippies also recognized its noninstrumental value as a moral way of living.[12] This ideology could easily be eroded with time and various hardships, but this was not the case for the individuals interviewed for this study. Their ethics of play seemed constant and intact, and leisure appeared to be central to their lives as older adults just as it did in their youth, if not more.

The manner by which they *practiced* the ethics of play was modified to fit their needs, abilities, and current circumstances. These modifications were evident in the central triad of the hippie ethics of play, namely, sex, drugs, and rock-n-roll, as well as in other leisure pursuits. Reporting an overall enduring involvement in most activities, study participants described modifications that varied according to the activity type. In some cases, such as sex and dope, there seemed to be some reduction in intensity. In others, such as music and other arts, gardening, and cooking (for men), involvement only grew with age and primarily upon retirement.

As relatively few talked about sex in their lives at present, one cannot generalize from their reports to the entire group of interviewees nor aging hippies and older adults as a whole. Yet, those who did share information about their sex life today reported decreased sexual activity. The reduction was significantly more evident when dope was discussed. Many quit using psychedelics, and those who still use it reported lower frequency. In addition, while most interviewees said that they still use cannabis and many of them said that they do so on a daily or almost daily basis, they testified that their use is somewhat less intense than it used to be in the past.

The reduced involvement in sex and dope use is consistent with previous research reporting a decline in leisure participation with advancing age. Various constraints, including health-related, psychological (e.g., decreased interest), and social (e.g., lack of partners) conditions, may explain these trends. In gardening, music, and other arts, however, there was considerable stability and even increased involvement. Moreover, some men adopted cooking as a new leisure activity and thus demonstrated innovation in leisure. Such expansions were facilitated by having more time, and in some cases, they were supported by other people and various technologies. Overall, they indicated a balancing mechanism according to which more involvement in some activities compensates for reduced participation in others.

Adjustments were reflected not only in the level of involvement, but also in the *meaning* attributed to the various activities. For some people, sex per se seemed to lose its significance somewhat, and they tended to prioritize friendship and emotional intimacy over physical pleasures. Although its social component remained stable, the spiritual meaning of dope dramatically decreased. Instead, it became a means for maintaining and even enhancing physical and psychological health. Rock, too, demonstrated some change in meaning. While it was still the most preferred genre and served as a means of self-expression, it no longer acted as a factor affecting people's aspirations.

The significance of walking and gardening – the two most common activities among study participants – seemed obvious. Still, in addition to their explicit physical, social, and uplifting benefits, they appeared to contribute to a sense of continuity. The love for nature and the wish to go back to the land were central to the hippie ethics of cultural opposition. They were also among the main motivations that study participants mentioned when they talked about joining The Farm commune in the 1970s. Living in a rural area and establishing an agricultural community that grows food on the land and exhibits self-sufficiency were dominant in the alternative posed by the commune to the mainstream way of life. Accordingly, by maintaining this lifestyle at least to some extent, study participants were still posing an alternative to mainstream society whether they still lived at The Farm or had left it decades ago. Consequently, they also preserved their hippie identity.

Walking and gardening were often complemented by cooking, which some study participants perceived as a leisure activity in itself. For some people, cooking was an enduring pursuit, and for others, it was a relatively new interest. Yet, the fact that most of them focused on vegan or vegetarian food suggests that cooking, too, contributed to the sense of continuity. Cooking supported the cooks and their families' lifelong diet and allowed them to keep manifesting the hippie admiration for nature and the natural. In addition, just like music and other arts, cooking enabled the expression of one's creativity.

The continuity of the ethics of play, in general, and of activities that maintained participants' identity, in particular, are consistent with previous research demonstrating a tendency for continuity in leisure in later life. Still, the present study emphasizes the importance of combining continuity and change. Allowing for modifications in both intensity and meaning may result in a leisure repertoire that better fits the older individual's interests and circumstances. This combination, along with (1) the dominance of physical and social activities that have a well-documented impact on wellbeing in later life,[13] and (2) the many "serious" leisure activities that are known to have significant psychological rewards,[14] suggest that to some extent, aging hippies can be a model for people who want to make the most of their later years.

# CHAPTER 7

# The Aging of the New Agers

S PIRITUALITY IS AN ELUSIVE, COMPLEX, highly subjective
concept, and one that is difficult to measure. Although many
confound it with religiosity, these somewhat overlapping concepts are not identical. Religion is a system of ideas or ideological beliefs
and commitments with external, institutionalized, formal, and doctrinal
aspects. Whereas spirituality may refer to individuals' subjective religious
experience, it can also be something that people define for themselves
that is free of the rules, regulations, and responsibilities associated with
religiosity.[1] Accordingly, it is often described in terms of relationship and
connectedness with self, others, nature, and a higher being.[2]

Although the hippies cannot be regarded as a homogeneous group,
many of them believed that spiritual awakening is essential to forming a
new and better world. Their search for spiritual development involved
the exploration and embracing of Native American and Eastern religions
and mysticism, and extensive use of dope, which was regarded as key to
spiritual insights. The outcomes of this quest were reflected in the hippie
ideology, which was highly associated with all domains of spirituality.[3]
This link may explain why popular culture's description of the hippie
movement's new way of thinking often uses the expression "The age of
Aquarius" – an astrological term referring to an era in which humanity
undergoes a revelation of truth and expansion of consciousness, popularized by the 1967 musical *Hair*.

Studies have shown that spirituality tends to grow during later adulthood.[4] Whereas human development theories provide different explanations for this tendency,[5] scholars agree that spirituality contributes
significantly to wellbeing in later life. The positive influence of older

adults' participation in spiritual activities and groups is expressed as reinforced faith, a greater sense of purpose and meaning in life, spiritual and tangible support, positive thinking, improved emotional wellbeing, more satisfaction with life, less depression, and more social capital that strengthens them physically, psychologically, and spiritually.[6]

Considering the human tendency for continuity,[7] one may assume that aging hippies have preserved some, if not all, aspects of spirituality they adopted in their youth and early adult life. Yet, as many of them were persistent seekers, they may have kept questioning everything, including their existing attitudes and beliefs, and consequently experienced various changes in spirituality during their life course. Such changes might include greater interest in spiritual issues as well as spiritual extension and development. However, it is just as probable that their aging involved disillusionment and even rejection of some spiritual tenets. Because The Farm was formed as a utopian spiritual commune, it is an ideal springboard for a study on continuity and change in aging hippies' spirituality. This chapter thus explores the spiritual journeys of the community's founding members from early adulthood to the present day.

## SPIRITUAL AWAKENING

Most of The Farm's founding members came from white, middle-class families that lived in suburban areas and exhibited rather conformist lifestyles. Typically, their families belonged to a specific church or synagogue (25–30 percent were Jewish – a surprisingly high rate given that Jews constituted only 2.5 percent of the U.S. population in the early 1970s). Regardless of their faith, however, most members came from nonconservative families, and their religious affiliation was often more social than religious (Figure 7.1), as Roger commented: "We were not really religious. Not unreligious, but not religious. We went to the temple on the High Holy Days. I went to the temple other times during the year for Shabbat and things like that. But not really religious, just a little bit."

Many study participants shared that they felt pretty estranged from their original families' religious orientation at some point in early adolescence. Some reported experimenting with other religions, such as

**7.1** A Jewish ornament outside a couple of study participants' home. Although most Farm members are not religious, they still identify somewhat with their religious roots.

Joe, who did a social studies project on Hinduism in the ninth grade, and "decided right away that I was a Hindu." The majority, however, simply realized that "Oh, this is not going to work for me. No, no, no, no, no" (Anna). The reasons for estrangement varied and included both internalization and radicalization of parents' attitudes ("My father would purposely eat bread during Passover" – Chris) and teenage rebellion ("I decided that whatever religion they [mother and stepfather] were? I wasn't!" – Shirley). Some noted that religion "really never struck me as important" (Dennis), "the whole idea of a personal god didn't really make much sense to me" (Andrew), "the whole guilt thing… it was like, 'Uh, I just can't buy that'" (Julia), and "it [religiosity] was less fun and uplifting than it would have, could have, should have been" (Albert). In addition, for some of the younger participants, who were teenagers when the Vietnam War started, hostility to formal religion came from social criticism, as Jerry said:

> All these teachings from the Church were "love thy neighbor as thyself and if somebody does you harm, turn the other cheek," and things didn't add up because young guys were being sent off to war and dying – Why? What for? Who's this about? Why don't we love our neighbors? And why don't we have a better way to figure out this conflict? So, I was really pushed away from the Church, and I knew there was a problem with it in terms of the way we were living our lives.

Most study participants testified that the spiritual void caused by rejecting religion triggered a long journey of seeking an alternative. For some of them, the journey started in high school. For others, it began in college (or in Vietnam) and even later. Regardless of the exact age and circumstances, the search typically involved three components: dope, books, and teachers. The order of the three elements varied. Sometimes the journey began with taking classes ("As soon as I became a freshman in college, I started enrolling in Eastern religion and philosophy classes" – Anna) and in others, it began with reading ("At 18, I started reading some of the wisdom texts of the 'I Ching' [ancient Chinese book]. This book was my earliest spiritual teacher" – Laura) or with dope use ("As my consciousness loosened up and expanded, I developed an interest in philosophy, religion, certain things that I hadn't really thought about much before" – Paul).

Although each personal journey was distinct, many of them intersected because of the extensive word-of-mouth information being shared among young people in the late 1960s. Andrew's interest in Hinduism, for example, was sparked when a friend told him that "he was a student of Baba Ram Dass[8]... and not too long after that, Baba Ram Dass was giving a series of lectures at the Unitarian Church in San Francisco. So, I went to that, and it blew my mind." Similarly, Paul's exploration of Eastern philosophy and LSD was initiated when a couple of friends invited him to join them for a lecture by Dr. Timothy Leary in Berkeley: "And basically what he did was connect the life of the Buddha to the evolution of a person's consciousness, and of course he mapped it to, you know, taking LSD."

Overall, the various personal journeys shared the feature of being part of a more general trend that was common to many, as Joe summarized it: "There was a whole spiritual renaissance going on, in which the drug culture and the spiritual culture to a certain degree overlapped." Bringing much excitement and a sense of growth, however, the abundance of texts, teachers, and experiences also yielded considerable confusion. Their search for something or someone, who would organize the flood of spiritual information and approaches, led study participants residing in San Francisco at the time to Gaskin's Monday night classes, following which they founded The Farm. Others, who joined The Farm a little later, explained that the commune being a spiritual community was one of its main attractions.

## THE COMMUNE MILESTONE: A SPIRITUAL COMMUNITY OR NEW AGE CULT?

The commune period was a milestone common to all spiritual journeys explored in this study. Formed in the meetings in San Francisco and refined during the Caravan, the commune's spiritual philosophy reflected the attempts of Gaskin and his "students" (as they called themselves) to make meaning of their psychedelic experiences and identify the "essential truths" that are common to all religions. Described in the two books of Gaskin's transcribed talks (*Monday night class* and *The Caravan*), the preliminary philosophy kept evolving throughout the commune period. Anna explained:

> Living there was an intensive learning experience on so many different levels. We were working it out moment by moment, day by day, in relationships, having children, delivering babies, building a town, running a town – and so, there was so much variety of how you could learn. There were also the weekly services where Steven would have a topic and just sort of pontificate about, and all these books that we were reading together. It was like a big giant book club.

Although the commune's spiritual philosophy continuously developed, it had three stable qualities that should be understood: *eclecticism, pluralism,* and *performance*. Its tenets (see Chapter 3) were not new ideas but rather an *eclectic* collection of basic understandings shared by all religions and viewed with a modern perspective. Traugot[9] exemplified this eclecticism by discussing one of the central tenets: "attention equals energy," along with its corollary, "what you pay attention to, you get more of." This belief was rooted in the Christian principle, "As ye sow, so shall ye reap," just as it corresponded with the Buddhist idea that people "create their own karma." Similarly, Tim explained that the aspiration to make the world a better place originated in the "Jewish people who have the 'Tikkun Olam,' you know, repair of the world." Debbie noted that the vow of poverty taken by all commune members was inspired by the detachment principle promoted in various Eastern religions: "The material plane comes and goes, and you don't want to be attached to the material plane."

The Farm commune had a structured set of "agreements" and "sacraments" that resembled the rules and services associated with religiosity. Yet, its spiritual philosophy was generally secular and pretty *pluralistic*. It legitimized any means that might help one be in touch with the "higher self" – an inner self that "knows what's right and what's wrong, what's going on, that knows it is part of something bigger,"[10] for example, being in nature (Figure 7.2). Completely splitting spirituality from traditional religiosity, commune members could hold and practice any faith and were generally not obliged to exercise any ritual they did not feel comfortable with, as Sam explained:

> You could be any denomination. You could follow Jesus or Ram Dass or Steven or nobody. I pretty much had my own philosophy, which I called "the Boy Scout motto." Yeah, honor, tell the truth, be fair, consistent, you know. Those were my life goals, and they weren't associated with the Sufis or Ram Dass. So, if you want to go to Sufi dancing, I would give you a ride there, but I wouldn't go in with you, or if you wanted to meditate and I may go to another room and play my guitar.

The Farm's spirituality was also more *performative* than philosophical, or, as Albert described it, "an eclectic combination of world religions applied to a practical situation." In the *40 Years on The Farm* documentary, one interviewee even stated, "What was being built here was the vision of the Aquarian age that was seen in Haight-Ashbury and put into actual

**7.2** The Farm has numerous sites where one can relax, reflect, and admire nature.

practice." Chris explained that unlike other spiritual communes, "where the first thing they do every morning is get up and meditate together... The Farm was more work-driven," and there was never enough time to "sit around when the kids are up, and there is so much work to do." He admitted that if he could have done it all over again, he would have wanted the commune to be more like other spiritual communes because "things could have maybe turned out differently." Similarly, Laura shared that she thought The Farm "became more of a 'look at us,' and got away from 'looking within' which is the only [spiritual] way. If I don't look within, I could be serving soup at the soup kitchen every day, and what's that going to do?"

Most members, however, found the commune's performative spirituality very appealing. Shirley, for example, said, "I always felt that activism to improve our country and spirituality were the very exact same thing, so I was attracted to that very much. There was some of my religiosity that I really felt was real." Harold clarified, "We used to say 'well, our work is our meditation, we have to learn how to work and be in good spirit and not get angry with each other.' We tried to practice our spiritual practices. Those were good things to learn." Anna added, "To be able to put our values into practice rather than just have them be theory was really exhilarating. In a group with so many different kinds of projects needed and so many different kinds of people doing pieces of it, it was just so fun!"

The qualities of eclecticism, pluralism, and performance and its spiritual tenets suggest that the commune's philosophy could be described as "New Age" thinking even though this term was hardly used in the late 1960s and early 1970s. New Age is an "umbrella term that includes a great variety of groups and identities" that share an "expectation of a major and universal change being primarily founded on the individual and collective development of human potential."[11] The New Age pursues a transcendent metaphysical reality. It is innovative because it does not follow a particular tradition or traditions but rather borrows eclectically from them. Unlike traditional religions, which are embedded in collective symbolism, the New Age emphasizes the principle of self-spirituality according to which one's experiences are the primary source of authority on spiritual matters, and personal growth is key to individual and collective development.[12] Manifesting a complex of spiritualities that emerges on the foundation of a pluralistic, secular society, New Age can be viewed as "secular religion."[13]

Despite its eclecticism and individualistic approach to spirituality, the New Age literature displays recurrent themes.[14] The most notable is the belief in divinity, namely, in something that is beyond the human level that may be described as a universal force or energy that consists of love and wisdom (often termed "mind," "consciousness," and "intelligence"). Intentional spiritual development may allow one to recognize and understand divinity, at least to some extent. In addition, because of the relationship between the human body *and* mind, individuals' spiritual development enables self-healing. It may even support the healing of others and the universe as a whole.

The Farm's spiritual philosophy was characterized by the eclecticism and individualism of New Age spirituality and corresponded with many of its central themes. The idea that we are all one and part of the universe, and the concept of different levels of consciousness, suggest a belief in divinity. Similarly, the basis for spiritual midwifery, for which The Farm is known to this day, is that the human body and mind are connected. Thus, considerable attention should be given to the emotional and spiritual aspects of giving birth. In addition, the belief that by setting an example, supporting people and communities in need, and protecting the environment, one can change the world is closely linked to the New Age expectation that universal change can occur thanks to individual and collective efforts.

Although the commune was pluralistic and viewed anything that helps us connect with our higher self as legitimate and blessed, it did not tolerate violation of the various sacraments (e.g., birth, marriage) and agreements (e.g., not harming the land, living in a voluntary peasantry, following a vegan diet, no smoking, no drinking, no psychedelics, no political involvement, no violence, no negativity, being honest and fair and compassionate with each other, all conflicts should be discussed and sorted). These strict institutionalized and doctrinal aspects made the commune an unusual phenomenon. Like other New Age streams, it was indeed a secular religion. Yet, its structure and behaviors were extraordinary, leading to a somewhat common perception of The Farm as a cult.

When I first met Cindy and invited her to participate in my study on aging, she asked me, "So, do you think we are a cult?" Her truly unexpected question made me realize how bothered commune members were and still are with the negative perception of The Farm as a cult. In addition, it clarified how unresolved this matter is. Although the cult-like qualities of The Farm commune have been discussed in numerous articles, memoirs, and interviews, it is hard to determine whether it was indeed a cult. Acknowledging that there was "a cult of personality in and around Stephen" (Cliff), most study participants did not regard the commune as a cult. Yet, Stephanie admitted that the "realization that it was a cult to get out of" was among the reasons that made her leave the commune, and Melvyn Stiriss, who wrote a memoir on The Farm, said in a recent interview,[15] "Hell yeah! Stephen was indeed a charismatic cult leader, and The Farm was a cult – a benign cult, nevertheless a cult."

Deciding whether the commune was a cult depends on the definition used. Applying the *Cambridge Dictionary*[16] definition, which states that a cult is "a religious group, often living together, whose ideas are considered extreme or strange by many people," might lead to a "Hell yeah!" announcement. Yet, using more complex definitions may yield an opposite or at least indecisive conclusion. The Cult Research and Information Center presents a list of over thirty characteristics associated with cults.[17] Some of these features clearly correlate with The Farm in its commune days, for example, excessive zealotry regarding the group's ideology and practices, the devotion of inordinate amounts of time, energy, and money to the group and its activities, charismatic leadership that functions as the ultimate authority and spokesman, efforts to bring new members, and even the application of mind-altering practices. Yet, there is no evidence in The Farm's history nor the study participants' testimonials to many other characteristics associated with cults, such as cutting ties with family and friends and associating with other group members only, participating in behaviors or activities considered reprehensible or unethical before joining the group, isolating members and penalizing them for leaving, and exempting the leader from accountability to the authorities (reminder: Gaskin went to prison when the police discovered that the commune was growing marijuana).

Some of the characteristics described by the Cult Research and Information Center are harder to associate or dissociate from The Farm commune, such as the polarized, us-versus-them mentality. Although "Gaskin said that everybody that has a belly button is our religion, which meant it includes everyone" (Shirley), the fact that the commune aspired to set an example to the world suggests that it perceived itself as distinct. Likewise, although questioning, doubt, and criticism were supposedly welcome, study participants' reports indicated that Gaskin was not always open to criticism, especially if it concerned his behavior.

Considering all of the above, it seems that Cindy's question cannot be addressed with a simple "yes" or "no" answer. The distinction between spiritual community and cult does not seem to be dichotomous. Instead, it can be viewed as a continuum, and The Farm in its commune days may be perceived as located somewhere along that scale. Exhibiting some of the qualities associated with cults, the commune was still pluralistic, inclusive, and full of good intentions. It can thus be regarded as a New Age community with some cultic components, or simply, as Stiriss described it – "a benign cult."

## FOUR TYPES OF POST-COMMUNE SPIRITUAL PATHS

Probing study participants' spiritual paths as they evolved after the commune era to this day revealed considerable heterogeneity. Nevertheless, participants could generally be divided into four groups that were of approximately the same size. The first is the group of people who, over time, became "somewhat less spiritual" and significantly less involved in previous spiritual activities. People in this group were typically not too high on the hippie spiritual dimension (see Chapter 4) to begin with. The spiritual aspect was relatively marginal in their decision to join The Farm in comparison to their fondness for the people and their wish to live close to the land. In addition, their participation in the commune's spiritual activities – the Sunday services in particular – seemed more social than spiritual. To some extent, therefore, they replicated in The Farm the very same patterns their original families demonstrated in their communities.

This less spiritual group included people with a pretty neutral, live-and-let-live attitude to spirituality, like Sam, who, as mentioned, had a personal spiritual philosophy (the Boy Scout motto), and Sarah, who noted "I went to church when I was a kid, and when I came here I went to the Sunday services, but now I'm just not motivated to meditate and the like... I'm a super peaceful, mellow, and chilled person anyway." However, some people in this group seemed to become quite skeptical and even critical of spirituality as a whole. Julia, for example, said that "anything that tells me that I need to know all those technical levels and sayings and writings and stuff, I'm like, 'No.'" Paul expanded:

> I'm pretty much an atheist now. I believe that God is a conceptual construct made by early males to dominate the female power in nature. So, when someone says that a beautiful sunset is God's beautiful artwork, I say, "no, that's nature's beautiful artwork." My spirituality is not really connected with much of anybody else. I really stay away from the "magical" things. I tell people I belong to the church of reality now. If it's real, we believe it.

The most cynical individuals in this group rejected the term "spiritual" altogether, as Rebecca explained, "I reverted from calling things 'spirituality' to saying, 'Well, I don't know if I want to put that name on it' because I'm an atheist. I don't use that word in defining things." Nevertheless, many still reported beliefs and practices that could be described as spiritual. Paul said, "I love Jesus as much as the next person, probably more than a lot of people, but organized Christianity is not anything I want to have anything to do with." Joe stated, "I'm interested in spirituality. I just depart from the other people when they latch on to some dogma like Kabbalah and numerology. To me, that's all just gobbledygook." Julia added, "I sit here, I look at you, and I look at the meadow outside my window every day, and that's my peaceful place, my holy place. And walking in the woods and keeping my mind empty of a lot of clutter. To me, that's my spiritual things."

The second group, which I labeled "forever Farmies," included those who, to a great extent, preserved the commune's spiritual beliefs and practices. In addition to speaking "a certain language of spirituality and energy and vibes and healings and that kind of stuff" (Gordon), individuals in this group still practiced many or most of The Farm "agreements," be it the vegan diet, the care for the environment, the attempt to change the world, or the avoidance of certain substances. Their lifelong spiritual view was often expressed without any solicitation from my side. Elizabeth, for example, demonstrated the "no negativity" agreement in her answer to my question about current reasons for worries and concerns: "Worry does not do anything except put negative energy into things, so that's not a good practice. I don't worry because I don't want to put that negative energy into the world. It's very important, especially now in the hard times that are happening on this planet, to put positive energy out all the time." Similarly, Henry disclosed his identification with The Farm's philosophy when he quoted a neighbor from whom The Swan Trust was trying to buy land: "He said, 'I'm a Christian, and you all are pagans... I believe God put everything here for us, and you believe that God is in everything and that there's a web of life and God is in all of that.' That's where we vary, and we couldn't argue with him."

The third group was very similar to the first in its adherence to the commune's spiritual philosophy. However, its members' involvement in previous spiritual activities increased with age, and many of them kept exploring and adopting new beliefs and practices. People in this group thus appeared to be "perpetual seekers." Joe, for example, shared that after completing his medical residency, he joined the Quaker Church and attended their meetings for about ten years. Then he "got into ecstatic dancing, which is kind of a spiritual, meditative dance, and I still do that, and I DJ some of the ecstatic dances." Anna adopted ecstatic dancing too and still does it three times a week. She also became involved in earthing, which is "what the Japanese call forest bathing, going and finding lands to lie on the ground... because we have so many natural resources here, it's just great for that." Chris shared that a Sufi spiritual teacher has "given me a set of prayer beads and a set of prayers that I do for 15 to 20 minutes every morning, right after I get up, to clean myself up." Sandra developed an interest in alternative medicine, and particularly in "hypnotherapy that included a script for a past life regression, and altered states of consciousness, and doing therapy in intentional relaxation." She became a certified hypnotherapist and "found that it was a skill and a calling for me... so I did that for many years and loved it." Similarly, Charles developed an interest in astrology: "There's some online chart software that you can use, and then the interpretation is up to me, although I use books for guidance. I've done many people's charts and done the reading for them, and that's kind of fun" (Figure 7.3).

The ongoing eclecticism resulted in pretty diverse personal repertoires of spiritual practices, which took an increasing share of participants' time. Despite the great diversity, they all reported more involvement in some type of meditation. Stating that during the commune era, they "didn't have a regular meditation practice except for the Sunday service" (Daniel), and even then, "Stephen would kind of overrun it with his personality" (Charles), everyone in this group said that now they meditate regularly by themselves or with a meditation group. Another communality was their openness and willingness to learn from a variety of sources and teachers. Yet, this group seemed to become pretty suspicious about overly charismatic leaders, as Lillian's story may exemplify:

We got involved with a man who was a roadman for the Native American Church, and we brought it to our community [in California]. We really liked it. It was really beautiful, and it was hard work because you have to

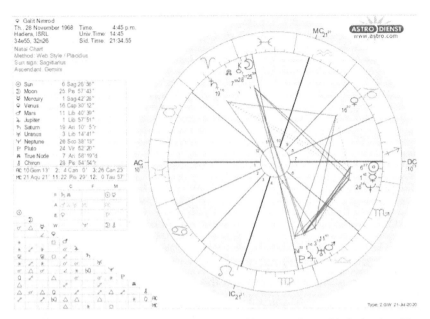

**7.3** When the moon is in the Eleventh House, and Mercury aligns with Sagittarius. The author's astrological chart created by Charles.

sit up in a teepee all night and drink this awful-tasting medicine [peyote]. And you would see yourself and the patterns of your thoughts. Anyway, several people of the [Farm] community got together with this. But then, the roadman had shortcomings, and this is like with women, you know, the same as Stephen. And so, when people saw that, it was like, "Oh, no. We don't want this. No way."

Interested in spiritual development but demonstrating greater caution, people in this group prefer to participate in spiritual activities guided by their peers. Accordingly, most current spiritual activities in The Farm are organized by the residents, and many former residents who live in California take part in activities directed by one of them. Some of them, for example, participate every week in a Zen meditation group led by someone who "had been on The Farm for a short time, and then left to join the San Francisco Zen Center and became a teacher himself" (Lillian). As many as 160 former and current residents are part of The Farm praying circle managed by Sandra, who said:

It's a wonderful, sweet, kind-hearted email group that prays for anyone who gives us permission to pray for them. There's chatter on that on a daily basis. Mostly, we send people love in all our different manners of doing so… you could line them up for blocks, the people who have been directly affected [by the prayers], so if someone is sick or whatever they write and ask us to pray for them. It's a beautiful thing. It really is. I love it very much.

The fourth group consisted of individuals whose involvement in spiritual activities significantly increased with age. Like the third group, many of them kept exploring and adopting new beliefs and practices throughout their lives. However, they differed from the perpetual seekers because they seemed to be done with seeking. In other words, they felt they had found the one path that was optimal for them. Their spiritual paths thus departed from the New Age eclecticism and represented a most "focused spirituality." Although spirituality was very significant to many study participants, individuals in this group also differed by making their chosen spiritual practice the most dominant component in their lives. The significance of these practices was reflected in the amount of time dedicated to them and their centrality in these individuals' identities.

FOCUSED SPIRITUALITY: SELECTION AND DISCOVERY The group exhibiting focused spirituality consisted of two subgroups. The people in the first subgroup demonstrated a high level of "spiritual selectivity" by making one aspect of its previous eclectic spirituality the center of their life and abandoning most or all other aspects. The people in the second subgroup, however, exhibited "spiritual discovery" by turning a new spiritual path, encountered and adopted relatively late in life, into their main practice. Six examples are provided to clarify the significance of the chosen spiritual path to the identity and daily life of people in these subgroups. The first three represent spiritual selectivity and the latter three exemplify spiritual discovery.

HAROLD'S CHOICE – BUDDHISM When I asked Harold about the primary sources of satisfaction in his life, he first talked about the joy of grandparenting and then moved on to discuss meditation and clarified,

"I got a lot of satisfaction out of that." At this point in the interview, it was clear that by "meditation," Harold referred to his lifelong interest in Buddhism, which was sparked even before joining The Farm ("I was doing yoga and meditation in my 20s, and then when I got to The Farm, you know, there was no time") but became the center of his life after early retirement at around the age of fifty.

Harold's daily routine nowadays includes practicing yoga and meditating for "anywhere from an hour and a half to two hours, sometimes three hours, but usually around one to three p.m. is my meditation period." After that, he typically spends some time reading "literature and philosophy and spiritual things." Explaining that "going back to formal meditation" was very important to him, Harold clarified that he follows the traditional Buddhist seven aids to awakening, of which Samādhi meditation is a significant component:

> You can focus, and you can expand. That's what Samādhi meditation is all about. You try to reach the point of no awareness of yourself or anybody else... and you can get into the state of absorption called Dhyāna. When you get to that level, you can bring the thought of someone else into your meditation and – they have these practices called the Metta practice in which you send these people love, so it becomes an inclusive kind of meditation. The passionate part of it is that you gain what they call "momentary awareness" and become aware all the way down to the atomic level. You can see how all life and everything is made up of atoms and cells and how we're all just part of this incredible flow of energy.

Although Buddhism to Harold is "like coming home in a real deep way," he noted that "it takes a lot of courage to face life" and that "learning how to take control of your mind" is a gradual and probably endless process: "I'm still growing. Yes, I'm still trying to pull some weeds out. I'm working on it." He added that the more he meditates, the more meaningful meditation becomes "because you go deeper and understand things in new ways and realize what's real and what's not," and that "there are things that you can easily change just by not worrying about them." In addition, he stressed the significance of meditation in old age:

Because we're all going to die, and you want to be prepared for that. I think it's important to prepare yourself for that in some way, even though you don't have any idea about when it's going to happen or what's going to be. It's good to have some sense of how to overcome fear and how to overcome these prejudices that we carry with us from our conditioning.

Harold's spiritual practices are usually solitary, but he often discusses his "meditation and stuff that I am experiencing" with another former resident of The Farm, who "has been meditating solidly every day for 50 years" and even teaches Samādhi meditation ("He's actually 10 years younger than I am, but he's my Dharma [right livelihood] teacher"). Harold also did "some retreats with people here who have spent a lot of time studying with meditation Masters in Southeast Asia." Moreover, he tried "to encourage young people to meditate, but they don't listen to me. Nobody wants to do these things, but, you know, maybe one day they will."

SHIRLEY'S CHOICE – ZEN As a young woman who moved to San Francisco in 1969, Shirley "tried all different types of classes and whatnot," from Kundalini yoga to Gestalt psychotherapy classes. She also visited the San Francisco Zen Center once, but "it was just too weird." Later, however, when Zen was brought up at a Monday night class, she "bought and read the book by Suzuki Roshi[18] and found that to be the most interesting philosophy that I'd ever, ever come across." In 1974, after living at The Farm for three years, she moved back to California and spent two years in a Zen monastery. Describing the strict monastic schedule that fully followed "the monastics in Japan, except it's women and men," Shirley referred to this period as life altering: "I went to the monastery with the belief that there was something wrong with me, and left it much more stable. I figured out that the only thing wrong with me was that I thought there was something wrong with me."

Ready to "start from scratch again," Shirley moved back to The Farm but eventually left in 1980, when she was already a single mother of one, because "The Farm was so poor then and I found myself walking in the woods looking for something to eat." She spent most of her adult life in Florida, where she completed her academic education, developed a successful career, and married twice. During these years, she "did some meditation but not regularly" and "went to some other meditation groups," but it was "nothing like the Zen monastery at all." In 2007, after a painful divorce from her second spouse, she thought she "could really use going back to Zen meditation." At about the same time, she was "asked about a Zen Master to start the Zen center," so she decided to take action.

Soon after that, Shirley bought "$3,000 worth of meditation cushions" and found a place in her town where she guided Zazen (Zen meditation) sessions every Sunday morning. When she moved back to The Farm in 2018, she designed the second floor of her house as a Zendō (meditation hall). She currently guides Zazen sessions at her place every Sunday morning and plans to offer evening sessions. Sharing that she is "hooked up" again with the "incredible people that run the San Francisco Zen Center," she clarified:

> The practice that I teach is not something that we go around telling people about. People have to get interested and come to it on their own and for themselves, because it's not about I'm going to tell you, it's about you're going to tell you. I don't want to sound arrogant about it, but I find the Zen really sophisticated because it's not about talking. It's about understanding yourself and trying to see those things about yourself that you can make better.

As I had never practiced Zazen before, I asked Shirley to join the next Sunday meditation. A few minutes before 8:00 a.m., I was at her door along with several older adults and two tattooed young persons, ready to experience a two-hour session that I later described in my journal as "real torture." Most of the meditation time was spent sitting on a cushion on the floor, in a position that caused my back and knees to hurt badly. In addition, I could not let go of the million thoughts I had and quit the "observer" position – a particularly frustrating state because we were facing the wall and closed our eyes, so there was nothing to observe. At the end of the session, when Shirley held a short discussion on the idea of "be a lamp onto yourself," I felt like a complete failure. Yet, when she read a beautiful short story about the different ways to accommodate the sounds of early morning rain, I felt the pain was worth it.

## EVELYN'S CHOICE – JUDAISM

Although most study participants do not consider themselves religious, they still express some identification with their religious roots. Whereas the ones who were Christian only occasionally mentioned God and Jesus, study participants of Jewish origin used related terminology and references quite often. Assuming that this tendency resulted from the fact that they knew that I am Israeli, I first regarded Evelyn's frequent mentions of Judaism as a form of bonding. Only at a later phase of the interview did I realize that Judaism was much more than a social lubricant in her case. It was her chosen spiritual path.

Just like me, Evelyn was born to a secular Jewish family. This may explain why her parents were shocked when she wanted to have a Bat Mitzvah:[19]

> I was raised very, you know, reformed of reformed. My family just gave it [Judaism] up. When I found out in 1963 that boys got $5,000 and girls got powder and nightgowns for Bar Mitzvah, you know what I did? I actually did that. It freaked my parents out, but in later life, they were like, "Oh, she was cool." They loved it.

Having a Bat Mitzvah triggered Evelyn's interest in Judaism and other religions and spiritual practices, including Buddhism, Hinduism, and Native American ceremonies. This interest could explain why Evelyn joined The Farm. Still, she stressed that for her, the main attraction was the commune's similarity to the Israeli Kibbutz ("I wanted to go to Israel, but I couldn't go where there is war"). The years Evelyn spent at The Farm were a period in which she "stuffed it [Judaism] down." She explained that "although there were a lot of Jews, it really wasn't celebrated," and added that she thought that Gaskin was "fairly anti-Israel in some things that he said to me when I asked him about it." Yet, she mentioned that it was actually Gaskin who taught her about the Baal Shem Tov,[20] and "it was like – you know, it really awakened something in my soul."

Many years after she left The Farm, when she was practicing medicine in a "Berkeleyish kind of town in California with a huge Jewish community," Evelyn "fell into Jewish renewal" and became fully devoted to Judaism. The change started while attending a communal candle lighting:

I lit a candle, and I prayed, and I was just blown away. I just felt like I came home. Aryeh Hirshfield [rabbi and musician] was there, and that was an instant rabbi love affair. He was my rabbi, and I was his doctor, and it was just incredible. I loved that I could bring the Buddhist practices that I treasured, and we were doing Sufi Dances of Universal Peace in Hebrew. I felt welcomed in that way. It was very different from the Aquarian minyan [quorum] – the hippies in Berkeley and San Francisco that were doing acid for Shabbat. Back then, I didn't really get any of that.

Today Evelyn lives in a remote place where she is "the only Jew doing Shabbat." Her current partner, however, shares her passion for Judaism: "He wasn't raised Jewish, but I think he has a Jewish soul... he's more into it than I am." Evelyn is also convinced that she spent her past life in Auschwitz ("It's a cool story I'd love to share with you some time") but states that she and her partner are still relatively liberal: "The orthodox in Israel would tell us we're full of shit, but to us, it's very powerful."

## NICHOLAS'S DISCOVERY – DANCE OF UNIVERSAL PEACE

Because Nicholas defines himself as a "lifelong spiritual seeker," it seems accurate to place him in the group of perpetual seekers. This classification may be supported by the fact that, for over twenty years, he has been organizing spiritual retreats aimed at "allowing people to open up within and see what type of guidance they can come up with on their own." His current project also implies an ongoing search:

I am interested in spiritual knowledge and truths, and since I am an author, I am interested in possibly developing a book that would be a handbook for sanity... so I created this Facebook group to talk about essential truths that all faiths and practices around the world shared... and then I transfer those discussions to a website. If I get enough into the website, where it's been edited and organized, then that will be transferred into possibly a book. That's just kind of personal interest.

Yet, an in-depth examination of his interview transcript and the texts he posts on various digital media suggests that Nicholas recently found a new practice that quickly became the center of his spiritual life. This pattern associates him with the group that exhibits focused spirituality.

Nicholas's new passion started about three years before we met. Looking for new ways to express himself musically, he discovered Kirtan[21] and started doing that at The Farm. Following a friend's advice, he realized that he could add dance to the singing and used YouTube to learn about the Dance of Universal Peace (DUP) – a spiritual practice of North American Sufi origin that employs singing and dancing to raise consciousness and promote peace. Soon after that, he "started going to other locations where people were doing the dances so that I could do them with people who were experienced, and it's just grown from there."

Today, Nicholas leads DUP sessions at The Farm twice a week and offers DUP workshops to the attendees of The Farm's spiritual retreats, as well as retreats fully dedicated to DUP. He also occasionally guides DUP sessions in remote locations such as Chattanooga and Atlanta and regularly travels to DUP events in the U.S. and abroad:

> There is a dance in Missouri every May and October. I have gone to that four times in a row. The one in Mexico is in February, so I have gone there three times. When I started, I went out west to a weeklong camp to get more in tune and trained. And then, the opportunity came to go to Turkey for a three-week dance leader training event, so I did that last September, and now I am just looking where I can go next.

The DUP events provide Nicholas with two complementary benefits. First, they enable enrichment of the dance repertoire and improvement of skills ("And then my wife and I come back and critique how I did, what worked, and what we could do better. There is still room for improvement"). Second, they allow interaction with other people who share his passion for DUP – individuals Nicholas describes as "my Sufi tribe" with whom he keeps in touch regularly via social media. Therefore, it seems that Nicholas's new spiritual path has a vital social component, both within and outside The Farm community. In addition, as his partner commented, it allows him to put into practice his natural leadership skills: "He pretty much started leading from day one."

JOAN'S DISCOVERY – NAHUA WEATHER WORKING AND HUICHOL HEALING Parallel to managing a big business and having a pretty busy life, Joan was always a spiritual seeker. In the late 1990s, however, her continuous searches proved fruitful and demonstrated the accuracy of the phrase "seek and ye shall find" (Matthew 7:7). Her studies of shamanism and mysticism led her to take classes in Plant Spirit Medicine for about a year and a half. Through that, she and her late spouse, "who was also very committed to spirituality," met people connected to different Mexican traditions, one of which was the Nahua weather-working[22] tradition:

> My husband was identified as being called to that path, so we came down
> [to Mexico] and met a man who, at that point, was in his late 80s, that was
> a weather-worker in the Nahuatl tribal tradition. And so, when he started
> talking to my husband, he turned to me and said that I was also connected
> and that I should be a weather worker as well. And so, we both became
> initiated into that tradition. A year and a half after that, our son was also
> initiated as a Nahua weather-worker, and we still do that today.

A couple of years after her initiation into weather work, Joan was also called to an apprenticeship into the Huichol tradition. Her calling to this was described as part of her Tonalli which is considered in Huichol to be part of your soul path. After nine years of apprenticeship and pilgrimages, she "was initiated as a Mara'akame in the Huichol tradition, which is a medicine person and ceremonial leader... and I'm seeing patients both here [The Farm] and in Nashville." She added:

> And then, part of that whole thing is associated with what is called *Sacred*
> *Fire*. In the Sacred Fire organization there are firekeepers trained and ini-
> tiated through that, and fires are being held in eight different countries at
> this point. So, I'm also part of that organization and I'm a firekeeper. It's
> a nondenominational, nonpolitical way of connecting. It's about having
> a connection to the natural world through the element of fire and recog-
> nizing that fire is a major source of inspiration for almost all traditions.

Being part of the Sacred Fire organization is very demanding, because Joan serves in its leadership – a role that utilizes her lifelong managerial skills and "takes as much time at least as the business, if not more." In addition, she organizes monthly community fires, where everybody interested "makes offerings to the fire, and by consecrating the fire with those offerings, you are now establishing the beginning of a relationship with fire."

Having had the opportunity to participate in the community fire, I can say that it was a rather festive multi-age social event. Yet, the ceremony was serious. It included walking around "grandfather fire" and, upon completion of every circle, praying and throwing one offering at a time into the fire: tobacco for wisdom, copal (a natural incense) for new beginnings, cocoa for abundance, and wood for healing. Joan explained that establishing a relationship with fire helps to connect with nature and thus makes the world a better place: "Spending time around sacred fires gets people to recognize that humans are not just part of the world, that we should be in a relationship with it, and that the disconnection that started happening hundreds of years ago is what got us into the mess that we're in now. Reconnecting can help us move forward." Dennis, Joan's current spouse, shared that when they "first got together, Joan tried for weeks to explain to me what she just briefly explained to you, and of course, most of that was just, 'What?'" Although he never "got into that," he supports Joan's spiritual practices and even brags: "I don't know too many people of our generation who are involved in a spiritual path like Joan has been working on for the last 20 years or so."

LAURA'S DISCOVERY – A COURSE IN MIRACLES Laura's spiritual journey included thorough study and intense practice of various religions and spiritual methods. She spent time at the San Francisco Zen Center, took philosophy and religion classes at the university, learned and practiced healing touch, and even did past-life regressions. However, it was clear from the beginning of the interview that all past explorations eventually brought Laura to a sole spiritual practice that became the center of her life. Moreover, the terms that she used throughout the interview (e.g., "forgiveness lessons," "separation makes us afraid") implied, even before she said it, that her journey led her to A Course in Miracles (ACIM).[23]

As Laura noted that "my spiritual path books have always led me to a deeper truth" and named many books she had read throughout the years, it was not surprising that her "true spiritual path" was realized when she browsed a friend's spiritual books library:

I asked her, "what do you think is the deepest book you have?" And she said, "*A course in miracles.*" And I never heard of that, even though I thought I had read all the spiritual texts that there were. I picked it up, and it was illuminated for me, and I read the table of contents, and I remember this voice all the time, it was like, "oh, here it is." Actually, 10 to 12 years before that, I had this very clear dream that I was carrying this blue book that was illuminated and that my role was to carry this book... so here I am and here's this blue book, and I'm starting to read it, and I'm going, "here it is."

Laura started to study ACIM and felt "in a wonderful place, full of peace." Only a year later, however, when she joined a weekly ACIM workshop led by "this older person whose wisdom went all the way," she understood that she "didn't know what this course was about." She explained: "I was totally reading that, but some part of me was afraid of reading the hard parts. I was like, 'no, let me get to the good part, peace and love, and I am as God created me.'"

For the past six years, Laura has been delving deeply into ACIM under the guidance of the workshop instructor ("after Stephen [Gaskin] I became allergic to spiritual teachers... so I watched him like a hawk for two years"). She also tried to convince some of her "old Farm friends" that ACIM is "what we were looking for when we went to The Farm, the highest spirituality that is going to take us all the way," but most of them were not interested. Yet, she mentioned that "there are Farm people who definitely know about the course, and it's nice because it's like we have another language that we can talk. Most of the people from The Farm don't follow."

Practicing on an almost daily basis, Laura described ACIM as "a very, very difficult path because the real practice is watching my own ego and action, and who wants to do that? Most of the time, if I'm honest, I don't want to do it either, but some part of me knows it's the only way." Stressing that "it's a lifelong process," Laura added that through the ACIM she "was a lot of times in a peaceful place that is beyond the world" and that it helped her "truly grow up" and even cope with anxiety:

I always knew I needed a psychiatrist, but I never found a psychiatrist that I knew would take me all the way. The course is that psychiatrist. It's not the book; it's the thought system. For me, it's what will lead me through and wherever I get. Its non-dualistic path teaches us we are awake, we are already awake in heaven, we're dreaming of exile. So, our real selves have nothing to worry about. But we have these classrooms called life, right?

## SUMMARY: NEW AGERS GROWING OLDER

The life-course perspective applied in this study sheds light on patterns of continuity and change among people who adopted New Age spirituality early in life. For some of these individuals, the interest in spiritual philosophies and mysticism seemed merely a phase. They experimented with spiritual ideas and activities, but they were not convinced or highly involved. Some of them even became more skeptical and cynical than they had been before. Questioning authority of any kind, these people rejected all spiritual frameworks even if they had some form of faith. This group, therefore, could be regarded as complete rebels.

Whereas the group of forever Farmies maintained the beliefs and practices they had adopted in the commune era and regarded them as their spiritual pillar of fire, they did not seem interested in expanding their spiritual world in later life. However, the other two groups demonstrated an increased sense of spirituality in later adulthood – a tendency also identified in previous research.[24] They also reported a variety of positive effects that resulted from their increased spirituality, of which a greater sense of meaning and satisfaction in life was dominant. This, too, was consistent with past studies.[25]

What seemed unique to aging hippies were two patterns, which could only occur among people who had adopted an eclectic spiritual philosophy early in life. The first pattern involved lifelong spiritual seeking and could be described as "spiritual innovation." This pattern was evident among both the perpetual seekers and the subgroup of focusers who exhibited spiritual discovery. However, the outcomes of the ongoing search differed. Whereas for the former, the constant seeking typically resulted in an even more varied spiritual repertoire, for the latter, it led to identifying a single spiritual path that they perceived as optimal.

The second pattern, which was apparent among all focusers, may be labeled "spiritual selectivity." Whereas some of them selected a single spiritual path out of an existing collection of beliefs and practices, others discovered a new spiritual direction that displaced most or all former ones. All focusers, however, shared the sense of finding the ultimate path and experienced a significant spiritual shift. Unlike the paradigm shift described by the Gerotranscendence Theory,[26] in which people move from a rational perspective to a transcendent view of life, the spiritual shift among the focusers was from eclectic to focused spirituality.

Both patterns align with behaviors described in studies of later life leisure – that of innovation[27] and that of selectivity,[28] which were found most beneficial to wellbeing in later life. Moreover, the group of focusers reported involvement in spirituality that resembled "serious leisure," which is characterized by six qualities: (a) perseverance; (b) significant effort toward developing skills and knowledge; (c) sense of development marked by turning points and stages; (d) unique ethos and social world; (e) realization of various personal and social benefits; and (f) strong identification with the chosen activity.[29] If we probe deeply into each of the focused spirituality examples presented above, we can see that they all demonstrate these six qualities. The focused spirituality may thus also be described as "serious spirituality."

These connections between spirituality and leisure suggest that among aging New Agers, the spiritual sphere is like a playground full of possibilities – an idea consistent with the ethics of play that characterized the hippie movement.[30] Moreover, many study participants felt that their spiritual practices affected others and the world at large, be it by including others in their meditation, participating in prayer circles, singing and dancing to raise consciousness and promote peace, or establishing a relationship with the sacred fire. This feeling suggests some overlap between aging hippies' spirituality and generativity (see Chapter 5). Overall, therefore, it seems that the initial aspiration to change the world and make it a better place is still a primary motivation evident in both the daily activities of aging hippies and their spiritual life.

## CHAPTER 8

# Lifelong Community

**T**HE ETHICS OF COMMUNITY was central to the hippie movement's ideology just as much, if not more, than the ethics of dope, sex, and rock. The aspiration to offer an alternative lifestyle, in which affinity and solidarity ruled, originated in the Native American tribal culture that the hippies admired and in the overwhelming sense of community that was provided by rock festivals, the social use of dope, and the combination of the two.[1] Only a couple of hundred of the numerous hippie communes, however, survived to this day. Although it has been reported that past commune members look back fondly at their experiences,[2] no study thus far has explored what remained, if anything, of their sense of community.

A psychological sense of community (PSOC) is "the sense that one is part of a readily available, mutually supportive network of relationships."[3] Many studies demonstrate that PSOC significantly associates with wellbeing among people of a wide age range and in various countries and community settings.[4] Hence, individuals who have a solid connection to their community (or communities, as one can be a member of multiple communities) are happier and more satisfied with their lives. Studies also revealed that people's PSOC and satisfaction with their social networks increase with age,[5] and that having a close and supportive network of family and friends promotes older adults' psychological wellbeing, cognitive function, and physical health.[6] It was even found to be a factor that delays mortality.[7]

A psychological explanation for increased PSOC with advancing age is offered by the Socio-Emotional Selectivity Theory,[8] which claims that older adults' shorter perceived future time motivates them to focus on emotionally rewarding interactions while trying to avoid conflicts or minimize their impact. A behavioral explanation is the older adults' tendency to gradually reduce the geographic range of their daily activities and become more dependent upon their residential area's physical and social context.[9] However, it should be noted that although "place" is a critical element in PSOC, older adults are increasingly engaged in communities of interest linked to friendships, ethnicity, professional and leisure pursuits, religious beliefs, political ideology, and so forth.[10] This trend is significantly catalyzed by their increasing spending power and their growing use of information and communication technology.

The Farm in its commune period was both a community of place and a community of interest that aspired to actualize a spiritual and communal back-to-the-land model of community life. After the changeover, however, most of the idealistic young people who had founded the commune had to leave it and search for an alternative-to-the-alternative to be able to support themselves and their families. This chapter aims to describe the transition of The Farm from a community of both place and interest to a multiplace community of interest and explore the PSOC among lifelong residents of The Farm in Tennessee, returning residents, and former residents. In so doing, this chapter not only highlights what has remained of the hippies' sense of community but also adds to the literature on PSOC across the lifespan.

## SEVERAL COMMUNITIES OF PLACE NESTED IN ONE COMMUNITY OF INTEREST

Residents of The Farm community in Tennessee often call it a "bubble." They describe it as a "hippie gated community" (Julia) of "lucky, mostly Caucasian, cloistered people" (Chris), that is "out of the mainstream, very non-American" (Cindy), thus making it a "gold mine" (Sarah) and a "sanctuary of peace, tranquility, nature, community, love, and communication" (Jane). This bubble is perceived as standing in contrast to both its immediate environment ("It's like a blue star in the middle of this red, red state" – Sarah) and what residents call "the real world," where it is "same old, same old, materialism, capitalism… and people are just still caught up in the whole material game and the rat race" (Nicholas).

It is not surprising that people who lived in a small rural community for most of their adult lives or moved back after years away from it strongly identify with their community and express a strong sense of belonging. It may be even more predictable among those who perceive their community as a utopian bubble of like-minded people. What seemed remarkable was that all founding members of The Farm – including people who only lived there for a few years and have not visited it since they left in the early 1980s – still regarded it as their community.

Current and former residents alike described The Farm people as their "tribe" and even their "family." Stating that they all still share the same ideals, they stressed that what keeps the community together is a strong sense of connectedness based on shared history and ongoing friendships. Harold explained:

> I feel deep closeness and love with those individuals. There are many nice people here, where I live, but there's nobody that I can sit down and talk about anything like I do with persons from The Farm. It's a very deep close relationship. We did something that brought us all together, and we're still all together even though we're not living like we used to. We still hold the same values of non-violence, community, honesty, and love. Those kinds of things are very deeply rooted in all of us, and because we went through powerful experiences together, we're just different. It turned us into something different. I mean, we're a tribe.

As such sentiments were common to most interviewees, they indicate that despite the geographical distance between its members and the passing of time, The Farm has remained a community of interest linked to relationships just as much as it is based on ideology.

Two main factors may explain the long-lasting existence of The Farm as a community of interest: (1) the formation of place-based communities of former residents; and (2) the emergence and widespread diffusion of digital media. After the changeover in 1983, those who left The Farm tended to move to the same areas, typically even to the same towns and neighborhoods. They helped each other find jobs and open businesses, sent their children to the same schools, and took turns watching over them. Some of them even shared houses and lived communally until they were able to sustain an independent household. Such communities of former residents evolved in different places around the country (e.g., Nashville, Asheville, Austin, San Diego, and Sonoma County, CA). Ranging in size from several families to "probably 300 alumni that live in the San Francisco's Bay Area" (Sandra), these local communities facilitated their members' transition back to mainstream America.

Most former residents who took part in this study live in such communities to this day. Many of them stated that members of their local Farm community make the core of their social network ("Farm friends that live here are still our best friends" – Karen; "They stayed our best friends all those years" – Julia; "Most of our closest friends are from The Farm" – Lillian). They also still spend a lot of time together in both structured activities (e.g., praying circle, singing groups, fundraising events) and informal socializing ("Just all kinds of community stuff going on all the time" – Carolyn; "There's always some party at somebody's house" – Charles; "We get together regularly and have a wonderful fun time" – Jerry).

All former residents, including the very few who lived in remote places where a local Farm community did not exist, reported keeping in touch with The Farm in Tennessee as well as with the rest of the "Farm diaspora" around the country. This network – which may be described as "a lifelong community of interest" because it has lasted for decades – is maintained by phone calls, occasional visits (especially around the annual reunion), as well as involvement in Plenty and other initiatives. However, what seemed to give it the greatest boost is the introduction of digital media in the mid-1990s. Rebecca explained how The Farm's digital revolution started:

> The Farm had a newsletter that went out in the mail… and I thought that an email list would work better, so I enlisted another guy, and we invited people to join. We had about 200 people, and it was very active, and I also did a website for it where we had everybody's name and pictures and little stories that people would send in, and I put up… and then a year later, I started a chat room for Farm people.

In 2004, when Facebook was founded, most of the group's communication moved to this platform. Gordon stated that currently, "there are maybe half a dozen Farm Facebook groups, but the main one that most everybody's involved with is The Farm Community Facebook group that is open to former and current members only." In addition, members maintain group and personal communication with each other via their own Facebook pages ("I have 564 Facebook friends of which probably 400 are from The Farm" – Andrew), Facebook groups dedicated to specific topics ("I run a Facebook book club with The Farm people" – Joe; "I have an art Facebook page that a number of Farm people are members of" – Gordon), and other digital media ranging from emails to video conference software such as Skype, Facetime, and Zoom.

## ADVOCATING THE ETHICS OF COMMUNITY
## IN THE DIGITAL ERA

The early and extensive adoption of digital technology among current and former Farm residents is reflected in numerous uses beyond social media. Although a few study participants reported pretty limited use (e.g., "I'm at the low end of the knowledge scale. I know there's a lot more I could do" – Ben), the majority described diverse, complex, and rather intense use of information and communication technology (Figure 8.1). Chris, for example, said:

> I have my iPhone, iPad, and laptop. I do everything online: Emailing, texting, Facebook. I've got a dish reception, so I have Wi-Fi. This is my communication to talk to my family. It's very simple. I've got some exercise apps. My iWatch records my steps. I have an old-fashioned iPod, and I had disks, and I have music on my phone. I can do all my banking. I don't get bills in the mail anymore. I can manage my retirement account. I can take money in and out. I can trade. I can do what I want.

The enthusiasm about technology among study participants may be surprising considering the common stereotype of the hippies as opposing modernity. However, there is no evidence of any general rejection of technology in the counterculture.[11] The hippies opposed technologies that had destructive effects on the planet or the people and animals living on it, but they embraced and even advanced helpful technologies.

Technological innovations were integral to The Farm's culture from its beginning. The commune's businesses incorporated computers as

**8.1** The Farm is pretty isolated and the cell phone signal is unstable, but residents are well connected to the internet via satellite dishes hidden in the woods and fiber optic cables.

early as the mid-1970s, and it is known to this day for inventions such as the first Doppler fetal pulse detector, a portable ionizing radiation detector, and passive solar-space-heating technology. Moreover, some of the people who left The Farm became key figures in the history of the internet.

Matthew McClure, soon joined by his Farm friends Cliff Figallo and John Coate, was the founding manager of WELL (an acronym for Whole Earth Lectronic Link) – the world's first online community. After that, he worked for several high-tech startups and was involved in developing many products and software, including a word processor ("kind of like Microsoft Word before Microsoft Word"), a mobile computer ("a portable Macintosh"), online television ("internet startup that took TV contents and put them on the web"), financial investment software ("It basically took a bunch of factors and massaged them and came up with an allocation"), and video-editing software. Figallo spent his post-WELL career planning, designing, and managing online communities for all organization sizes and types – from enterprises to small nonprofit startups. He was also a very prolific writer who authored articles and books about online communities and knowledge management. Coate established SFGate – the online version of the *San Francisco Chronicle* newspaper and the first big news website in the world. Later, a company that produced an online gaming environment hired him, and currently, he works for Edgeryders, a Europe-based network of experts aiming to solve significant social problems through collective intelligence dynamics.

Nancy Rhine, another former member of The Farm, worked for WELL as its first customer support person and served as a consultant for several websites, including SeniorNet, the first online community for seniors. Then, along with Ellen Pack, she founded WIRE (Women's Information Retrieval and Exchange, later Women.com), the first online space and first internet company to focus on women's interests and educate women about this burgeoning communications technology. Later, America Online (AOL) hired her to create the first online women's television channel – again focusing on women's interests (e.g., women's health, loans for women-owned businesses, scholarships, parenting, etc.). She moved on to serve as Business Development Director for AOL and the Tribune Company's Digital City – San Francisco branch – and later was Vice President, Communities at PlanetRx that operated health-related online communities (e.g., www.diabetes.com, www.Alzheimer.com, and www.obesity.com). Rhine co-authored with Figallo a book on knowledge management networks. Her prominent contributions to the cyberculture were documented in Claire Evans's book:[12] *Broad band: The untold story of the women who made the internet.*

Judging by my interviews with McClure, Coate, and Rhine, the marks they have left on the digital world stemmed from the years they spent at The Farm. Coate explained:

> I wasn't done with communities after leaving The Farm. A hundred percent of my career came from living at The Farm. It was all about the relationships, so I did everything that I could to serve that, everything. My whole life was consumed by it. I had a hunger for it. Why would Farm people be suited to this kind of work? It had everything to do with the daily experience of living with and working with and working things out with all sorts of different people where you have to come to some harmonious

resolution, or you're not going to be able to continue. You couldn't use the word community [for online communities] unless it had that kind of truth at its core. To me, it was a blend of personal and professional interactions that created this kind of bonding. To me, that's what a real village is; that's a community, and when the people themselves declare that for themselves, then that's what it is.

Similarly, Rhine stated, "I think that the kind of group dynamics that we learned on The Farm, how to get along, how to interact, how to collaborate was something that we really developed a lot of muscles about." McClure added that written computer-mediated communication might be pretty challenging because "there are no non-verbal cues that help with understanding humor and sarcasm, so there are lots of opportunities for misunderstanding, and that can lead to flame wars." Emphasizing that "the main thing that we learned on The Farm was to be open and compassionate," he described how the same attitude was applied in the online communities to "extinguish occasional flames as quickly as possible."

Overall, these study participants believed that their experiences at The Farm trained them and many other Farm members to do what they later did in the high-tech industry. Because many of their actions involved forming online communities and networks, they practically advocated the hippie ethics of community in the digital sphere and thereby considerably affected one of the world's most remarkable revolutions in the past decades.

## A LIFELONG PSYCHOLOGICAL SENSE OF COMMUNITY

In the years after the changeover, most commune members were focused on surviving. The people who stayed in Tennessee had to figure out how to make a living and cover the community's financial debt, and those who left had to start over from scratch somewhere else. "It took about 10 years for things to settle down" (Ben), and during this period, people's sense of community resulted mainly from interactions with the community of place they had with Farm friends and others, be it in Tennessee or elsewhere. Some of the former residents admitted that they also had pretty negative emotions towards The Farm community at large in these first years. Stephanie, for example, said: "I was burned pretty badly, and I did not communicate with anybody from The Farm except two or three people for the next many years," and Cliff shared, "For a while, my wife had a fairly strong reaction, like she was there too long and really didn't want anything to do with it for a pretty good while." However, as the years went by, and mainly thanks to digital media, the tribe reconnected, and the sense of being part of a larger community gradually returned.

A datum point for understanding PSOC is McMillan and Chavis's model,[13] according to which this construct consists of four elements: membership, influence, integration and fulfillment of needs, and shared emotional connection. *Membership* represents a sense of belonging and proposes that the community has clear boundaries. *Influence* relates to members' feeling that they make a difference in the community and that the community matters to them. *Integration and fulfillment of needs* refers to the benefits that members gain from being part of the community. *Shared emotional connection*, the most important element, is the idea that members feel a bond and identify with other community members and with the community itself. This element relies on the sense that community members have shared and will continue to share a history of negative and positive events and experiences.

Probing study participants' reports suggested that most of them have a strong PSOC related to both their local Farm community and the Farm tribe as a whole. Yet, there were some notable differences among lifelong, returning, and former residents: Whereas the dimensions of *membership* and *shared emotional connection* were similar, *integration and fulfillment of needs* seemed stronger among Farm residents, and *influence* was most substantial among returning residents.

MEMBERSHIP Although some study participants talked about negative emotions, reservations, and even criticism of certain Farm people or The Farm community in general, most of them expressed a strong sense of belonging. Often, they used the family metaphor to clarify this feeling ("It's a bigger family in a way" – Julia; "It's just a spiritual family feeling" – Jane; "We call it Farmily" – Elizabeth). Some even went as far as describing their belonging to The Farm as marriage. Gordon, for example, said, "It is a huge group marriage, we're all married together at a level, and it's a pretty deep level." Similarly, Carolyn stated, "It's like you're married to hundreds of people. Yeah, it's like one big happy sort of dysfunctional family."

The sense of marriage to the community may have had to do with the high divorce rate among Farm members (see Chapters 1 and 3) and the fact that many of them remarried other community members. Most study participants, who married more than once following divorce or spousal loss, had a new partner from The Farm. It even happened quite often that while interviewing someone, I discovered they had previously been married to a person I had already interviewed. The multiple marriages within The Farm resulted in numerous family ties that strengthened the tribe feeling, as Henry commented: "Hippies and Indians are the same. By blood and marriage, and I can explain this, I'm related to 50 people here, and us living together in extended families is the same way the Indians did it."

To provide a sense of belonging, communities must have clear boundaries that define who is part of the community and who is not. In the case of The Farm community of interest, the boundaries are very clear: To be part of the community, one must be a current or former resident of The Farm in Tennessee. Although the community in Tennessee warmly welcomes visitors and new residents, the process of receiving full member status is long and exhausting (see Chapter 3). Similarly, some of the activities organized by former Farm residents are only intended for other former residents, and even those that are open to the public are typically only attended by such members ("We always try to get as many as we can [to the annual fundraising event – see Figure 8.2], but it's usually just Farm people that come" – Sandra).

The community's boundaries are drawn in the online sphere, too. Some of the online groups and activities that target the greater Farm community are limited to current and former residents. The online prayer circle, for example, is "an offshoot of Farm people, part of it was you had to live on The Farm" (Lillian). Similarly, The Farm community Facebook group is "a closed group limited to people that have lived on or in some way have a direct connection to The Farm. This might include spouses of former members or those from the second generation, as

**8.2** An eighty-seven-year-old Farm member dancing at the annual fundraising event in California. Although it is open to the public, most attendees are "Farmies."

well as their children" (quoted from the group's description). When I asked for permission to join this group as part of this study, I was politely directed – like anyone else who does not meet the group's criteria – to the open Friends of The Farm Tennessee Facebook group.

SHARED EMOTIONAL CONNECTION The sense of belonging went hand in hand with a strong sense of emotional connection among tribe members. Tim explained, "It's just that feeling of connected, it's like a tribal identity, and I've been on Native American reservations, and there's a little bit of that feeling," and Debbie joked, "We call this the 'res,' the reservation." Quite a few highlighted that the emotional connection is what bridges over time and distance ("There's just that connection, so even if we don't talk to each other, when we do, it's just like we saw each other five minutes ago" – Evelyn) and facilitates communication ("It's not just physical, it's spiritual. We have that basic understanding that makes it like we're already at the second base when we try to communicate" – Stephanie, "I feel like there's an understanding that I have with those people that I wouldn't have with anybody else" – Joe).

Study participants identified with the community and felt a strong bond with other community members. Many of them stressed that this bonding lasted their entire adult life. Laura, for example, described her friendship with other women from The Farm as "lifelong sisterhood," and Albert said, "We were our brothers' keepers, and that doesn't go away. Decades later, the feeling is there. It's great." Elizabeth explained, "Living this way in a community creates bonds for a lifetime... we still have that bond even though we haven't seen some of the people in 25 years."

Similar to Elizabeth, most interviewees agreed that the shared history created a lifetime emotional connection, and most of them discussed both positive and negative bonding experiences ("We shared so much karma, good and bad, blood, sweat and tears" – Dennis). However, their portrayals of the commune period ranged from relating to it as "living in summer camp year-round with your best friends and so that doesn't go away" (Sandra) to comparing it to military service. Paul said, "It's a shared experience that was really powerful. Sometimes we say it was sort of like army buddies, except it had nothing to do with violence or war or that kind of stuff." Evelyn stated, "Something really happened in those early years, you know... we have bonded like people who have been in the military together, and we kept the '60s thing going." Andrew summarized, "We shared our lives in such an intimate way that you don't go back from that intimacy."

The strong bonding and intense shared history made The Farm a central component in community members' identity and led them to feel part of something extraordinary. Sam said, "The Farm is not for everybody, it really isn't," Elizabeth stated, "We are a unique group of people on this planet," and Julia argued, "Nobody else is like us, we've held this way of thinking, and it's just this headspace I think for forever." Few individuals voiced reservations about this sense of distinctiveness. Laura, for example, said, "My thought system now is really different in a lot of ways to this, 'oh, The Farm is so special.' I don't see it that way anymore." Yet, even she admitted, "But you know, I got like maybe 500 Facebook friends, but these are all people I know from The Farm. These are people I delivered their baby, or they were at my birth. These are not just people I know online. They are some of my deepest friends in this life."

INTEGRATION AND FULFILLMENT OF NEEDS If I were to explain the essence of The Farm community in three words, I would describe it as a "culture of helping." The interviews with study participants and my own experiences while visiting the community in Tennessee led me to the conclusion that members constantly help others, be it their parents, partners, children and grandchildren, other community members, local residents, and, of course, communities in need (see Chapter 5 regarding Plenty). The solidarity and mutual help among community members are truly astonishing and reflected in instrumental and emotional support alike.

Even without getting into the numerous help stories told in the interviews – some of which were shared incidentally – I witnessed quite a lot of instrumental help with my own eyes. One morning, when I was about to leave my hosts' house to meet and interview Henry, Sarah gave me a brown bag with breakfast for him and explained he had not had a chance to eat that morning. Touched by this sweet gesture, I asked Henry why he had not had breakfast, and he explained that he was busy with his next-door neighbor, who has Alzheimer's disease and sometimes "gets emotional." Sarah, therefore, was helping the helper. On another occasion, while participating in a DUP session, one of the older community members told everyone that her ride to an appointment with an eye doctor in Columbia the next day had been canceled. Although it takes about forty minutes to drive from The Farm to Columbia, it did not take long before a young woman said, "No problem, I'll take you there," and added, "I can find things to do in the city" to make the other person feel comfortable.

Another individual, who was supposed to be interviewed for this study, fell and had a concussion before my visit. While talking with some community members, I found out that they took turns cooking for her and her partner. Brian, for example, said he made them "a wonderful vegetable soup and hard custard bread" and that his spouse "went over there and delivered the food and stayed for a couple of hours." He clarified:

> Other people were doing that too, and that's not the first instance that that's happened. Other people have different situations develop, and people rally around them and help support them until they get through the difficult period. People really rally around the folks when there is a need, and it's a very supportive community. We rally around each other, and we support each other, and it's good for that level.

As may be understood, the support in time of need is not only instrumental but also emotional. Sarah, who went through a family crisis that lasted years, said that what helped her cope with it was "talking to my friends… it was eating me up inside, but everyone said that they thought things would come around and get better." James shared that after his spouse passed away, he "moved in with some friends because I didn't want to be by myself." After a month or so, these friends traveled to Guatemala, so he joined them and "lived there with them for six weeks… and started healing up, started feeling better about life and myself, and by the time it was up, I felt like I could go back and stay in my house."

The frequent exchange of instrumental and emotional support resulted in knowing that if needed, there would always be someone there for you, or, as Cliff put it, in realizing that "there is one place on this planet where we have a bunch of really good friends." In addition, being able to support others provided a sense of meaning and satisfaction, as Tim stated: "Hippies are usually not so individually oriented about their own needs but rather look out for other people and help them out. That gives you satisfaction, you know. I mean, it's kind of a Buddhist thing too that if you're helping, If you're doing something for somebody else that makes you feel good." Julia, however, confessed that in later life, the satisfaction comes with some frustration because "I always feel like, 'well, I'd like to do more,' but right now, this is all I can handle. Somewhere in there, you got to be realistic with yourself while still striving to do better."

Although all study participants reported giving and receiving support from other community members, the exchange seemed more frequent and intense among those residing at The Farm in Tennessee. A possible explanation for that may be that former residents were members of multiple communities where they lived, as Stephanie highlighted: "I diversified my social support system to where it's as safe as I can make it as far as having local people plus the distant people." Such diversification was less common at The Farm, as Elizabeth explained, "One of the beauties about living in this community is that I have good friends handy. At most, I have to drive a mile." Similarly, Jane said that the geographical factor was one of the main reasons to move back to The Farm:

> The traffic in California was so bad that it took me 45 minutes to get to see my son or my best friends... and here it is like, "I'm just going to walk over to Debbie's house," or "I'm just going to go out for a walk and stop at Sarah's house," or, "Come on over tonight, we're having wine and playing games."

Indeed, the spontaneous interactions among residents seemed very frequent and occurred while taking a walk, shopping at The Farm's store, or attending community events. It also happened quite a lot that while I was interviewing one person, another dropped by for a visit without prior notice. For someone like me, who has lived in a big city for many years, this was inconceivable.

INFLUENCE All study participants shared the feeling that The Farm was a significant part of their lives and the time they spent there – whether it was several years or their entire adult lives – and the friendships formed during that time were of great value. Andrew, for example, said, "I think we all have the feeling the community is valuable and that the community that we built and the sense of community that we built, is very valuable." Paul declared, "The thing that I most wanted was the community itself, and I have that. I have it now. I will never not have it. It can never be taken away. It is of incomparable value."

Past and current residents alike also felt that, as the founding members of The Farm, they influenced the formation of the community. Still, when it came to the present, there were notable differences among the three groups. The first difference was evident between current and former residents: Whereas the first had a formal community to manage, the latter maintained an informal social community with both local and far friends. Relying on online communication, the local diasporic communities also held some physical events and activities. Some people, therefore, stepped forward and took a role in organizing them and thus had more influence than others. However, as Andrew confessed, "it wasn't the same." Describing a recent stay in a Zen monastery, where he worked with the monks and felt "the same harmony that we used to have in The Farm," he shared that he really missed this kind of collaboration, which cannot be experienced in mainstream America.

In contrast to the diasporic communities, The Farm in Tennessee required daily management and had more positions to fill, of which many were formal operational roles rather than just social. Current residents served on the community's Board of Directors, were involved in various committees (e.g., planning, membership, finance, housing, land use, archive), and even initiated new committees (e.g., conflict resolution), task forces (e.g., dues collection), and community events (e.g., weekly potluck, monthly community fire). The various formal roles were described as pretty challenging and time-consuming work, which could occasionally be satisfying. Yet, it also involved unpleasant aspects such as tedious paperwork and nasty conflicts ("You get two people, you get three political parties" – Chris). The residents felt that they must take up such roles because "someone's got to do it... if you live in a community, you've got to have people take turns of doing this" (Debbie) and "make sure the wheels are greased, and people are complying, and everything is working" (Jane). There were, however, considerable differences between the lifelong and the returning residents, as the latter were significantly more involved in community roles.

Sam and Bill may exemplify this difference. After moving back to The Farm, Sam took up several community roles. He served on the board for seven years, managed the community's budget, and supervised all teams (e.g., welcome center, swimming hole) and projects (e.g., renovating the water tower). Sam also served as the chairman of the land use and the planning committees (Figure 8.3). Overall, he dedicated about twenty hours a week to these roles. Although taking up managerial positions corresponded with his pre-retirement career in construction, which may have prepared him for being the target of occasional criticism, he felt somewhat uncomfortable with having "some people on The Farm say

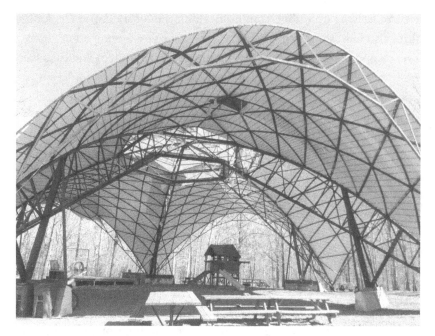

**8.3** During the summer, many of The Farm community's events (e.g., concerts, parties, market days) are held under "The dome." According to Sam, fixing it "is a $125,000 project, so I have to plan for that: Get engineers, get my crew together, have meetings and then come to the Board on a long term."

I have too much power or too much control." He explained, "I never really asked for any of these jobs, the Board asked me to do them, and I would say, 'Yes.'" However, his motivation to fill these roles was intrinsic: "There were things that I thought could be done better. I wanted to put us into the twenty-first century, move us forward."

Bill, who was involved in such roles from the early days of the commune until recently, said that at some point, he realized it was too stressful for him:

> I was the chair of the board. I was involved in everything on The Farm
> until I was losing weight. My stomach hurt all the time because I was too
> involved... I'm no use to anybody if I'm not healthy, and I don't seem to
> have the capacity to do too much of this. Now Sam has come in and taken
> all of that side. I love Sam because he can do that, and I can be a resource
> for Sam. We have great conversations, but I don't want to do it because I
> just find I get too much stress. Some people thrive on conflict, and they

thrive on the tension that happens in interactions. I don't. I wouldn't say that Sam is one of those, but he certainly can absorb more.

Returning residents also participated much more in the various community activities, whereas the lifelong residents were pretty selective. Many of them skipped the multiple activities held weekly and mainly took part in occasional community meetings and events such as meet-and-greets for new members, concerts, market days, blueberry picking, and the like. Cindy explained:

> I am not as active as some people are. The new folks seem to be more active because that's how they get to meet people. I'm sort of over all that. After years of going to everything, I go to some things, but I don't go to everything. Some people, especially the people that used to live here in the old days and came back, are not as tired of all the community activities and things as we might be, and so, yeah, it just depends on who they are, I guess.

In contrast, Ben, who "decided to come back and re-energize what we're doing here, taking care of here," said that although there are many community activities that "cover a lot of different areas and interests... part of the magic of back in the days was the people coming together and making things happen and having shared experiences. We need more of that."

## CONFLICTS AND PEACE MAKING

When Douglas Stevenson and I talked about the portrayal of The Farm in the media, he said that journalists writing about the community are typically interested in a "feel-good, warm and fuzzy, touchy-feely story to balance the usual bad news and scandals." Accordingly, he makes sure that they will only interview "good talkers" that he "could trust not to say something stupid or air a bunch of dirty laundry." He admitted, "we also have problems," and based on the interviews with study participants, it seems that the problems are many, varied, and long-lasting.

Despite the "no negativity" agreement, resentments, tensions, and conflicts among community members occur just as they do in any other group of people. This has happened throughout the community's history. However, when it comes to the present, there is a notable difference between residents and former residents as the former report many more conflicts than the latter. It seems that when a group of people live together on the same land and have to operate a physical community with many collective assets and functions, it results not only in a greater sense of community, but also in various conflicts that are common in organizations, namely, *task, value,* and *relationship* conflicts.[14]

*Task conflicts* in The Farm revolve around operational issues such as fair workload, due payment, bylaw updates, or a tree cut without community permission. Such conflicts were mainly reported by people who took up formal community roles. Henry, for example, said, "Being a trustee put a target on my back," and Sam noted, "You get a lot of flak, some people say, 'Who gives you the right to do this or that?'" Dennis explained, "when you are elected [to a formal role], you get into politics because then you have to have opinions and you have to make decisions, and people may not like your decisions." Jane argued that the politics is precisely why some lifelong residents do not take up community roles anymore: "They are saying, 'Oh, I'm tired of politics. I don't want to do that anymore.' And I come back and say, 'What? No! We got to do this! No, hey! What are you guys doing? You're slacking!'"

Although study participants continuously claimed that sharing the same ideals kept the tribe together, they also reported quite a few *value conflicts.* Sarah, for example, was furious at members that did not pay the $105 monthly tax to cover the community services (e.g., roads, water, garbage): "I was raised very strong that you have to pay your bills, then you cover yourself and help out. It is annoying to deal with these people that don't understand it. But really, we're doing it for them." Another example is a value conflict around the ostensible contradiction between materiality and spirituality, reported by some of the more well-to-do residents. Julia said:

> Early on, we thought you had to be poor to be spiritual. There are still people on The Farm who believe you are more spiritual if you have less money, and it's hard to be around them. You know, we went out and worked really hard. Nobody gave us anything. Now, we have a nice house,

we have a nice car, we bought a little used camper, but does that mean we're not spiritual?

Most reports, however, referred to *relational conflicts*, of which some were relatively subtle. In contrast, other conflicts developed into horrible fights ending with people not speaking to each other and even initiating petitions to remove the other person from the community. Study participants described numerous such tensions and conflicts and provided two explanations for their proliferation, the first being the community's small size. Carolyn argued, "People think that in a small town like this everybody is like 'lovey, lovey, lovey,' and they don't know that some people look down on others and don't treat them very nicely." Henry explained that in small communities, "if we're having a problem and somebody else is in that problem, it goes around, everybody starts talking about it until it's a bigger problem than it really is, because we're like in the same room and it just keeps going around."

The second explanation was the long history Farm residents shared, and in that regard, it did not matter if the history was good or bad. Sarah, for example, shared that she had a lifetime of good relationships with everyone in the community. However, during the extended family crisis that she experienced, she was genuinely offended by some people who were "picking their nose into others' business" and "criticizing me big time" to the extent that "it made my stomach turn." She explained:

> People were really saying, "Oh, yeah. They were really right. They weren't making things up." You know, that's the part that hurt, "Come on! Who are you going to believe? I've been here all through this. I mean, I'm not a bullshitter. You've never ever had any problems with me. And now you're going to believe this stuff that this psychopath is saying?"

In contrast to Sarah, Carolyn felt that she was always "a bit of a controversial figure" at The Farm. It started during the Caravan when her babies were crying a lot, which inconvenienced all the single people. Later, throughout the commune days, she was perceived as a "California girl" because she had married three times already and was looked down on by "all these young, bright, beautiful, happy hippies with no baggage, and here we [family] were with just all this baggage." After the changeover, she and her spouse were shamed for being "debtors." When they left, they were harshly criticized for renting out their house ("People started calling us 'absentee landlords,' whereas the truth was we could barely get enough rent to keep the maintenance going on our house"). After moving back to The Farm several years ago, Carolyn hoped to start over but ran into some cold shoulders:

> There are still a few people who don't give me the time of day. There's a couple of people that didn't even say, "Welcome back," and act like I'm not in the room. I really don't know why. In fact, lately I was thinking, "I'm going to have to talk to these couple of people." But I had to get over feeling like, "Well, I'm just a second-class citizen there," you know?

In a later correspondence, Carolyn wondered if she was just "over-sensitive" and "take people's disinterest in me too personally." She also suggested that "some people get overwhelmed with everyone coming through here, and don't reach out to people." Yet, her tendency to talk to the people who ignored her is an excellent example of the community's long tradition of conflict resolution via "sort-it-out" sessions in which all parties were committed to "mental nudity" (see Chapter 3). In the past, cases of acute conflict were brought to Gaskin, and members accepted his rulings. Today, community members have the option of applying to the Community Conflict Resolution Team (CCRT) and asking for a facilitated meeting. When I asked Sarah if she would consider asking the CCRT to help with her family and social issues, she said, "It makes my skin crawl to even think about it." However, her spouse Bill thought that "the mediation group has had a tremendous impact on the local community because instead of going to court, people are mediating with each other to find some level of agreement."

The CCRT was formed and trained by Elizabeth, who had extensive professional experience managing reconciliation and mediation programs in Tennessee, through which "we had 10,500 referrals, 95% of which came to mediation and contract, and we taught 30,000 kids conflict resolution and anger management, and we did anger management classes for the communities." Elizabeth explained that for the mediation to be successful, the parties should be ready to hear each other, and the mediators must have "the right temperament that enables being neutral and unbiased." Reporting that in the past two years the CCRT had "at least 50 facilitated meetings," Elizabeth stated:

> Humans have conflicts. In fact, I got a book that says, "Problems are doors to peace," so you can change your view of them from obstacles to opportunities. There is always an obstacle that you have to overcome, but the idea that "somebody has to win, somebody has to lose" is a wrong idea. It [conflict management] is more of a lateral management kind of style where everybody can win.

Overall, community members agreed that forgiveness is key to community sustainability ("Forgiveness is really an essential part of a community, and so just let stuff go" – Henry, "If you can't forgive or have a hard time with stuff like that, you're going to have a hard time here" – Sam). In addition, they seemed to make an intentional effort to prevent conflicts from developing, or, as Ben put it: "Not to react and respond to different situations that we find ourselves in is really important. To be able to get more of an immediate resolution and not to escalate – that's the peace that we can work it on an everyday level."

While visiting The Farm, I witnessed two incidents in which the parties tried to prevent conflicts from developing. The first occurred during the meeting of The Swan Trust's board of directors, when the attendees discussed the purchase of an additional 138 acres of land. Although it was already agreed to take a bank loan to cover this purchase in the hope to later get a grant for it, Cindy had second thoughts. Explaining that an electricity line that crosses the property decreases the chance of getting a grant and that reliance only on donations is risky, she asked to postpone the purchase contract signing. Henry objected to such a delay because he was confident that funding would be found, and the argument started to heat up. A younger person, serving as the board chair, tried to intervene by explaining to Cindy that Henry was afraid of losing the deal, but this only made Henry more upset and even hostile towards that person ("In how many such deals were you involved, exactly?"). Another person then took a mediator role and gently told Henry that he was not listening to Cindy. Following that remark, the whole atmosphere in the room changed. Henry took a deep breath, talked about the need to have faith, and suggested alternative funding solutions. Cindy softened and admitted that a lot of her hesitance resulted from her dislike of "begging for donations." Soon after that, the board was able to move to the next item on the agenda.

Whereas this conflict could be described as a small-scale *task* conflict, the second incident – which occurred during the general community meeting – could have developed into a large-scale *value* conflict. In this case, the agenda item that caused considerable turmoil was a proposal to issue a local hunting club a permit to hunt deer on The Farm's land. Because of the nonviolence ideology and veganism, many Farm members strongly objected to this suggestion. They were thus presented with four arguments that supported it: (1) The Farm's land has no borders and no enforcement abilities; (2) people from the area hunt on The Farm anyway, so it is better to have the club regulate the hunting than just letting anyone in; (3) in contrast to the local hunters (who "use heavy weapons and bring alcohol and girls, which is something that we do not support"), the club is of "father and son" type, has stringent rules, and even donates one-third of the catch to the poor; and (4) the deer population in Tennessee has grown from 2,000 in 1948 to 2 million today, and has become a risk to the natural equilibrium. They also put humans in danger because they cause numerous car accidents. As these arguments were logically and respectfully presented while allowing for questions and discussion, the objectors were eventually convinced that issuing the hunting permit was the best possible solution under the circumstances.

Former residents of The Farm hardly mentioned present conflicts. Like the current residents, many such interviewees discussed problematic dynamics and conflicts in the past, but only two of them disclosed recent issues and negative emotions towards the community. Rebecca, who, similar to Carolyn, "always felt kind of second-class at The Farm," had a period of feeling "in the middle of the things" when she managed The Farm's email list. However, after divorcing her spouse and forming a relationship with another former resident who is transman ("He is somebody who was identified female as birth but has always identified as male"), she no longer felt welcome: "Women, who I thought were my friends, kind of dropped me, dumped me and they no longer want to include me in those things we used to do together." Currently, she is "not very friendly with more than a couple of Farm people" and feels "on the outskirts of the community, again." Describing Farm people as conservative, noninclusive transphobes, who are also pretty "smug, self-satisfied and self-congratulatory," Rebecca seemed to accept that "people are very much like school, there's the in-crowd, the out-crowd, and people who don't fit in." Yet, she was deeply hurt by her close friends' behavior and "just don't still have all the warm fuzzy feelings that I used to have for The Farm."

The second former resident expressing current issues with the community was Gordon, who defined himself as "the black sheep of The Farm" and explained that he was "raised by a hot-headed Italian" and thus has "some anger tendencies to be concerned about stuff and not to be as emotionally calm as some people can be in certain situations." Gordon described quite a few conflicts with Farm people – both in the past and more recently in the digital sphere – following which he had "blocked some Farmies on Facebook because I'm tired of how they treat me and they're talking baloney as far as I'm concerned." He was also asked to leave the community's Facebook page because he was the "kind of guy that would look at the dirt under Stephen's [Gaskin] fingernails… and would go ahead and expose the shortcomings of the guru, and they didn't really want to hear it and wanted it [Facebook page] to be a pristine presentation of the community to the world." Despite the various conflicts, however, Gordon stressed, "I still have some good friends there for sure" and "we're family no matter what, even if I'm a bad uncle or something like that. We still have that underlying cement that holds us together."

## THE NEXT GENERATION

When discussing The Farm community – both the physical community and the tribe spread around the country – study participants included the younger generation, namely, children born on The Farm and their children. Some persons shared that their children complained about the way they had been raised. Cliff, for example, said that one of his daughters "feels that it was a bad start on her life and she blames my wife and me for being here, and she blames The Farm for various distortions in her life." Most interviewees, however, argued that their children feel grateful for The Farm and have a strong feeling of belonging to the community ("That sense of community, many of our second-generation kids feel the same way" – Andrew).

Some of the former residents said their children "didn't really want to leave The Farm" (Roger), and others described some post-leaving estrangement that disappeared over time. Paul, for example, shared that when his daughter "was a teenager, she wasn't really interested in The Farm, but later she became more connected." He explained: "For her, just like for me, just like for anybody who is part of it, the tribe is always there. It's always available. She's not the only one who didn't really want to have a relationship with it [after leaving] and then did. And it was completely available to her, just like that. Right away. Bam."

A strong sense of community was reported even when discussing children who had left The Farm at a very young age or were born after their parents had left it. Sandra's son, for example, was three years old when his family left The Farm, and her daughter was an infant. Nevertheless, "they can't believe how just because they were born on The Farm they're part of the family, and it didn't matter that they didn't grow up there. They were just included, and that's a wonderful thing for them." Karen added, "our kids are still very tight with their old Farm friends," and Chris said that his daughter "got lots of old friends here too, she loves the community." Moreover, several people reported that their children married other "Farm kids."

The younger generation was described as part of the tribe and the *future* of The Farm community in Tennessee. Children who never left and those who left at a young age or left for college and then returned make the core of the younger cohort at The Farm. In addition, a number of young couples with no family ties to The Farm have joined the community in the past decade (Figure 8.4). An even greater number of young families are interested in doing so but still have to go through the membership process ("We're a living, thriving community, and more people are interested in joining. It goes in spells but right now, it's on the upswing" – Sam).

Farm residents distinguished between the second generation and the new people who had never lived at The Farm. They were excited about having their children take over their place. Joan, for example, said, "I'm shaping the business up to move it to the next generations, including my son who came to work there," and Henry shared, "In the last three years,

**8.4** The Farm school nowadays is not as populated as it used to be in the commune era, but the number of young families in the community is gradually growing.

I've been enjoying work more. I'm savoring it. I'm with my son and my grandson, and I'm still very important to the company. I'm old but not in the way, and it's a wonderful thing." Douglas Stevenson even wrote in The Farm's newsletter for October 2020:

> Sustainability is about more than solar panels and energy-efficient homes. It's about how you pass on your values to the next generation. Because we are here on this earth for only a short while. It is through our personal relationships that the work we start continues after we're gone. It may take a new direction, but the foundation is put in place through love, and we are thrilled and excited to share this adventure with the grandkids.

Study participants felt confident that their values were well transferred to the second generation, and based on my conversations with some of their children, this certainty seemed justified. One of them, for example, told me that as a son of "the original Caravaners" he always has an internal pressure to save the world, and that every day that passes without doing so makes him feel guilty.

The interviewees' sentiments regarding the new people were some-what more complex. Stressing that "we really need youth here," Carolyn was excited that "we have young people come here and they look like we did and it always amazes me. It's like, really, they're still hippies?" Sam, however, was concerned about "the fact that we have changed while bringing all the new folks to come in" because "sometimes there's a gap between what we tried to establish then and had worked all these years philosophically and now, it's a little different." He exemplified the dif-ference by describing The Farm's culture of conflict resolution in con-trast to the typical American manner: "Let's say if you lived in Chicago all your life and you come here at 25, you have a different philosophy because of how you were raised, so if somebody let the air out of your tire, you called the police. We would never call the police." Similarly, Bill said that some new people "talked about bringing cattle here because they are not vegetarians, and that's been hard for me because I'm really not into killing animals."

However, all residents interviewed for this study agreed that it is bet-ter to have the community change a little rather than seeing their life's work "boarded up and gone like the Shakers" (Sam). Daniel explained:

> The Farm really does change, and each one got to accept that the young people will not be exactly the same as it's already not exactly the same as we started it. So, hopefully, a lot of what we have will transmit and go forth, but we have no guarantee, and you can't go back. You've got to go forward.

Accepting that "after we're gone, the next generation may do all kinds of things that we might not agree with, but that's their choice," Bill said that "some people on The Farm that are very conservative don't want to see new people and don't want to cut those trees to build a house... but it's not a tree Farm, it's a people Farm, and we've got millions of trees."

## SUMMARY: LIFELONG COMMUNITY

Although one cannot generalize from The Farm community to all hip-pie communes that proliferated in the heyday of the counterculture, the present study suggests that the hippies maintained the ethics of community throughout their lives. This continuity was observed among those who had lived in the same place for several decades and individuals who left it and went back to mainstream America, but chose to reside in enclaves of like-minded people with whom they shared history and ideology. Moreover, the hippies embraced new technologies that enabled alternative ways of participating in a community and were even among the driving forces that led to the development and prevalent adoption of such technologies.

The findings support previous notions regarding PSOC, according to which it associates with wellbeing in later life.[15] Obviously, when people are members of a group with which they identify and fulfill various needs by exchanging instrumental and emotional support, they are more satisfied with their lives. It seems, however, that PSOC and satisfaction with social networks do not necessarily increase with age, as previously found.[16] When people are involved in forming an intentional community at a young age and dedicate their entire lives to that community, their PSOC is very strong to begin with and thus does not change much with age. Such people may even experience some level of "community burnout" that makes them more selective about the community activities they are involved in and the people they associate with. They are also notably less inclined to take up community roles, which have the advantage of having an influence but may embroil them in potential conflicts. Therefore, the socio-emotional selectivity theory[17] does not only explain increased PSOC with advancing age, it also explains some balancing mechanisms that older community members activate to make their interactions emotionally rewarding while trying to avoid conflict.

Demonstrating that strong PSOC may be maintained by belonging to a community of interest, even one mainly sustained by digital media, the present study indicates variations in PSOC in later life. Generally, it suggests that PSOC associated with a community of place is more substantial than PSOC related to a community of interest, because there are more frequent encounters and immediate exchanges of emotional and instrumental assistance in communities of place. Such exchanges enhance residents' social capital[18] and promote the community's collective efficacy.[19] There is, however, a notable difference between lifelong and returning/new residents. The latter experience more influence thanks to their higher social and civic participation.

Lastly, the study suggests that PSOC is a sense that may be "inherited" by one's children and grandchildren – a phenomenon that in itself is a source of satisfaction in later life. However, the next generation is also a source of worry, especially if the number of children who continue to live in the community they grew up in is relatively small. Opening the community to newcomers is challenging, as it requires openness to inevitable changes and their acceptance. Yet, it is a mandatory step if the aging residents wish their community to be sustainable and their legacy to last.

# CHAPTER 9

# Alternative End of Life

A GING INEVITABLY MEANS GETTING CLOSER to the end of life and may increase awareness of mortality and fear of death. Psychologists suggest that "fear of death" is a multidimensional construct involving a host of fears, including *fear of encountering* the dead and the dying, *fear of end of life* that is connected with the inevitability of death and a sense of helplessness about it, *fear of mortality* which makes it impossible to achieve specific goals, fulfill obligations, take care of loved ones, and experience anything, *fear of the physical destruction* of the body after death, *fear of the process of dying* that may be accompanied by suffering and pain, and *fear of life after death* that manifests itself in uncertainty about afterlife existence or perception of life after death as a terrifying reality.[1]

Although everybody realizes that death cannot be averted forever, people's fear of death varies considerably according to demographics, personality, and contextual features. Three factors in particular were found to decrease fear, the first being perceived social support. Having more social support provides a greater sense of security and reduces fear of the unknown.[2] The second factor is religiosity, but its impact depends on the content of one's belief. If the faith stresses the love of God and an idyllic afterlife, it is related to less fear of death, but notions of punishment in the afterlife may increase fear.[3] It was also found that the consistency and intensity of one's spiritual beliefs and practices, rather than religiousness per se, decreases fear of death in old age.[4] The third factor is people's sense of control over their environment. Experiencing more control produces a feeling of greater security and reduces fear of death.[5]

Internal locus of control is a relatively stable personality trait associated with individuals' belief that rewards or outcomes in life result from their own efforts.[6] However, planning for the future is a life management strategy that people may adopt and develop regardless of their personality and consequently promote a sense of control and structure in their lives. Although future planning tends to decrease with age, its positive effects on individuals' sense of direction, control, and wellbeing are more prominent among older adults than in younger age groups.[7] Consequently, aging people who make plans for their later years and end of life may experience more sense of control and less fear of dying and death.

Later years and end-of-life planning may include various actions such as making a change in residence, writing a will, and filling out Advance Care Planning (ACP) forms. Changes in housing arrangements may be moving into a smaller house in the same community, relocating closer to adult children who have moved away, or transitioning into a retirement community with assisted living facilities. Writing a will may provide instructions regarding distributing one's possessions after death, passing on responsibilities (such as custody of dependents), and preferred body disposal (e.g., cremation, burial) and memorial service. In consultation with family members and healthcare professionals, ACP is a process whereby older people make individual decisions about their future healthcare in advance of anticipated impairment in decision-making capability. This process may be challenging as a result of a reluctance to talk about death as well as difficulty discussing the unknown, projecting unpleasant circumstances, and making decisions about an uncertain "future self." However, ACP significantly improves the quality of the dying process and allows older people and their families to maintain a sense of control and better cope with their fear of death.[8]

As the present study aimed to explore the current realities of aging hippies, I did not ask study participants about concerns related to advanced age and end of life. The only future-oriented question I asked referred to their plans for the next ten years, and this typically triggered thoughts about specific activities or civic engagement. Nevertheless, quite a few participants talked about later years and end-of-life considerations without any solicitation. This chapter summarizes the reflections, experiences, and materials they shared with me and suggests that the hippies offer a somewhat alternative approach even when it comes to the end of life.

## LATER YEARS AND END-OF-LIFE PLANNING

The Farm was established by young people who were typically in their early twenties. Young families populated it for many years, and more than half of its population were children. Nevertheless, the community has a long experience of caring for the aged. It started decades ago when Plenty brought some older people to live at The Farm and became more common when members' parents were getting older, and quite a few of them moved in with their children. Brian explained that caring for the older generation is part of the hippie ideology:

> It [hippiedom] is a matter of ideals and beliefs and treating each other with respect and in a loving way, taking care of your parents. We brought our parents here when they were getting feeble. There have been a number of parents who have lived with us and have passed on through the community. In fact, my mother-in-law lived with us here for nine years until she passed away, and she was a member of a group of elderly folks that would get together every week and have meals together. There were maybe 10 folks who were octogenarians and sadly, they're all passed away at this point.

Watching their parents age and eventually die prompted community members' contemplation about their own aging and initiated discussions about the future. Particularly at The Farm in Tennessee, where 90 of the 200 adult residents are over sixty, members felt that they should *collectively* think about the future even if financially each is on their own. Healthcare was not of significant concern, as all members aged sixty-five or over are on Medicare, the national health insurance program for senior citizens. Many of them also have supplemental coverage through Farm Bureau, a regional nonprofit insurance provider. Moreover, many community members are health professionals, so there is always someone around to offer medical advice and first aid in emergencies. Other issues, however, were yet to be resolved.

To meet the needs of its aging population, the community recently established a new committee that aims at "figuring out how we can get old and make this transition graceful and compassionate" (Ben). One of the first things done by this committee was the introduction of Five Wishes to community members. Five Wishes is a short and easy-to-fill ACP document developed by Aging with Dignity – a nonprofit organization aspiring to protect the human dignity of every person who faces the challenges and opportunities of aging or serious illness. With five sections of up to two pages each, the document allows people to express the following wishes:

Wish 1 – The person I want to make healthcare decisions for me when I can't make them for myself.
Wish 2 – My wish for the kind of medical treatment I want or don't want.
Wish 3 – My wish for how comfortable I want to be.
Wish 4 – My wish for how I want people to treat me.
Wish 5 – My wish for what I want my loved ones to know.

Filling out the Five Wishes form is easy and encourages open communication with healthcare providers, family members, and other loved ones. Once it is filled out and signed in the presence of two witnesses, the document is valid under the laws of almost all states. In most states, including Tennessee, notarization is not required. Individuals who fill out the document are advised to keep it in an accessible place in their homes and give copies to their healthcare agent and family. They are also provided with a wallet card they should carry with them so that others know where they keep their Five Wishes.

Parallel to encouraging community members to fill out the Five Wishes document, the committee has recently begun to discuss possible housing arrangements. Ben, who considered joining the committee but eventually decided to run for the board of directors "with hopes of getting this and some other projects moving," envisioned building or turning an existing residential building into a home for The Farm's elders. He explained:

It's about circling the wagons a little bit, and it's going to be interesting because it's different when you have the experience of living with folks. I asked my mother about it a few years ago because she's got several older friends living alone, but it was not something that they wanted to do. They all appreciated their independence and living their lives without other people around. But I think that here it's going to be a little more accepted. We'll see. Folks with more resources may stay in their single-family dwelling and get the help they need. Some folks will probably go live with their kids in other places. But I think as a community, it would be wonderful to have a facility here.

Carolyn agreed that going back to communal living may be a good housing arrangement for the older people on The Farm:

People are saying we're going to need to live together when we're older… So, we could end up living together again. It will probably make this easier for us to take turns cooking the meals as we did back then. So, you still have some space for yourself to take care of your health and do your little routines. Yeah, I would consider doing that. I think it would be easier now that we've known each other this long. We can kind of feel out where the chemistry feels best.

Existing residential buildings that may be turned into a home for older community members are the big houses built during the commune days that hosted thirty to forty residents. Tim and Debbie, who live in such a house, thought it could be easily turned into a home for seniors. They gave me a tour of the place and showed me how it could work. The upper floor had seven spacious rooms, and each could host a person or a couple. The ground floor had a large kitchen, dining area, a living room, and a specious entrance hall that could be merged into a common area. A door from the dining area led to a separate, relatively new unit that Tim had built for Debbie's mother, who lived with them for five years until she passed away. That unit, they thought, could serve the staff that would take care of the residents, and thus installing an internal elevator between the two floors was the main change required. Tim even showed me exactly how an elevator could fit in a space near the staircase. Yet, the couple also had other ideas for the place, such as turning it into a center for workshops and retreats where Tim would teach carpentry, Debbie would educate about vegan cooking, and others would give yoga sessions and the like.

Another collective aging-related consideration reported by the study participants was a change in the community's bylaws. Sam, who initiated this change, explained that The Farm's vision significantly differs from the fundamental values of Western property law. As the community is committed to respect and protect the environment, the land is owned by The Farm's Land Trust. This unusual arrangement is described in the trust's orientation manual as "an intersection between feudal property law, principles of Haudenosaunee [an indigenousconfederacy in northeast North America, also known as Six Nations] respect for the land, and our hippie ways developed in the past 50 years." De facto, it means that Farm members hold the land collectively but do not legally own or have a deed to their homes. Accordingly, as Sam put it, "when you pass away the bylaws, as they read, were that whoever inherits your house had one year until they become a member or sell the house at the best offer." Arguing that this arrangement was "wacky," Sam organized a series of meetings that ended up with the board changing the bylaws "in one word, from 'one' year to 'three' years." He clarified:

> The Farm didn't want people that weren't members to come in and take over houses, but you couldn't even become a member in one year, and families got to have a longer time to figure out what they want to do. If I pass on and my daughters inherit this house, they have to pay the dues from day one. They can rent it out, but it's not like the Farm will lose any money. And I wouldn't advise any family to decide to sell a house in one year if you just had a deceased family member. You're not even over it in a year.

Like Sam, some other community members had aging-related initiatives, but their ideas did not require collective decisions to be made. Accordingly, they just moved on and tried to realize them. Not surprisingly, the pioneer to do so was Stephen Gaskin – The Farm commune's leader, who remained a community member until his passing in 2014.

After the changeover in 1983, Gaskin maintained his involvement in Plenty and kept writing books and giving lectures. He also continued advocating hippie ideals such as the legalization of marijuana and even ran against Ralph Nader in an unsuccessful bid for the Green Party's presidential nomination. In 1996, he came up with what was probably the first enterprise ever to target aging hippies – a retirement village for the "60s idealists who 'sold out' in the 1980s and 1990s – the ones who went out and got real jobs," who are "poised to turn on, tune in and drop out once again."[9]

Certain that many ex-hippies would be interested in returning to their early selves and lifestyle, Gaskin formed a new nonprofit organization named *Rocinante* (pronounced "ro-see-NON-te") after "Don Quixote's horse and John Steinbeck's pickup truck, so it's a vehicle for an incurable idealist."[10] In his letter to the Internal Revenue Serviceapplying for charitablestatus,[11] he wrote:

> Our intention is the creation of an infrastructure to facilitate the co-operation of expectant and new mothers, old and fragile people, and people in the final stage of life, in a manner to hold down costs and to improve their quality of life...It is our intention to raise funds to build low-cost, energy-efficient housing for people who might otherwise be homeless. Also, qualified people are given the chance to help build themselves a cabin on our land, which will be their home for their life span and then will revert to Rocinante to be offered to another old or fragile person who might not have been able to build a cabin.

Rocinante's goal was to offer residents an opportunity to live cheaply in a multi-age, rural environment that facilitates both birth and death. Accordingly, it was planned to include a complete senior community (with adult daycare, assisted living, and a hospice for the dying) and a birth center with a midwifery training facility. This combination was supposed to provide the old residents with the option to become involved in the midwifery center by taking care of the children of expectant mothers – an arrangement that could be beneficial to all parties involved.

To this end, Rocinante bought 100 acres adjacent to The Farm and brought in electricity and phone lines, drilled and cased a well, installed pumping equipment, and began road work. Gaskin was planning to build a community center with a clinic, kitchen, laundromat, and media room with computers and internet access at a later stage. He also intended to staff an office to mediate communications between residents and their legal and medical support. None of this, however, came to fruition. After having several cabins built on the land, the development of Rocinante terminated. The reasons for this are unknown, but as far as I could understand from my conversations with Farm members, it was a combination of little demand, difficulty in getting grants, and poor management.

Gaskin's family still owns the land, and the cabins are rented. When I tried to visit the place, I saw at the entrance a sign with the following warning: "PRIVATE PROPERTY. Trespassers will be shot. Survivors will be shot again." Although this sign may have been some kind of twisted joke that I could not understand, I decided not to take the risk, turned the car, and drove away. Anyway, the aspiration to present "an inexpensive and graceful paradigm that can serve as a model for health care for the next century...and therefore be of significant value to the planet"[12] clearly failed.

Other, less ambitious but more successful individual initiatives came long after Rocinante ceased to exist. One such initiative was transforming a house on The Farm into a fully accessible home for people with disabilities, including ramps for wheelchairs, accessible baths and the like, and room for a caregiver. This house was built by a community member with quadriplegia, and since his passing, it has been rented to people in need. Another initiative was made by Chris, who built a hospice unit at his house (Figure 9.1). When Chris showed it to me, I wondered why he did that, as earlier he had told me that he had retired from hospice care because this work was too stressful and took an enormous emotional and physical toll on him. He explained that someone else would do the actual caregiving, and he would only supervise. Yet, after having "had the good grace to be a hospice nurse and help people die comfortably for almost 10 years," he was hoping to make community members' end of life more comfortable, relaxed, and dignified.

**9.1** The home hospice unit in Chris's house.

## DYING DIFFERENTLY

One evening, my hosts at The Farm got home quite late after visiting a friend dying of cancer. They said that the visit went pretty well even though it became emotional at times, especially when they told their friend how meaningful he was in their lives. The following morning, when I finally interviewed Bill, he reflected more on it: "The worst thing about aging is seeing your friends get sick and pass away. We've seen more and more of that. I guess this is our time to go. But on the other hand, we're all going on together, as I'm holding your hands as you jump off the cliff, and I'm glad for that." He added that because the founding members of The Farm were at about the same age, they always thought that they would "die together like popcorn," namely, in a rhythm that gets faster and then slows down until it stops. He vocally demonstrated it to me: "Pik.......... pik.......... pik.......... pik...... pik...... pik, pik, pik, pik, pik, pik, pik, pik, pik, pik, pik...... pik.......... pik.......... pik."

"Dying together" is not only a possible prospect; it is also a practice in the sense that Farm people usually do not die by themselves but rather surrounded by family and friends. Quite a few study participants reported visiting and taking care of friends who were about to leave the world. Daniel explained, "Materially, everybody is on their own, but spiritually there is a lot of help," and Stephanie shared, "Recently, a Farm sister died. She was so well supported by the tribe that it was extremely moving. It was phenomenal. We had to have a schedule because too many people wanted to sit with her while she was dying."

When needed, Farm people host their dying friends for the last period of life and arrange home hospice for them. Rebecca shared: "My friend who was dying died in my house with hospice. It was a bit better location than her house, and all Farm women were coming in to help take care of her, and... a couple of weeks before she died we had a circle around her with candles and some singing and stuff like that." Andrew added that Farm people are not alone even after passing: "Recently a Farm woman passed away. The day after she passed away, the Farm couple who had her stay with them said, 'Come see her.' So probably 150 people came because she was a good friend."

Some of the women interviewees compared dying with birth. Anna, for example, said:

> I was taking care of my best friend and was with her when she died, and I realized that the energy felt so much the same as at birth. It was so peaceful, and there was a sense of time stopping, and a sense of one foot in a different realm and one foot here, and it was so beautiful.

After having a series of such experiences following the death of her parents and two more friends, Anna felt that "the universe was kind of saying, 'do you want to experience this? This is you, you know.'" Perceiving hospice counselors as the ones who "really help the most," she decided to go back to school and get a Master's degree in Counseling Psychology. With time, she realized that preparation for death is "not about the last six months... it is more about our greater awareness of our mortality and our impermanence as we get older." She thus became a counselor working with older people and their families around these topics.

Another woman who made a career change after realizing the similarity between birth and death was Charlotte, who in her first email to me mentioned that she had been "a birth midwife for 36 years (now retired from that) and now a death midwife and end of life doula." When we met, she told me that when her mother died, she was the one who took her off life support, and then, a year later, her stepson got sick, and she "midwifed him through his dying." After receiving help through this process from the Core Council for Final Passages, a local nonprofit which provides education about conscious dying and home and family funerals, she decided to join it. She recently did their end-of-life doula training and has already organized fifteen home funerals. When I asked her why she chose to become an end-of-life doula, she explained:

> I got to do 12-hour shifts with a woman I had known for 28 years at her end of life and other people I've visited. It's a very sacred threshold, and it requires the same kind of energy as birth midwifery, where I am holding space for the sacred, being sensitive to the energies of the family and the person, and guiding them back to themselves. So, if there's the opportunity to resolve any unfinished business, I'm in support of that... I feel very, very blessed to have gotten to be a guardian of the gates.

In an email exchange, she added, "Witnessing death is humbling, reminding me of my own mortality and enabling me to discuss it honestly with my adult children (am in that process now) and my grandchildren."

Death was always one of the sacraments in the spiritual philosophy of The Farm. It was regarded as bringing a "strong connection with the profound" and "a period of internal reflection and contemplation."[13] This approach seems to last to this day. Moreover, discussions of death with study participants suggested that many believe in the afterlife and reincarnation. Some people mentioned reading a lot about it, and Warren Jefferson even went as far as conducting a two-year research on reincarnation and near-death experiences among Native Americans. That study turned into a fascinating book titled *Reincarnation beliefs of North American Indians: Soul journeys, metamorphoses and near-death experiences* (2008). Other people, however, reported first-hand experiences related to reincarnation. Cliff, for example, spoke about a trip to Kentucky he had taken many years ago:

> I've never in my life been there. And my wife and I are driving along, and I'm all going, "Wow! It's all so familiar!" and I would describe to her what was going to come, and there it was. And at some point, I said, "The road's going to bend to the right, and around the bend on the left is a yellow farmhouse with white trim," and I told her the name of the real estate company sign that was in front of that, and she said, "Okay, now you're freaking me out." I had seen this stuff! What it said to me was that the consciousness is not necessarily tied to the body because my body had never been there. I suppose it leaves open a possibility of some kind of life after death.

Whereas Cliff's experience was unintentional, some people deliberately explored their previous reincarnations by having sessions of past life regressions. Laura told me that in one such regression, she found out that in an early reincarnation, she was a young man in ancient Greece, where her ex-spouse – another Farm member – was her best friend and lover ("we were in this civilization where homosexuality was totally accepted"). Laura also recalled that on the night before going into the last battle, she (as that young man) knew she would die, but she still "made an appointment [with her lover] to be together again." This insight helped her "put together why I was with him in this lifetime" and heal from their painful divorce.

Sandra shared that many years ago, while visiting a library, "a book literally dropped off the shelf on the floor in front of me." When she picked the book up, she saw that it was about hypnotherapy and included a script for a past life regression. Sandra got curious and "kind of did it in my meditation to myself, and got some things that were fascinating and interesting and insightful for me, for what was going on in my life in the present." Following that experience, Sandra participated in special training in New York and became a certified hypnotherapist. She shared that she had "done past life regressions with a number of Farm people. We were in so many lifetimes together, let me tell you. You were probably there, Galit." Albert agreed, "That's right. You should have a session with Sandra. It's in there."

The only person that expressed blatant skepticism regarding the possibility of afterlife and reincarnation was Gordon:

A lot of hippies are totally into reincarnation. I'm really pretty well convinced that when you die, you're dead, and that's the end of the story. I don't know, of course, but I suspect that the energy that a person is made out of basically dissolves into the great pull of energy, and some other combination gets made from all those parts to make the next generation of people. Like the grass. In 10 years, it's all different grass, but it's still grass, and it's made up of all the old grass that died and then became like this.

Gordon somewhat mocked other hippies and their past life beliefs: "They always have great stories. 'I was this in the previous incarnation.' Not many people really go around saying, 'Well, yeah, I was a pitiful peon in my previous life in the fifteenth century or something.'" Yet, he added he could "understand why a whole lot of people just cannot grasp or cannot deal with the idea that when it's done, it's done, and they're gone, and it's done. It's over. That's it."

## POST-DEATH

Chris was the first person I interviewed at The Farm. We were sitting at his kitchen table and talking about his family when he looked at the woods outside the window and said that his second spouse was buried there. When I asked where, he explained, "That's the cemetery, and I can see her headstone from here." He added that people that tour The Farm and visit the cemetery say they wish they could be buried there and that it is "a really unique place, really special." However, other than noting that "it is pretty free form about where the graves are," he did not clarify what made the cemetery so special.

In the next few days, I heard from several people – old and young alike – how they wanted to be buried in The Farm, but the main reason for that was their wish to "be buried with my friends" (Sam). Julie also mentioned that former residents are allowed and sometimes choose to be buried at The Farm. She spoke about a recent passing of a former resident who lived in California, whose "body was flown back, and we had a funeral here, and people came in, and that was a big event."

The wish to be buried with friends and in a place of great significance in one's life was easy to understand. Yet, I was puzzled by the occasional visitors' reaction to the cemetery. So, early one morning I decided to visit the place. It took me some time to find it because it is literally inside the woods, but I understood its magic as soon as I got there. This cemetery was like nothing I have seen before. Gravestones were scattered around the place in no particular order, and they significantly varied in size, material, and shape. Many of them were artworks, some included artifacts (e.g., shells, flags, quartz crystals, statues from India and South America), and all of them were personalized (Figure 9.2).

Some gravestones were as big as a medium-sized plate, and others were bigger, but only a few were of regular or large size. Some did not have any text or had a name and date of passing only. Others had a short text that said something about the deceased (e.g., "She was an effective mother, educator, feminist and activist," "A beautiful spirit, always with a song in her heart," "Nature-loving humanitarian, ambassador for peace") or carried a general message ("My love is always free," "All that you have is what you give away," "You don't have to live forever, you just have to live"). The largest and most "formal" was Stephen Gaskin's gravestone, which had a long text providing quite a lot of information about him and his contributions to the community and the world. Yet, at its bottom, there was also a Zen Ensō circle (symbolizing enlightenment and infinity) followed by "What a long strange trip it's been" (the title of an album by The Grateful Dead).

People buried in the cemetery are community members, residents' parents who spent their final days at The Farm, and residents' children who did not survive birth or died at a young age. Stephen Gaskin, however, was not buried under the gravestone placed in the cemetery in his memory by the community. After his death, based on his explicit request, he was buried somewhere in the woods without any marker (though the coordinates are mentioned at the bottom of the gravestone at the cemetery). This unusual body disposal may have been an inspiration for Ben, who during the meeting of the Swan Trust suggested that the funding for the purchase of additional land would come from "having an area for green burials[14] for people that want to be buried here." Later, when we talked about it, he said that this

**9.2** Some of the gravestones at The Farm's cemetery. (The one in the upper-left corner is in honor of Stephen Gaskin, who is not buried in the graveyard.)

idea was "bouncing around my head" for some time and that the priority was to have an option for green burial at The Farm. Yet, if The Farm does not "entertain that idea," then the "Swan Trust would definitely be a second choice." Another idea that Ben brought up at that meeting was "memorial donation" – suggesting that donors buy an acre of land for the trust and acknowledging this donation by placing there a bench in memory of the donors or a person they wish to commemorate.

On the back of one of the gravestones, I found the following poem:

> The day you were born was as warm as your passing.
>
> And all the while I was crying, you flow above me laughing.
>
> Your hands push my steps towards everything,
>
> and your voice comes through in every song I sing.
>
> You bring your light upon my breath,
>
> and you were born into the day you left.

Later, I found out that poetry writing was among the more common methods Farm people use for commemorating loved ones who had passed away. Constance Miles, who admitted "death inspires me to write," even gave me a book of "death poems" she had written. She explained that writing such poems is an Asian tradition and that "the local Zen center has an evening of writing these annually, close to the New Year." Her beautiful poems suggested a philosophical view on death ("Aren't we each transient, like a burble of laughter?") and related to others' passing as well as her own expected death ("Can I script my dying? One last sniff of a newborn's head… One last morsel of dark chocolate… the comforting hand squeeze and snuggles of my daughters… Then I am ready").

Constance also wrote a series of "grief poems" following the death at the age of thirty-five of an opiate overdose of the son of two of her clients. In one of the poems, Constance, the midwife who helped bring his son to the world, tried to ease the grieving father's sense of guilt. She did so by describing the death by overdose as "ancestral trauma" because of "addiction snaking its way through the matrilineal line as well, coiling tightly around his great-grandfather, long ago, lost to heroin." She ended this poem by stating, "This is so much bigger than you, my friend. Your son is gone, but you are not to blame."

Constance described another poem I found particularly touching as a "home funeral inspired poem." To me, it demonstrated the earlier mentioned perception of dying as a sacred moment and an opportunity to resolve "unfinished businesses":

Bill's daughter speaks of his trauma.
She tells me his mother had severe
postpartum depression after he was
born. She was sent to a sanatorium,
subjected to shock treatments –
Mama–baby bonding interrupted,
he was sent to live with an aunt.

A year later, returning to his mother,
he saw her with another baby in her
arms. He asked, "Mama, why don't
you ever hold me?" His mother's arms
were full of someone else. For Bill,
an emptiness that engulfed him.

Seventy years later, as I enter the
room where he has died, in the arms
of his son and daughter, I see two
signs, his words from two days ago,
when he was still lucid. "You don't
need to talk," in big letters, and, in
smaller ones, "But you can." The
boldly lettered sign hanging from
his hospital bed says, "JUST HOLD ME."

(Constance Miles, November 29, 2020)

In an online Sunday service held in July 2020, during the COVID-19 pandemic, Douglas Stevenson presented a slide show honoring all "tribe members" who had passed away the previous year. After saying a few words about each of them, he took his guitar and sang a song he had written about separating from loved ones. The song's main message was that those who leave continue to exist in the hearts of those who remain behind. This song, he explained, was first sung at the funeral of his grandson, who died when he was only two years old of "a tiny bug called E-coli."

This tragic death was mentioned in several columns that Stevenson wrote for The Farm's newsletter. In one column (from April 2021), he wrote about the altar he had created in his bedroom as "a point of

**9.3** The altar at Douglas Stevenson's home. The heron represents his grandchild, who died when he was two years old. (Photo from The Farm's newsletter for April 2021.)

reflection," that he filled with "objects that represented a significant point or person in my life" (Figure 9.3). He explained that the wood carving of a heron at its center was there because when he lost his grandson, "herons [which represent stillness and tranquility] came into my life and my consciousness, appearing before me in the forest along the creeks, at the beginning and end of significant journeys and travels." In The Farm's newsletter for November 2019, Stevenson described how his grandson explored the forests and streams at The Farm and felt a "growing connection to the land." He shared that in his grief, he returned to "this woodland sanctuary" and "felt his [grandson's] spirit, and the spirit of the land, and the energy of countless others who had traveled to this sacred space for healing and celebration." This experience led to a lifetime commitment: "In his memory, I committed my life to saving this forest from devastation for children of future generations."

Overall, Farm members' ways of commemorating their family and friends are varied and include creativity, spirituality, and even civic engagement. In addition, there is a list of all people who have ever lived at The Farm and passed away that includes the exact locations of their graves. The community in Tennessee also honors the dead with frequent visits to the cemetery while taking walks, and congregating there on an evening close to or on Halloween, when "the veil is lifted between this world, and, you know" (Daniel). On that evening, the community members follow a tradition common in Latin American countries. They light candles inside brown paper bags and place them on all graves. The candles' glow reminds them that "we are not alone; we carry the memories of our loved ones in our hearts and minds."[15] Later that night, around a fire, they share stories of those who have left the world.

## SUMMARY: SOCIAL SUPPORT, SPIRITUALITY, AND CONTROL IN THE FACE OF DEATH

Study participants did not discuss fear of death, but this does not mean that they were not afraid of death like any other human being. Most probably, the topic was not considered because none of my questions referred to death-related worries. Yet, the information that community members shared with me (or with the world) suggests that the three factors that were found particularly useful in decreasing fear of death – social support, spirituality, and sense of control – were quite present in their lives. Accordingly, they may have been somewhat less fearful of death than older adults who were not part of the hippie tribe.

Apparently, the value of the social support provided by a lifelong community (see Chapter 8) is reflected throughout life, including its end. Based on their own and other community members' behavior, study participants seemed to know that their friends would comfort them in times of grief and visit, pray, and care for them if they became terminally ill or were unable to take care of themselves. The practice of being with and caring for Farm friends who are about to leave the world suggests that community members are not very fearful of *encountering* the dead and the dying. This practice may have also alleviated their fear of the *process* of dying when their time comes.[16]

The value of the lifelong community is reflected even after life is over. Again, based on their own and others' actions, study participants could be confident that their friends and family would commemorate them in a meaningful manner. Moreover, residents of The Farm in Tennessee found the idea of being buried with their friends comforting and could rest assured that after they pass away, the community will gather around their graves and fondly talk about them at least once a year, on Halloween. The expected companionship – of deceased and living community members alike – may have made the imagined post-death loneliness more bearable.

Although some study participants reported decreased spirituality in later life (see Chapter 7), spirituality was present in many discussions related to the end of life, such as in portraying dying as sacred and dying persons as existing simultaneously in two worlds. Spiritual components were also reflected in commemorations of the dead, be it in the text on their graves, poems written and music composed in their memory, or symbols put on the home altar of someone who loved them. Moreover, most study participants believed or at least entertained the idea of the afterlife and reincarnation. Reading, researching, and even experimenting with past life regressions may have reduced their fear of *mortality*, which relates to a fear of not experiencing anything after this life is over.[17] In addition, they did not seem to fear *life after death*. None of them suggested a possibility of terrifying after-death reality or reincarnation, and their perceptions and beliefs appeared to have a relaxing rather than a frightening impact.[18]

Lifelong and returning residents of The Farm could also benefit from collective and individual efforts to plan for their future. The change in the bylaws, which allows family members more time to make decisions about the house they inherited, may have reduced the older residents' worries about the future of their loved ones. Having an option to die peacefully at Chris's hospice unit may have decreased their fear of the process of dying, and those who had filled out the Five Wishes document surely felt less anxious about the quality of that process.[19] Therefore, the various community and individual efforts may have given them a greater sense of control and made them feel less helpless about the end of life.[20]

Thanks to plenty of social support that promotes a sense of security, spiritual beliefs that foster optimism about the afterlife, and planning that enhances a sense of control, study participants may have been less fearful and more accepting of death than other people of their age. Almost all fears composing the general construct of fear of death[21] seemed to be addressed in one way or another by these factors. The sole fear that did not appear to be tackled is the fear of the *physical destruction* of the body after death. Yet, the fact that some people were considering a green burial may suggest that they were not troubled by the expected demolition of their bodies.

Moreover, participants' thoughts, experiences, and initiatives indicate a somewhat alternative approach to death. The handprint of their former spiritual leader, Stephen Gaskin, who was as unorthodox in his later life as he was in the 1960s, could be recognized in some of their initiatives (e.g., the idea to live communally again and the suggestion to have a green burial area). Yet, it is clear that their alternative approach to death was not shaped by a single person but rather by a lifetime of maintaining the hippie values of community, spirituality, environmental awareness, and creativity.

# CHAPTER 10

# Aging Differently

P EOPLE WHO ARE SIXTY-FIVE YEARS OLD and over constitute the most heterogeneous segment of humanity. At one end of the continuum, there are those who have no or only a few and minor physical, emotional, and cognitive limitations, who are capable and highly motivated to live an active and fulfilling post-work life. At the other end, we can find the physically, emotionally, and cognitively frail individuals, and in between these ends, there are numerous variations of objective conditions and personal lifestyle choices. Chronological age per se is scarcely able to explain variations in the objective and subjective wellbeing of older adults.[1] Accordingly, social gerontologists constantly offer and test theories and models that explain why some people age better than others.

In their book *Cultures of ageing*, Gilleard and Higgs argued that the welfare mechanisms that helped shape later life in the nineteenth and twentieth centuries have begun to fragment, and, consequently, a variety of cultures, or subcultures, is emerging within which older adulthood can be lived.[2] Suggesting that this segmentation is also linked to processes of hypercommodification – the marketing, selling, and distribution of lifestyle choices – with which retirees are increasingly engaging, they criticized scholarly and consumerist advocates of "do-it-yourself" anti-aging lifestyles. Still, they recognized that such positions are important reflections of the social and cultural realities that reconstruct later life in the twenty-first century.

Hippiedom may be considered a specific culture or subculture within which some older Americans live their later years. As the 1960s hippie movement had an international influence (see Chapter 2), hippiedom as a culture of aging may also be discussed globally and refer to older individuals from many countries. Yet, one should be cautious in discussing the findings of the present study. The group of aging American hippies interviewed for this research cannot speak for aging hippies in other cultural contexts. It does not even represent American hippies as a whole because the hippies were a rather heterogeneous group even at a young age. At most, the study participants can be regarded as good representatives of the segment described as "visionaries," namely, the idealist hippies that aimed at posing an alternative to existing society.[3]

As one of the hippie communities that still exist today, The Farm offered an optimal context for studying aging visionaries. Having lifelong, returning, and former residents, The Farm also enabled a comparison between the visionaries who allegedly "remained" hippies and those who "reentered" mainstream America. As the differences among these groups were eventually marginal, the study yielded some general insights about the aging experiences of hippies. However, the extent to which hippies age differently or better than other older adults is yet to be discussed.

The qualitative approach applied in this study cannot offer a solid scientific basis for any comparative claim according to which hippies age differently or better than others. To support such a claim, I should have studied similar yet nonhippie communities and used quantitative techniques such as large-scale surveys. Nevertheless, I believe that two subjective perspectives, which will be discussed in this chapter, may shed light on the unique qualities of hippie aging. The first is the viewpoint of the study participants, and the second is my own.

Although some of the interviewees, especially Farm residents, felt that they lived in a bubble, all of them were well aware of other circumstances of aging in the U.S. and elsewhere. Accordingly, they were able to compare their experiences with those of other older adults and discuss who, in their opinion, aged better. Because subjective evaluations of wellbeing in later life are strongly correlated with objective measures,[4] the interviewees' perspectives offer a pretty reliable indication of their actual condition. In addition, as a scholar who has studied wellbeing in old age for more than two decades and in a large variety of national and cultural contexts, I have a certain degree of accumulated knowledge that enables me to reflect on the unique experiences of the aging hippies interviewed for this book.

## AGING DIFFERENTLY: THE AGING HIPPIES' PERSPECTIVE

Study participants hesitated about comparing hippies to other older adults. Perceiving the hippies as a diverse group, they felt somewhat uncomfortable generalizing about them ("There's a wide variance" – Joe; "It's such a mixed group of people at this point" – Jerry; "It's a mix like everybody else" – Rebecca; "It's like the normal bell curve. Some yes [age better] and some no, and then everybody is in-between" – Sandra). Overall, they thought that the hippies are not immune to the challenges of aging ("The challenges of aging are the same for all, regardless of who and where you are" – Bill; "We know so many people in a constant state of getting sick and dying that I'm not sure" – Julie).

Several interviewees even claimed that the hippies do not do as well as others in some aspects, especially the financial ones ("A lot of people who have done things that I consider less interesting got more money than I do. For all of the 70s, I made nothing. I had nothing" – Paul), and are more susceptible to poor health ("Poor people don't have good health. Poor people don't make good health choices. They are also more stressed and don't rock and roll as well" – Evelyn; "A certain amount of that subculture went off the deep end and got into hard drugs and all that" – Joe). In addition, they acknowledged that many other people are involved in good deeds ("A lot of good people are involved in a lot of good organizations and efforts to make good things happen" – Ben), have a supportive community ("People have their church communities, and that's their community, and they cover for each other" – Debbie), and live their form of a more authentic life ("A lot of people in my area led their own parallel version of an alternate lifestyle" – Paul).

Despite such reservations, most study participants thought that the hippies aged differently. Comparing themselves to others – their parents when they were their age, their siblings, their neighbors, and various nonhippie peers they have met through school, work, and the like – they also felt that they have aged much better overall. Although these sentiments originated in subjective evaluations, many interviewees supported them by quoting external, objective perspectives. They mentioned numerous comments made by laypeople (e.g., "I have a friend who's in her mid-50s, and we were walking the other day, and I said I was 70. She goes, 'What, you're 70? Oh my god. I want to look like you when I'm 70'" – Karen; "I went to my high school 50th reunion, and one guy, who I hadn't seen in years, went, 'You look like a million bucks'" – Dennis). Often, they strengthened these comments by citing professionals. Elizabeth, for example, shared, "The nurse practitioner in my primary care doctor's offices said, 'What is that about you people from The Farm? You all look great!'" Similarly, Carolyn quoted her daughter, a massage therapist working with "very high class, wealthy people," who said, "There's no comparison to how you guys are so much more youthful than the people that I take care of."

The most common support for the claims about better aging was the study participants' relatively young-looking appearance. It seems, therefore, that while deemphasizing the centrality of the hippie look (see Chapter 4), they still valued a youthful look. The magic number, mentioned by many, was ten years. Joan said, "You can look at some people that are our age, and they look 10 years older than us," and Nicholas stated, "I look at squares, and they often look about 10 years older. Being a hippie keeps you young mentally, and then that's reflected outwardly." The interviewees also offered many explanations for the hippies' better aging and discussed the factors that, in their opinion, help them age well. These factors could generally be classified into three categories: health, engagement, and social support (Figure 10.1).

HEALTHY LIFESTYLE CHOICES Study participants often argued that they, their Farm friends, and other hippies were generally healthier than the average American at their age. They listed several factors explaining their better health, of which the most prominent were their *plant-based diet, high involvement in physical activities, life in nature, low level of stress,* and *use of dope.* Often, these factors were discussed as being interrelated. Evelyn, for example, said, "I was a doctor in a hippie-ish town, where people have embraced natural healing, healthy eating,

**10.1** Map of The Farm: The road to wellbeing?

exercise, meditation, and all the stuff… they look fabulous and are doing incredibly well." Cindy declared, "I think we're generally healthier," and explained:

> A lot of the people I see at the gym [outside The Farm] are all overweight. I'm looking at them, and I'm thinking, "If you do this exercise thing, how can you be overweight?" Well, it must be their eating habits. You can hardly see overweight people here, and you'll see many people biking and walking. People walk or bike to work, to the post office, and to the store. And we are surrounded by all these wonderful woods. It's like living in a park, and you can get down there easily and walk around. Living close to nature is also more peaceful – it helps your head. If you have been watching too much TV or reading horrible things on the news, or your phone, or everything, put that away and just go down in the woods.

Living in or close to nature was associated not only with lower stress but also with "having cleaner air and water than many people do" (Bill). Similarly, having less stress was related to a less competitive lifestyle than in "urban environments, where it's just kind of a little dog eat dog, everybody is kind of alpha" (Ben). It was also presented as the result of frequent meditation practice ("I do meditation every day, that's helpful, and I do introspection during that period" – Brian; "Some people are maintaining that meditative state and seem happy enough" – Evelyn). Dope use, too, was associated with better health and less stress (see Chapters 5 and 6). Some people, like Jane, even described it as maintaining youth:

> Smoking pot makes you realize that there's more to life. You're like, "Oh," and all of a sudden, you're nicer, you're more creative, you can see things you didn't see before, or you can see it in ways that you might not have seen before. And because your view of life is different, your experience of later life is different. Once you've opened your mind and received the love and put out the love, I think that helps you stay young. Love makes everything better.

The interviewees stressed that maintaining a healthy lifestyle is a matter of personal choice. Dennis argued that such a choice should have been made at a young age: "It depends how you took care of yourself when you were younger." In contrast, Ben thought that this was a choice made daily and that it was never too late to improve: "I implement these principles in my life, the healthy eating, the exercising, and the positive thinking, but I can always do better. I don't do as good as I could." Chris added that healthy lifestyle choices include both dos and don'ts:

> I was shopping for folding chairs and saw a chair that's for 300-pound people. I couldn't believe it. It's like, "Are you kidding me?" It's got to be the soda, diet, poor food choices, television, lack of exercise, and stress... I don't smoke. I don't drink alcohol. I try to take good care of myself, get good sleep. Most deaths are lifestyle choices. Lifestyle choices are everything. Genetics, stress, and all of those other things sure come into the mix, but this is part of my strategy to try to age in place. I'd like to break a 100 with style.

**PURPOSEFUL ENGAGEMENT** Study participants attributed a good part of the hippies' better aging to their high engagement in various activities. Brian said, "As aging hippies, we still like to party, we still like to get together, still like to have fun, we still like to dance." Chris stated, "Living here is a mitzvah. It's a blessing. I mean, take a look: This is heaven! I get to walk, I get to ride, I get to dance, I get to be with good friends, we get to eat a potluck. Life is good here." Joan suggested: "I think it [better aging] has to do with lifestyle and with engagement with life in general. People who don't stay engaged or interested tend to start withdrawing, and their world gets smaller, and it starts to shut. I would absolutely love to be 140."

Several interviewees stressed that by "engagement," they primarily meant *making a difference*, as Elizabeth put it: "You could say that it is about having more purpose in life, and there's always an opportunity for good work." Albert explained that in the case of aging hippies, purposeful engagement is a constant throughout their lives: "I think if folks maintain those principles – the spirituality, the liberal thinking, the brotherhood, the resistance – they'll come up on top of the average American who is somewhat spiritually lost and uptight and freaked out at the state of the world. You got to cut through all that, and those hippie practices help." Similarly, Julia stated, "Hippies age better because they never bought into things that were not important for social reasons or political reasons. That's always been the way. If I get too involved, I have problems with a lot of judgments, but I have a lot too." Sandra agreed: "Because of spirituality, I think that aging without a sense that life has a meaning or a purpose must be very challenging, and sad, and difficult. If you have a sense that your life does have a purpose and a meaning, then you're probably going to age a lot happier."

Making a difference did not have to be grandiose. It could be pretty *modest*, as Chris explained: "I tried to focus on doing something right every day, and I tell my friends, 'Do something good. Help somebody. It'll make your life better.'" Sam approved, "I don't think any of my contributions are more important than anybody else's. We all get involved with niches that we have interest in." Yet, he seemed pretty proud of some of his Farm friends who were "out there" changing the world on a *larger scale.* "One of them is now the mayor of Kalamazoo, Michigan, and another guy is now a liaison in Washington, DC for democratic senator. They still hold The Farm values in their lifestyle, even though it might be some other place." Daniel, too, talked about people who try to profoundly change the world, such as Bernie Sanders and Elizabeth Warren. He argued that thanks to such efforts, his generation presents a new model of old age:

> The hippies changed the face of later life. In traditional cultures, not that many people lived really long, and the people who did were considered wise people. And now we're going to have lots and lots of people living long lives and hopefully will have accumulated enough wisdom to help calm the world down a little bit. We, humans, got to stop playing with each other and work on things like global warming. We have to learn to share because if we don't, we're going to blow each other up and wreck it. So, it's crucial right now that those still alive try to hang in and be active.

SUPPORTIVE SOCIAL NETWORK The third group of factors mentioned as explanations for the hippies' better aging was their supportive social networks. Yet, it was clear that in this case, study participants were referring to The Farm community rather than to hippies in general. They stressed that having a supportive social network improved their wellbeing because it provided a sense of *safety*. Cindy said, "Hopefully, I can age in the community. As we always say, we're going to take care of each other." Carolyn argued, "People are already taking care of each other. You can feel that here," and Henry stated, "My neighbor that has Alzheimer's is a good example. There's no plan for her, but she's quite safe because there will always be people around to take care of her."

In addition to the safety, several participants presented the community as a fountain of youth ("It keeps my brain young and my body young, and I will age gracefully in the community" – Nicholas) and argued that it is a source of great happiness. Bill explained:

> I heard Jane Fonda, who is now over 80, talk about how she was happier now than she'd ever been. Well, I am. I really am. Even though I got various [health] things going on, I'm really glad to have a community of supportive people. The community is a resource. People know that there are people that will help take care of them. So the fact that you were able to sustain this community and actually live most of your adult life with your

friends and maintain friendships is a positive factor in aging. I don't think there's any question that a community contributes to even something as longevity. I expect that most of us will live longer than our parents, and my mother lived to be 97!

Such claims were made not only by The Farm residents but also by former residents. Stephanie, for example, said:

> We have a community of people who take care of each other still, and I look around and don't see that happening in too many places. It is a spiritual community still, and spirit has no geographic limitations. We have seen that, and it is invaluable to have that family, that tribe. We know it now because we're older. Older people who are isolated do not do well, and it's easy to get isolated, especially now, hello. I know it's up to me to rescue myself. I'm not saying anybody is going to rescue me from anything. But I know someones who would walk their path with me, who know the same things I do, and that is just amazing.

The interviewees offered three comparisons to support their arguments: *urban environments, retirement communities*, and *other rural communities*. They claimed that older people in cities are isolated and may thus be pretty lonely ("To be an old person in the city by yourself, to me, that's like – I don't want to be alone in the city somewhere" – Jane; "In the city, I am not in the community. I know people. I am friendly with people, but they are not my peeps" – Cliff). Some residents joked that The Farm "is much like a retirement community with the exception we're not that old" (Bill). Still, they thought it is entirely different because the residents in retirement communities are "strangers rather than lifetime friends" (Jane). In addition, "they are all old, whereas here I'm living in a community with my grandchildren and my extended family... so, my family experience is at least half of my community experiences" (Henry). Agreeing that residents of small, rural communities may have a good community life, they argued that it is not the same because The Farm community "is just more intimate, it's your family" (Henry), "we have so many similarities that you feel completely at ease" (Bill), "we have a commitment to being spiritual and taking care of the land" (Jane), and "we all have the hippie ethos" (Joe).

## AGING DIFFERENTLY: THE RESEARCHER'S PERSPECTIVE

My view of aging hippies' later years does not contradict the study participants' perceptions. Overall, I agree that they age differently and, yes, probably better than many other older adults in the U.S. and other countries. Based on the analysis presented in this book, however, my framing of the factors that make hippie aging unique is different. As I see it, aging hippies hold five keys to wellbeing in later life, and these keys share two overarching qualities: *ideology* and *adaptability*. It should be stressed that none of the keys nor their qualities are new. All of them and their positive impacts on older adults' wellbeing have been well documented in the field of aging studies. What I find unique to aging hippies is their integration and intense application, which I never witnessed in my previous studies or in others' research.

## THE FIVE HIPPIE KEYS TO WELLBEING IN OLDER AGE

Healthy lifestyle choices, purposeful engagement, and supportive social networks undoubtedly enhance aging hippies' physical, psychological, social, and spiritual wellbeing. Yet, the present study pointed to five keys to wellbeing in later life widespread among this particular culture of aging.

CREATIVE IDENTITY WORK Although the physical and social changes associated with old age may challenge everyone's identity, they could be particularly intimidating to those who used to say: "Never trust anyone over 30." The alleged contradiction between old age and hippiedom could make aging hippies prone to identity degradation. Yet, this study suggests that by creative application of several identity work strategies that bridge between internal self-identity and external social identity,[5] they maintained a consistent and positive self-perception.

The main strategies relied on the perception of hippiedom as a complex construct composed of multiple components and the differentiation between the hippie essence, behavior, and look. The first strategy was attributing greater importance to the hippie essence while deemphasizing the centrality of look and behavior. This strategy was based on the centrality of love – which is resilient to age-related changes – to the hippie essence. The second strategy was turning hippiedom from a dichotomous construct to a host of continuums referring to both external and internal components of the hippie identity. This perception suggested that individuals can be low on one continuum and high on another. They can even move up and down on the various continuums according to the circumstances. Both strategies represent *identity balance*[6] that enabled incorporating age-related changes without turning into a nonhippie.

Additional common strategies included using the relative term "older" instead of the definitive word "old," which may be regarded as *identity accommodation*,[7] and a general tendency to avoid all forms of age disguising. This tendency is consistent with the hippie love of nature and the natural. It may also be considered *resistance*,[8] as it opposes the anti-aging culture prevalent in Western societies. Overall, the various strategies seemed to effectively preserve study participants' identity as authentic, hippie individuals who always dare to pose an alternative to the mainstream, regardless of their age.

MULTILAYERED GENERATIVITY Aspiring to change the world and make it a better place, the people who participated in the study reported an outstanding involvement in generative activities, namely, activities aiming to guarantee the wellbeing of future generations.[9] Although generativity is typically more prominent in later life,[10] they were highly involved in such activities throughout their lives. Moreover, their generativity scripts were pretty thick as they were made of three synergetic layers: the individual, the community, and the generation.

Study participants were involved in various generative activities at the individual level, both in private and public domains. Many of them worked in jobs and businesses that promoted goals that aligned with their ideals. They also volunteered and donated money to various actions that endorsed such purposes, and quite a few even initiated and led nonprofit organizations and programs. In addition, they took part in and, accordingly, felt ownership of The Farm and the hippie movement's contributions to the world. They described all three layers, including the individual layer, as mutual efforts and suggested that all layers had similar goals.

Like the work done concerning their identity, the interviewees found ways to accept their generation's failures in changing the world, especially in the political realm. Explaining that human nature is hard to change and that the hippies were only part of several counterculture movements and tended not to be political, they emphasized their cohort's many notable successes. Overall, they were proud of their own, The Farm's, and their generation's achievements. This pride resulted in a dominant generativity theme in their narratives and strengthened their sense of meaning in life.

MEANINGFUL PLAY Leisure, too, was described as a significant source of meaning. Adhering to the hippie ethics of play, study participants had pretty diverse leisure repertoires adapted to their needs, abilities, and circumstances. Despite the considerable variety, their leisure activities had some commonalities. First, they included many social and physical activities – two activity types that contribute significantly to wellbeing in later life.[11] Second, almost all interviewees reported taking long walks and gardening. These activities, which may be regarded as healthy lifestyle choices, seemed particularly beneficial as they combined social, physical, therapeutic, and spiritual elements. Moreover, both fostered a connection with nature and had roots in the commune era, when study participants grew their food and usually walked to get from one place to another. Accordingly, these activities contributed to a sense of continuity and may have preserved the hippie (or "Farmie") back-to-the-land identity.

Continuity was also maintained through ongoing involvement in sex, dope, and rock. Although some adaptations were reported, both in intensity and meaning, this hippie triad was still well present in study participants' lives. Rock music, in particular, seemed to preserve its significance. For some people, it even became a form of "serious leisure" characterized by considerable efforts but offering many durable rewards.[12] Additional serious leisure activities included various arts (visual arts in particular) and cooking, and some people described gardening as a serious involvement.

Having serious leisure activities was typically reported by individuals less involved in generative and spiritual activities. In addition, all interviewees described reduced involvement in some activities and increased participation in others. These findings indicate a balancing mechanism according to which more participation in some activities compensates for reduced or lower involvement in others. Many also provided examples of activities in which they simultaneously realized several desires (e.g., nature photography). Accordingly, it seems that study participants both deeply understood the value of leisure[13] and used it brilliantly to make their later lives meaningful and enjoyable.

CUSTOMIZED SPIRITUALITY A certain level of playfulness was evident in the interviewees' approach to spirituality. This does not mean that they did not relate to spiritual matters seriously. On the contrary, the majority reported a lifetime of thorough spiritual study and practice and felt that sacred principles guided everything they did. Yet, their approach to spirituality allowed for ongoing explorations and experimentations that, just like in children's play, enabled a deeper understanding of their inner world and external realities.[14]

The outcome of the ongoing explorations was that each study participant had a unique spiritual journey leading eventually to a set of beliefs and practices that fit them best. For half of the participants, such customized spirituality was pretty eclectic and could be described as New Age spirituality.[15] Others reported a more focused spirituality in their later years. They either selected one path out of previously explored directions or discovered a new road to fulfillment and made it the center of their spiritual lives.

Whereas the group that exhibited focused spirituality and the perpetual seekers became more involved in spiritual activity with age, some interviewees did not report any spiritual growth but rather maintained beliefs and practices adopted early in life. Nevertheless, they all seemed to have enhanced wellbeing thanks to their spirituality,[16] which was reflected in having a sense of meaning and satisfaction in life and even in being less fearful of death. Interestingly, some study participants became somewhat less involved in previous spiritual activities. Yet, most of them still reported beliefs and practices that may be regarded as spirituality. Rejecting formal religions and alternative spirituality alike, they were questioning all spiritual authorities. By so doing, they maintained the hippie ethics of cultural opposition[17] and a high level of authenticity.

STRONG PSYCHOLOGICAL SENSE OF COMMUNITY The last but not least critical key to wellbeing in later life is the hippie PSOC. Despite some differences among lifelong, returning, and former residents of The Farm in Tennessee, all study participants reported a very strong PSOC. It included all elements related to PSOC, namely, membership, influence, integration and fulfillment of needs, and shared emotional connection.[18] The positive impact of PSOC on older adults' wellbeing is well documented.[19] Therefore, it is no wonder that a supportive social network was a central justification that the interviewees gave for their argument that hippies age better than other people.

Despite the considerable geographical distance between some community members and the long time that had passed since the commune period, The Farm is a lifelong community of interest perceived by its members as a "tribe" and even a "family." The strong sense of connectedness was maintained thanks to numerous local communities of former residents scattered around the country and the digital revolution that offered community members a simple and available means to stay connected. As a result, all community members know that their tribe and its "culture of helping" will always be there for them: for better, for worse, for richer, for poorer, in sickness and in health, in life, near the end of life, and even after death.

Study participants did not only practice the hippie ethics of community, they also developed a rather helpful system for conflict resolution, which is mandatory for community sustainability and aligns with their ideology of peace and nonviolence. Some of them even dedicated their post-commune career to advocating the ethics of community in the digital sphere. Moreover, it seemed that the "inherited Farm-related PSOC" of their children and grandchildren was one of their most significant sources of happiness and pride. Knowing that the second generation made the core of the younger cohort in The Farm reassured them that although it may take new directions, their legacy will last after they are gone.

## THE TWO OVERARCHING QUALITIES OF THE HIPPIE KEYS TO WELLBEING

Healthy lifestyle choices, purposeful engagement, and supportive social networks may enhance the wellbeing of all aging individuals. However, some of the five hippie keys to wellbeing in later life identified in this study (specifically, the identity work strategies and multilayered generativity) are less likely to apply to people growing older today. Nevertheless, these five keys share two qualities relevant to every person. These qualities were evident in every one of the forty extraordinary life stories I was fortunate to hear, and could be easily tracked on each page of this book.

IDEOLOGY-BASED LIVES The hippie ideology (see Chapter 2) has guided the study participants' lives from a very young age to the present. Seeming constant and intact, it also offered them a solid basis to accommodate the changes associated with aging. Just as it did in their youth, the ideology was first used to highlight what they were not: not traditional, not materialistic, not part of the anti-aging culture, but also not "old." Then, it was applied in shaping an alternative "older" age characterized by love, generativity, play, spirituality, and community.

The ideological tenets of the hippie movement were reflected in all hippie keys to wellbeing in later life. The centrality of love, peace, and nonviolence was evident in the identity work done by the study participants and motivated their generative actions. The play ethics was mainly apparent in their meaningful leisure but also seemed to affect their spirituality. The ethics of dope was preserved as a leisure practice and in some of their generative initiatives. The ethics of community resulted in the strong PSOC and added two layers – community and generation – to their generative scripts. Certain overlaps were also found between their spirituality and generativity as they felt that their spiritual practices affected the world, and between their sense of community and generativity because they aimed to set an example for the next generation. Their love for nature influenced their appearance, leisure activities, and environment-focused generativity, and the ethics of cultural opposition affected their identity work and spirituality.

Overall, the hippie ideology served as a pillar of fire that shaped study participants' identity, daily activities, and wellbeing throughout their lives, including their later life (Figure 10.2). Like in their youth, their particular culture of aging is an external expression of numerous, complex, and diverse ideological principles. While being fairly stable, the diversity of the hippie ideology allows for some flexibility and customization.

**10.2** A sign outside the home of one of the study participants.

Accordingly, it helps aging hippies maintain a consistent and positive self-perception and make their later lives meaningful and enjoyable.

LATER-LIFE ADAPTATIONS Study participants neither denied their age nor perceived it as a problem. They accepted being "older" as part of who they were, and a high level of continuity characterized their experiences of aging and keys to wellbeing in later life. This continuity resulted from the fact that they "have remained true to the hippie spirit."[20] It was reflected in their identity, generative efforts, leisure activities, spirituality, and sense of community. Nevertheless, study participants applied various behavioral and cognitive mechanisms that helped them adapt to the challenges associated with older age and the changes in their needs, abilities, and circumstances.

*Behavioral adaptations* included being selective about the activities in which they participated and the goals they wanted to promote (e.g., social and environmental, but not political), reducing involvement in certain activities (e.g., psychedelics, sex) while expanding involvement in others (e.g., rock, gardening, and serious leisure pursuits) and allowing for a certain degree of innovation (e.g., new spiritual paths, individual generative initiatives). *Cognitive mechanisms* included attributing more importance to some aspects while deemphasizing others (e.g., essence versus behavior and look, achievements versus failures, the advantages of community versus its downsides), and adapting the meaning of certain elements (e.g., sex, dope, rock, and age).

Overall, the delicate juggling between continuity and change has enabled both to exist. Considering the contribution of continuity,[21] selectivity,[22] and innovation[23] to wellbeing in old age, it seems that the aging hippies interviewed for the present study benefited from all three. They sought and found ways to preserve significant elements in their identity and lifestyles, let go or reduced involvement in less fulfilling activities, and were still open to new opportunities for personal, social, and spiritual growth. All in all, the people who sought more meaningful and authentic lives in their youth seemed to find them in their later years, too.

## A TAKE-HOME MESSAGE ABOUT COMMITMENT

A year and a half after my first visit to The Farm, I traveled to the U.S. again to spend a couple of weeks with the people whom by then I called "my hippie friends." I first stayed at The Farm and then traveled to California to visit the former residents, who until then I had only met online. In California, I also participated in the PeaceRoots Alliance annual fund-raising event – a full-day festival attended mostly by former residents. This trip allowed me to spend some time with most study participants, either one on one or in small groups. Accordingly, I could catch up on what had happened in their lives since they were interviewed, tell them about the study insights, and get their feedback.

In addition to the warm encounters and exciting conversations, we also shared numerous fun moments. Among other things, I participated in Sarah's birthday party, bought vegetables with Bill from the Amish residing close to The Farm, visited the house Cliff was building and saw his artwork, went for a morning walk with Chris and Tim, checked the RV that Nicholas and his spouse had bought and heard about their many travels during the COVID-19 pandemic, met Henry's new girlfriend,

**10.3** The Farm's fiftieth anniversary was not celebrated because of the COVID-19 pandemic.

explored the ecological house and garden of Joan's daughter, traveled to a redwood forest and the ocean with Rebecca, played with Andrew's new puppy, toured Charlotte's four-acre garden, and shared food and drinks with almost everyone. At the annual event, I also had the opportunity to see the Best Witches, the Farm Band, and other groups perform, watch Karen and Jerry dance, sort Lillian's exquisite tie-die clothes, participate in a raffle for one of her quilts, and meet many more founding members of The Farm, as well as quite a few of the second generation. By the end of my trip, I had even visited the Haight-Ashbury district with a woman who has lived there since the 1960s.

September 1, 2021, was when The Farm officially turned fifty (Figure 10.3). On that date, fifty years ago, the land became formally owned by the community's founding members, and they could drive their buses into the property. Because of the pandemic in Tennessee the event was not celebrated, but the day turned out to be most meaningful to me. After several days of rain, the sun came out, so Ben picked me up with his four-wheeler for a tour of the Big Swan Headwaters Preserve. At my request, our first stop was Stephen Gaskin's unmarked grave in the middle of the woods, where I spent some time thanking him for the miracles he had made by founding The Farm and for all the gifts he had given to this world and me, even without knowing about my existence. Before leaving the place, I also put a stone on his grave (a Jewish tradition) to express my respect.

From there, Ben and I went for a ride around the preserve and reached its borders in all four cardinal directions. We went up on the mountains and down to the creeks, made our way through the woods and the water, visited several waterfalls and ponds, watched birds, examined invasive species, and collected some spearheads. We chatted about various topics, but most of the time, we were quiet and appreciated the beauty. And the beauty was breathtaking. After several hours of an experience that some would describe as *spiritual*, I told Ben that I finally understood what everyone was talking about when they discussed the land: how it is part of the community just like the people, why they feel that they have a relationship with it, and why they want to be buried in it. Until that day, I could only understand it rationally. On that day, I could also *feel* it.

I was about to leave The Farm to travel to California in the afternoon of the following day. As I woke up early, I decided to spend my last hours at The Farm experiencing the land again and drove down to the swimming hole. No one else was there so early in the morning, so I could just sit next to the water and quietly enjoy nature. I imagined how, throughout the years, the place had silently witnessed the community in all its stages and the community members in all life phases. More than any book or film, it could probably best tell about the long-haired, colorfully dressed idealistic young people who had come there fifty years ago, built a community, raised their families, changed the world in a variety of ways, and now set an example for graceful aging. Imagining my hippie friends swimming there at different stages of their lives, I felt that no visit to The Farm would be complete without doing the same. Therefore, despite the chilly temperature outside and the freezing water, I decided to go in for a swim. After some vigorous laps that helped me adjust to the cold, I could stop for a peaceful float and absorb the beauty again.

Knowing that I would cross the gate on my way out in a few hours, I thought about the early rainy morning on which I had left The Farm after my first visit, and reflected on the personal journey this study had offered me. I remembered how, while driving to Nashville Airport, I had pretty mixed feelings. I was full of awe, excitement, and gratitude for having the experience of visiting the community and meeting the fascinating people who are part of it. Simultaneously, however, I felt a sense of loss. It may sound a bit weird, but I truly regretted not being born in the right place and time to be involved in the 1960s counterculture. I felt sorry for not having been part of the cultural revolution and having such an extraordinary life as the individuals I had met.

Moreover, I thought about a study that a colleague and I had conducted several years ago, which explored older people's perceptions of successful aging as a process. The central theme that emerged from our interviews with 207 individuals aged sixty-five to ninety-two was: "Investments at early stages are profitable."[24] All our interviewees thought that there are many steps one may take in advance to age well. They often described such steps as "investments" made at a young age from which people profit in future years. They also suggested that the primary investment areas should be health (e.g., healthy nutrition and regular physical activity), material safety (e.g., comfortable housing and sufficient income), relationships (e.g., family and friends), and self (e.g., interests and good memories). While driving to the airport, I regretted not making similar "investments" to the ones that the founding members of The Farm had made at a young age, as it was clear that these investments were very fruitful.

In the following months, I had many more such moments of regret that made me question the entire research project. Although I paid considerable attention to the difficulties that the study participants faced throughout their lives, including today, it was clear that this book describes an unusual case of good aging that resulted from a remarkable life. I thus asked myself, "If you had to be a hippie all your life to have a hippie old age, what is the point of this book? Am I writing it to make people feel bad about not being part of the hippie movement or lucky enough to be among the founding members of The Farm community? Is that the emotion that I want to leave with the readers?"

As the writing of the book progressed, however, my worries abated and eventually disappeared. The clearer the hippie keys to wellbeing in later life and their overarching qualities became, the more convinced I was: *We all can make our golden years meaningful, satisfying, and "hippie" to an extent.* Sure, it cannot hurt to start planning our old age when we are in our twenties, but most young people focus on the near future and do not think about aging at all. It can also be beneficial to maintain a healthy lifestyle and have a stable financial condition, some faith and ideology, a close community of like-minded people, and a diverse repertoire of generative, creative, and hedonic activities. Yet, I think that there is one thing that we can learn from the hippies and, hopefully, adopt.

The greatest lesson that the visionary hippies interviewed for this book taught us can eventually be summarized in one word – commitment. Commitment includes *commitment to other people* and *commitment to ideals.* Other people do not have to be a tribe of several hundred individuals with whom we spent many years of intense adventures. A few warm and caring relationships can be more than enough. The people in our closer social circle may be our family, lifetime and new friends, members of our religious community, or neighbors living in the same apartment building as we do. Similarly, our ideals do not have to have a deep spiritual foundation or be based on a complex philosophical paradigm. Believing in simple principles such as "Do no harm" and its complimentary tenet "Do good" may be enough to guide ideology-based lives.

When our commitment to people and ideals lies at the heart of our lives, age-related losses may be somewhat easier to accept, and adaptations may be slightly simpler to make. If we emphasize the significance of the goal, we may attribute less importance to the means. Accordingly, if one of our resources is temporarily or permanently unavailable, we may be more willing to replace it with alternative ones. We may then be happy to talk on the phone with an old friend if a face-to-face meeting is not possible, post on Facebook if we do not have the energy to demonstrate in the streets, take a walk instead of jogging if our knees hurt, cultivate several planters rather than an entire garden if we move into a retirement home, and so forth. Such adjustments may support our self-preservation and make our lives as purposeful and meaningful as possible, even in times of extreme constraint. Moreover, our commitment to people and ideals may result in a sense of community, personal spirituality, and relative control that will make us live in greater peace with the certainty of the end of life, any life, hippie and nonhippie alike.

# Appendix

## STUDY PARTICIPANTS

Table A.1 provides more information about the forty individuals interviewed for the study.

**Table A.1**

| Name | Age | Family status | Children* | Higher education | Work status | Main occupation |
|---|---|---|---|---|---|---|
| Lifelong residents – lived at The Farm for most of their adult lives | | | | | | |
| Joan | 67 | Widowed twice, married | 2 | – | Working | Business management |
| Elizabeth | 67 | Divorced twice, married | 3 | MA | Retired | Education |
| Sarah | 67 | Divorced, married | 2 | BA | Retired | Healthcare |
| Cindy | 70 | Married | 4 | MA | Retired | Education |
| Debbie | 70 | Married | 3 | Incomplete BA | Working | Administration |
| Carolyn | 75 | Divorced three times, married | 3 | BA | Retired | Healthcare |
| Nicholas | 67 | Married | 2 | – | Retired | Media |
| Henry | 68 | Divorced, separated | 2 | – | Working | Business management |
| Tim | 69 | Married | 3 | BA | Working | Business management |
| Daniel | 75 | Divorced, married | 5 | PhD | Semi-retired | Education |
| Bill | 75 | Divorced twice, married | 3 | BA | Retired | Media |
| Chris | 76 | Divorced four times, in a relationship | 3 | BA | Retired | Healthcare |
| Brian | 77 | Married | 4 | BA | Semi-retired | Media |
| Returning residents – left The Farm for a long period (>20 years) and moved back | | | | | | |
| Julie | 66 | Married | 4 | MA | Working | Education |
| Shirley | 72 | Divorced twice | 1 (2) | BA | Semi-retired | Law |
| Jane | 74 | Divorced | 3 | BA | Retired | Administration |
| Julia | 75 | Married | 2 | BA | Retired | Healthcare |

| Name | Age | Family status | Children* | Higher education | Work status | Main occupation |
|------|-----|---------------|-----------|------------------|-------------|-----------------|
| Cliff | 70 | Married | 3 | Incomplete BA | Retired | Manual craftmanship |
| Ben | 70 | Widowed, divorced, in a relationship | 4 | – | Retired | Manual craftmanship |
| Dennis | 72 | Widowed, married | 2 | BA | Retired | Public service |
| Sam | 73 | Divorced, widowed | 2 | BA | Semi-retired | Manual craftmanship |
| James | 75 | Widowed, in a relationship | 3 | – | Retired | Manual craftmanship |
| *Former residents – left The Farm* | | | | | | |
| Evelyn | 70 | In a relationship | 0 | MD | Retired | Medicine |
| Rebecca | 70 | Divorced, in a relationship | 2 | Incomplete BA | Semi-retired | Administration |
| Anna | 70 | Divorced, married | 3 | MA | Working | Media |
| Laura | 71 | Divorced | 4 | MA | Working | Public service |
| Stephanie | 71 | Divorced, in a relationship | 2 | MD | Retired | Medicine |
| Karen | 71 | Married | 4 | BA | Retired | Education |
| Charlotte | 74 | Divorced, married | 4 | BA | Retired | Healthcare |
| Sandra | 74 | Married | 3 | Incomplete BA | Retired | Childcare |
| Lillian | 78 | Divorced twice, married | 4 | BA | Retired | Healthcare |
| Paul | 69 | Divorced, married | 3 (3) | – | Semi-retired | Media |
| Roger | 73 | Divorced | 2 (1) | BA | Semi-retired | Manual craftmanship |
| Gordon | 71 | Divorced, in a relationship | 2 | – | Retired | Manual craftmanship |
| Joe | 71 | Divorced twice, in a relationship | 2 (2) | MD | Retired | Medicine |
| Jerry | 71 | Married | 4 | MD | Working | Medicine |
| Albert | 74 | Married | 3 | BA | Semi-retired | Marketing |
| Andrew | 74 | Divorced twice | 2 | BA | Retired | Media |
| Harold | 76 | Divorced, married | 6 (1) | Incomplete BA | Retired | Marketing |
| Charles | 76 | Divorced, married | 2 (2) | Incomplete BA | Retired | Administration |

Note: * Children – biological and/or adopted (in parenthesis – partner's children in whose upbringing participants were involved).

## DATA COLLECTION

Interviews with lifelong and returning residents were conducted in person, typically at the respondents' homes. Conversations with former residents took place online via software such as FaceTime and Zoom.

Recruitment of both groups was based on snowball sampling: The man who answered my first email to The Farm, who later became my host, helped me recruit many of the residents, and some of them suggested additional community members. Later on, when I decided to interview founding members no longer living at The Farm, I wrote to those already interviewed and asked them to connect me with such individuals.

After being informed about the project's aims, each study participant signed a consent form (or expressed oral consent that was recorded). The semi-structured interviews began with exploring the participants' background: when and where they were born and spent their childhood, what they did before joining The Farm, what brought them there, and their roles in the community in its early days when it was a commune. The interview then moved to review the participants' lives from the 1980s to the present, briefly covering topics such as work, family, leisure, community roles, and significant life events. Then, we focused on participants' current realities, discussing daily activities they were involved in and probing sources of joy and satisfaction on the one hand, and worries and dissatisfaction on the other. The interview then moved to participants' understanding of the term "hippie," whether and why they still considered themselves hippies, the assumed contradiction between being a hippie and being old, specific values and behaviors associated with the hippie movement (e.g., nonviolence, spirituality, drug use, liberated sexuality), and their relevance to the participants' present realities. We concluded by discussing the hippies' impact on the world.

Whereas the interviews with people who reside at The Farm were conducted in February 2020, just before the onset of the COVID-19 pandemic, the online conversations with former residents took place in July 2020, when most of them were self-sequestering and could not keep their regular routines. Accordingly, when discussing their present activities, they were asked to refer to their lives before the pandemic. These persons were also asked if and how they kept in touch with The Farm. Together we tried to evaluate how the years they had spent there shaped the rest of their lives, including their present activities.

The interviews lasted an average of almost two hours, ranging from seventy-five minutes to three and half hours. The sample included seven couples, six of whom were interviewed together – a process that typically took longer than individual interviews. All interviews were audio recorded and then transcribed verbatim, yielding almost 2,000 pages of text. All participants were invited to keep in touch with me, and some did. Our follow-up conversations and email exchanges were included in the primary corpus of data.

## DATA ANALYSIS

Each one of the life stories shared with me deserves an individual book. Yet, the study aimed at exploring what study participants had *in common* as far as later life is concerned – a task that required meticulous analysis of the primary data. As the first step of this process, the transcriptions and email exchanges were carefully read to explore the broad context characterizing the respondents' lives. This review allowed me to build a personal profile for each participant to obtain a combined picture of their life story and current circumstances. Then, the entire dataset was analyzed by drawing mainly on an inductive rather than a deductive approach. Open coding was used to let the data "speak," thus avoiding the imposition of pre-existing concepts. The codes were then grouped into categories based on the key concepts identified and their relationships with the coded data. Reflexive and theoretical notations as well as constant comparison strategies (Strauss & Corbin, 1998) were used throughout the process. These strategies included shifting back and forth between preliminary subgroupings and revised versions, as well as ongoing comparisons among different participants and circumstances. Analysis was supported by the qualitative data analysis software Atlas.ti7.

# Notes

## 1 INTRODUCTION

1  Gerald Holtom originally designed the peace sign for the British nuclear disarmament movement in 1958. Later, it was adopted as a generic peace sign associated primarily with the hippie movement and with opposition to the Vietnam War (Kolsbun & Sweeney, 2008).

2  "Yaldei hayareah" ("Children of the moon"), words by Ehud Manor, music by Shlomo Ydov.

3  The film *Hair* (director: Miloš Forman) was based on the 1968 Broadway musical *Hair: The American tribal love-rock musical*.

4  Participant observation is a qualitative research method used in various disciplines to collect data about people, processes, and cultures. When conducting such observations, the researchers participate in the setting under study, but not to the extent that they become too absorbed to observe and analyze what is happening (Kawulich, 2005).

5  Thick description is an approach to cultural analysis popularized by anthropologist Clifford Geertz. It involves both detailed descriptions and interpretations of observed human behaviors, which aim to reveal their underlying cultural significance (Harrison, 2013).

6  Online observations (also called netnography, or online ethnography) usually aim at understanding social interactions in digital environments (Kozinets, 2010). In the present study, they were predominantly used to deepen my understanding of The Farm community at large.

7  Method triangulation involves using multiple data collection methods or multiple data sources about the same phenomenon (Polit & Beck, 2012). This type of triangulation, frequently used in qualitative studies, enables a comprehensive understanding of phenomena.

8  "Flower child" as a synonym for "hippie" originated in the hippie custom of carrying or wearing flowers as symbols of peace and love.

9  Old age has many biological, social, and cultural definitions, but most simply, it can be defined according to one's chronological age. Most developed Western countries set the age of 60–65 as the official definition for old age, depending on the minimum age at which one is entitled to a pension and other benefits.

10  Miller, 2011.

## 2   THE HIPPIES

1   Roszak, 1969.

2   Bach, 2013; Issitt, 2009; Moretta, 2017. The summary presented in this chapter is based on an integration of these references.

3   Bach, 2013.

4   In 1965, when the counterculture movement began to converge in the Haight-Ashbury district, the term *hippie* was applied by local journalists to describe this new flamboyant subculture and differentiate them from the visibly drab, introverted, and cynical beatniks. This term derives from the word *hip* that first surfaced in slang around the beginning of the twentieth century and meant "aware" and "in the know." In the 1950s, "hip" was commonly applied to describe the beats and meant up-to-date and fashionable. The San Francisco journalists turned it from an adjective to a noun (that could be descriptive or derogatory), but the youths did not initially use it to describe themselves. Even later, when it was widely adopted, some hippies called themselves by other names, including "dropouts," "seekers," "heads," and "freaks."

5   Ken Kesey and the Merry Pranksters' acid tests were held between December 1965 through January 1966. At all events, LSD was supplied, the Warlocks – soon to be the Grateful Dead – played the music, and tripping hippies danced. The last event, which took place at the Fillmore auditorium in San Francisco, lasted three days and hosted 2,000 participants.

6   The Love Pageant Rally was the first major outdoor hippie gathering (later called "be-ins" or "love-ins") held on October 6, 1966, the day California outlawed LSD. To protest against the criminalization of LSD, a few thousand people gathered at the Golden Gate Park. The Grateful Dead and Big Brother played, and when the master of ceremonies read a manifesto, hundreds swallowed a tab of acid at the same time.

7   The dancehall concerts were social happenings where the hip community came together, used psychedelic drugs, engaged in various forms of artistic expression, and danced while bands played loud rock music. These events took place in the San Francisco dancehalls such as Fillmore, Avalon, Winterland, and Matrix.

8   To differentiate themselves from the mainstream and express their unique values, the counterculture developed an eclectic, flamboyant, multi-ethnic style of dress, ranging from workmen's overalls to tie-dyed T-shirts or "Granny dresses." They also promoted a natural appearance: For men, this meant long hair, beards, or mustaches, while for women, it involved rejecting hairdos and makeup, heels, bras, and even the shaving of armpits and legs. Since many hippies believed that their movement was an homage to tribal people, some had tattoos, ear and nose piercing, and other forms of bodily alterations. Condemning materialism, expensive jewelry was also "out" and replaced by cheap love beads and various primitive necklaces, rings, and bracelets. To show their disapproval of the war in Vietnam, the hippies also wore all sorts of military items and shirts and jackets showing the American flag.

9   Coined by Marshall McLuhan and popularized by Timothy Leary, "Turn on, tune in, and drop out" is a phrase that the hippies adopted as one of their slogans. "Turn on" meant develop consciousness (possibly by the use of psychedelics), "Tune in" advised harmonious interaction with the world, and "Drop out" suggested abandoning any involuntary or unconscious commitments. Many, however, interpreted it as get high and quit all constructive activity.

10  The Newark riots occurred in July 1967 after two white police officers violently arrested an afro-American cab driver for no justified reason. Over four days of rioting, burgling, and property destruction, twenty-six people died and hundreds were injured. These riots were one of 159 race riots that took place in the U.S. during that summer. Although only a minority of African-Americans joined the hippie movement, the hippies strongly supported the civil rights movement's struggle to end racial discrimination in the U.S.

11  After the war expanded into Cambodia, protests erupted, and hundreds of thousands of students at over 700 colleges demonstrated. At Kent State in Ohio, rioters fire-bombed one of the buildings, forcing the governor to call out the National Guard. On May 4, troops opened fire on students, killing four and wounding eleven others. In the week after Kent State, 4 million students contributed to demonstrations that overwhelmed over 50 percent of the nation's campuses. About 100,000 students also marched to the White House.

12  The largest environmental demonstration of the 1960s era was the first Earth Day on April 22, 1970, celebrated by 20 million people and 4,000 ecology groups.

13  Inspired by Art Nouveau, Dada, and Pop Art, the 1960s Psychedelic Art movement was characterized by flashy colors in sharp contrasts, highly symmetrical compositions, and collage elements, typically accompanied by inexplicable iconography and overly elaborated writing.

14  They also discussed the legitimacy of all sorts of unconventional marriages (group, polyandrous, polygamic), an idea partially and unsuccessfully applied in The Farm in its early years.

15  Miller, 2011.

16  Bach, 2013.

17  Howard, 1969.

18  Davis & Munoz, 1968.

19  Weiner & Stillman, 1979.

20  A video shared by one of the study participants.

21  Howard, 1969.

22  Moretta, 2017, p. 6.

23  Miller, 2015.

24  Aidala & Zablocki, 1991; Dunn-Froebig, 2006.

25  Weisner, 2001.

26  Hoffman, 2010.

27  Schick et al., 2010.

28  Adams & Harmon, 2014.

29  Gurvis, 2009, p. 242.

## 3   THE FARM

1   Miller, 2015, p. 18.
2   Bach, 2013, p. 285.
3   Moretta, 2017, p. 228.
4   Miller, 2015; Moretta, 2017; Stevenson, 2014a, 2014b; Stiriss, 2018; Traugot, 2019.
5   The production of soy products started as a necessity. Soybeans are rich in essential amino acids and protein and thus could replace meat and dairy products to support The Farm's vegan diet.
6   To be a minister in Tennessee, one had to have a congregation and services, so Gaskin became a minister, and the marriages he performed were legal.
7   Miller, 2011.
8   Traugot, 2019, p. 24.
9   Stevenson, 2014a, p. 103.
10   Traugot, 2019, p. 20.
11   To join the community today, individuals must first live at The Farm for one year, after which they can apply for Provisional Member status. After at least one year in that status, they can apply for Full Member status and be voted in by two-thirds of the current voting members. New members must prove they have a means of making a living, which is still challenging to do in rural Tennessee, and commit to paying monthly dues and following other community rules, including the agreement to be nonviolent. The process is identical to former residents (unless they are already Permanent Members because they helped pay the debt after the changeover). In their case, however, the process is shorter.

## 4   ONCE A HIPPIE, ALWAYS A HIPPIE

1   Chonody & Teater, 2016.
2   Barnhart & Peñaloza, 2012; Tosun et al., 2011.
3   Watson, 2008.
4   Identity Process Theory (Whitbourne & Weinstock, 1986) proposes three processes that operate continuously over time. In *identity assimilation*, older adults maintain a sense of continuity by interpreting age-related experiences according to previously established schemas about the self. *Identity accommodation*, the second process, involves a change in identity in response to experiences that contradict an existing sense of self. In *identity balance*, the third process, individuals make changes in their identities to incorporate age-relevant experiences but nevertheless maintain a consistent view of the self. Similarly, Chonody and Teater (2016) suggest that individuals deal with their move to the out-group of older adults in one of three ways, the first being *social mobility* that involves refusing or denying age by trying to remain in the in-group (young group) as much as possible. The second mechanism is *social creativity*, in which the individuals embrace old age and reshape their own identity by focusing on positive traits. The third is *social competition* – the individuals accept their new membership within the out-group but also actively advocate for equal rights and challenge neg-

ative stereotypes and attitudes. This strategy, also described as "resistance," involves stepping out of the box provided for older people through deeply ingrained cultural messages (Cruikshank, 2008).

5  Jung, 1934/1967; McAdams, 1993.
6  Biggs, 2005; Featherstone & Hepworth, 1991.
7  Rozario & Derienzis, 2009; Westerhof et al., 2012.
8  Gilleard, 1996; Gilleard et al., 2005; Thorpe, 2018.
9  Biggs, 2005; Woodward, 1991.
10  Davis & Munoz, 1968.
11  Howard, 1969.
12  Miller, 2011.
13  Jung, 1934/1967; McAdams, 1993.
14  Whitbourne & Weinstock, 1986.
15  Chonody & Teater, 2016.
16  Chonody & Teater, 2016.
17  Cruikshank, 2008.
18  Whitbourne & Weinstock, 1986.

## 5  STILL CHANGING THE WORLD

1  Erikson, 1963.
2  Newton et al., 2020; Villar, 2012.
3  Kleiber & Nimrod, 2008; Stewart & Vandewater, 1998.
4  Moieni et al., 2020; Villar, 2012.
5  McAdams & Logan, 2004.
6  Moran, 1988.
7  Keyes & Ryff, 1998; Kleiber & Nimrod, 2008, Villar, 2012.
8  Coyote, 2007.
9  Natural Health Movement, 2020.
10  Suarez, 1993, p. 364.
11  Plenty International website, 2020: https://plenty.org.
12  Ibid.
13  McAdams & Logan, 2004.
14  In their model of generativity, McAdams and de St. Aubin (1992) point out that the concern for the next generations may be derived from both cultural demand and inner desire, and claim that generativity is expressed in the actions of *offering* (giving of self or self's products), *creating* (products, projects, new ideas), and *maintaining* (sustaining product, project, or tradition). Each one of the generative actions described above can be classified according to one of these categories. All volunteer activities and donations, for example, reflected offering, all individual initiatives were certainly creating, and many actions were clearly directed at maintaining, be it the environment, people's health, or The Farm's story. Moreover, just as the model suggests, the involvement in generative actions resulted in a generativity script in the study participants' narratives.

15  Kleiber & Nimrod, 2008; Stewart & Vandewater, 1998.
16  Atchley, 1999.
17  Bakan, 1966, Kleiber & Nimrod, 2008; Newton et al., 2020.
18  Moieni et al., 2020; Villar, 2012.

## 6  SEX, DRUGS, AND ROCK-N-ROLL?

1  Miller, 2011.
2  In an attempt to combine these different concepts, Kelly (1996, p. 22) described leisure as the "quality of activity defined by relative freedom and intrinsic satisfaction."
   This definition concentrates on the experience, but in the context of an activity that
   occurs in a time and a place. Similarly, Kleiber (1999, p. 3) defined leisure as a "combination of free time and the expectation of preferred experience." He recognized
   the context of leisure as time perceived as free and suggested that leisure experiences
   occur in intrinsically rather than extrinsically motivated activities. Applying a somewhat "hippie" approach, Godbey (2008, p. 14) defined leisure as: "Living in relative
   freedom from the external compulsive forces of one's culture and physical environment so as to be able to act from internally compelling love in ways that are personally
   pleasing, intuitively worthwhile, and provide a basis for faith."
3  For reviews, see Gibson & Singleton, 2012, Smallfield & Molitor, 2018.
4  Nimrod & Janke, 2012.
5  Van der Meer, 2008.
6  Nimrod, 2016.
7  Nimrod & Janke, 2012.
8  Meaney & Rye, 2007.
9  Meston & Buss, 2007.
10  For decades, marijuana growers, sellers, and consumers have classified cannabis strains
   as indica or sativa to explain the type of effect they have when consumed. Indica was
   described as physically relaxing and having a soothing effect, and sativa as energizing
   and providing a head-high. Although this dichotomy was debunked, it is still widely
   used. For more information, see: www.insider.com/why-theres-no-difference-between-
   indica-and-sativa-marijuana-strains-2020-4
11  Stebbins, 2020.
12  Miller, 2011.
13  Gibson & Singleton, 2012, Smallfield & Molitor, 2018.
14  Stebbins, 2020.

## 7  THE AGING OF THE NEW AGERS

1  Hill & Pargament, 2008.
2  Fisher (2010) defined these four spirituality domains as follows: *Personal* spirituality
   refers to intra-personal processes concerning values, purpose, and meaning in life.

These processes reflect the human spirit's search for identity and self-worth and are driven by self-awareness. *Communal* spirituality involves an aspiration for quality and depth of interpersonal relationships relating to morality, culture, and religion. These are expressed in love, forgiveness, trust, hope, and faith in humanity. *Environmental* spirituality relates to care and nurture for the physical and biological world, including a sense of awe and unity with the environment. *Transcendental* spirituality is the relationship between oneself and some being beyond the human level (i.e., ultimate concern, cosmic force, transcendent reality, or God). It involves faith, adoration, and worship of the source of the mystery of the universe.

3 The rejection of mainstream culture and traditional values in favor of a simple, less materialistic life correlated with the *personal* dimension; the ethics of peace, love, and community correlated with the *communal* dimension; the appreciation of nature and the natural correlated with the *environmental* dimension; and the adoption of various concepts (e.g., karma, energy) and practices (e.g., meditation, yoga) certainly reflected the *transcendental* dimension.

4 Koenig, 1995; Wink & Dillon, 2002.

5 Human development theories such as Erikson's Model of Psychosocial Development (1982) suggested that this tendency is triggered by the need for personal autonomy and awareness that typically develops around midlife. Simultaneously experiencing a reduction in external responsibility (e.g., childcare, work) and starting to face the challenges of aging, middle-aged individuals devote more time and attention to issues of spirituality. From the Continuity Theory perspective (Atchley, 1999), greater spirituality in old age may be regarded as an extension and development of a lifelong search for spiritual meaning. Yet, Gerotranscendence Theory (Tornstam, 1996) proposes that a paradigm shift occurs as people age, in which they move from a materialistic and rational outlook on life to one that is more cosmic and transcendent.

6 Lifshitz et al., 2019; Malone & Dadswell, 2018; Okun & Nimrod, 2020; Shaw et al., 2016.

7 Atchley, 1999.

8 Ram Dass (originally named Richard Alpert) was an American psychologist who significantly promoted young Americans' interest in Eastern spirituality during the 1960s. He authored or co-authored more than twelve books, of which the most influential was *Be here now* (1971).

9 Traugot, 2019, p. 6.

10 Traugot, 2019, p. 4.

11 York, 1995, pp. 1–2.

12 Pike, 2004.

13 Hanegraaff, 1999.

14 Hanegraaff, 1996.

15 Tucker, 2018.

16 *Cambridge Dictionary*, 2021.

17 The Cult Research and Information Center was founded by Dr. Janja Lalich of California State University, Chico. The center offers a variety of resources and consulting

services. The list of cult characteristics presented on its website is based on a book by Lalich and Tobias (2006).

18  Shunryu Suzuki, known as Suzuki Roshi, was a Zen monk of the Sōtō school, the largest Zen sect in Japanese Buddhism. He moved from Japan to San Francisco in 1959 and founded the San Francisco Zen Center, which became one of the most influential Zen organizations in the U.S. The book Shirley was referring to was probably the one of his transcribed lectures – *Zen mind, beginner's mind* (Suzuki, 1970).

19  Bat Mitzvah is the equivalent of Bar Mitzvah for girls. Among orthodox and conservative Jews, boys celebrate their Bar Mitzvah at the age of thirteen while girls have their Bat Mitzvah celebration at twelve. Among the reform Jews, however, both genders celebrate it at the age of thirteen.

20  Baal Shem Tov was a Jewish mystic and healer from Poland who is regarded as the founder of Hasidic Judaism. A central component of his teaching was the direct connection with the divine through prayer and every human activity. Most information about his life and practices came from oral traditions handed down by his students and numerous legendary tales.

21  Kirtan is a musical tradition common in Indian religions, wherein multiple singers express spiritual ideas and dedication to a divinity.

22  The Nahua weather-working tradition includes a series of ceremonies aimed at bringing rain and limiting the destructive effects of intense storms.

23  *A course in miracles* is a book written by Helen Schucman (1975), a psychologist and professor at Columbia University, New York, who claimed that the book was dictated to her by Christ. The book offers a complete self-study of spiritual philosophy that stresses the healing power of love and forgiveness. It includes 365 lessons, an exercise for each day of the year.

24  E.g., Koenig, 1995; Wink & Dillon, 2002.

25  E.g., Lifshitz et al., 2019; Malone & Dadswell, 2018.

26  Tornstam, 1996.

27  Nimrod & Kleiber, 2007.

28  Kleiber et al., 2008.

29  Stebbins, 2020.

30  Miller, 2011.

## 8   LIFELONG COMMUNITY

1  Miller, 2011.

2  Miller, 2015.

3  Sarason, 1974, p. 1.

4  Stewart & Townley, 2020.

5  Luong et al., 2011; Ross et al., 2019.

6  Kelly et al., 2017; Roth, 2020, Wang et al., 2018.

7  Pantell et al., 2013.

8  Carstensen et al., 1999.

9   Cagney & Cornwell, 2010.

10   Means & Evans, 2012.

11   Bach, 2013.

12   Evans, 2018.

13   McMillan & Chavis, 1986.

14   Shonk, 2020.

15   Wang et al., 2018.

16   Luong et al., 2011; Ross et al., 2019.

17   Carstensen et al., 1999.

18   "Social capital" is defined as the "aggregate of the actual or potential resources which are linked to possession of a durable network of more or less institutionalized relationships" (Bourdieu, 1983, p. 249).

19   As a set of social resources to draw upon in times of need, people's social capital is essential to the community's "collective efficacy," namely, its social cohesion and informal social control. Communities with a high level of collective efficacy are communities whose members are willing to intervene on one another's behalf (Cagney & Cornwell, 2010).

## 9   ALTERNATIVE END OF LIFE

1   Jastrzębski et al., 2020.

2   Besser & Priel, 2008; Cicirelli, 1999, 2002.

3   Ellis et al., 2013.

4   Ellis & Wahab, 2013; Wink & Scott, 2005.

5   Aqajani & Samadifard, 2017.

6   Aqajani & Samadifard, 2017.

7   Prenda & Lachman, 2001.

8   Weathers et al., 2016; Zwakman et al., 2018.

9   Lattin, 2003.

10   Moretta, 2017, p. 248.

11   In Traugot, 2019, p. 55.

12   Gaskin, 1999.

13   Stevenson, 2014b, p. 188.

14   Green (or natural) burial is a way of caring for the dead with minimal environmental impact. Typically, it means that the body is neither cremated nor prepared with toxic chemicals such as embalming fluids. It is simply placed in a biodegradable coffin or shroud and interred without a concrete burial vault. The grave site is a natural setting, and if there is a gravestone, it is a rock or a piece of rough-cut limestone that is flat on the side. The goal is complete decomposition of the body and its natural return to the soil. Only then can a burial truly be "ashes to ashes, dust to dust."

15   Stevenson, 2014a, p. 148.

16   Jastrzębski et al., 2020.

17   Jastrzębski et al., 2020.

18 Ellis et al., 2013.
19 Weathers et al., 2016; Zwakman et al., 2018.
20 Aqajani & Samadifard, 2017; Jastrzębski et al., 2020.
21 Jastrzębski et al., 2020.

## 10   AGING DIFFERENTLY

1 Lowsky et al., 2014; Steptoe et al., 2015.
2 Gilleard & Higgs, 2014.
3 Howard, 1969.
4 Oswald & Wu, 2010.
5 Watson, 2008.
6 Whitbourne & Weinstock, 1986.
7 Whitbourne & Weinstock, 1986.
8 Cruikshank, 2008.
9 Newton et al., 2020; Villar, 2012.
10 Kleiber & Nimrod, 2008; Stewart & Vandewater, 1998.
11 Gibson & Singleton, 2012.
12 Stebbins, 2020.
13 Nimrod & Janke, 2012; Smallfield & Molitor, 2018.
14 Caper, 1996.
15 York, 1995.
16 Lifshitz et al., 2019; Malone & Dadswell, 2018.
17 Miller, 2011.
18 McMillan & Chavis, 1986.
19 Kelly et al., 2017; Roth, 2020.
20 Moretta, 2017, p. 6.
21 Atchley, 1999.
22 Carstensen et al., 1999.
23 Nimrod & Kleiber, 2007.
24 Nimrod & Ben-Shem, 2015, p. 817.

# References

Adams, R. G., & Harmon, J. (2014). The long strange trip continues: Aging Deadheads. In C. L. Harrington, D. D. Bielby, & A. R. Bardo (Eds.), *Aging, media, and culture* (pp. 83–95). Lexington.

Aidala, A. A., & Zablocki, B. D. (1991). The communes of the 1970s: Who joined and why? *Marriage & Family Review, 17*(1–2), 87–116.

Aqajani, S., & Samadifard, H. (2017). The role of cognitive fusion, locus of control and cognitive avoidance in the prediction of death anxiety in the elderly. *Journal of Health and Care, 19*(1), 62–74.

Atchley, R. (1999). *Continuity and adaptation in aging.* Johns Hopkins University.

Bach, D. (2013). The rise and fall of the American counterculture: A history of the hippies and other cultural dissidents (Doctoral dissertation). Texas A&M University.

Bakan, D. (1966). *The duality of human existence: Isolation and communion in Western man.* Beacon.

Barnhart, M., & Peñaloza, L. (2012). Who are you calling old? Negotiating old age identity in the elderly consumption ensemble. *Journal of Consumer Research, 39*(6), 1133–1153.

Besser, A., & Priel, B. (2008). Attachment, depression, and fear of death in older adults: The roles of neediness and perceived availability of social support. *Personality and Individual Differences, 44*(8), 1711–1725.

Biggs, S. (2005). Beyond appearances: Perspectives on identity in later life and some implications for method. *Journals of Gerontology Series B: Psychological Sciences and Social Sciences, 60*(3), 118–128.

Bourdieu, P. (1983). Forms of capital. In J. G. Richardson (Ed.), *Handbook of theory and research for the sociology of education* (pp. 241–258). Greenwood.

Cagney, K. A., & Cornwell, E. Y. (2010). Neighborhoods and health in later life: The intersection of biology and community. *Annual Review of Gerontology and Geriatrics, 30*(1), 323–348.

*Cambridge Dictionary* (2021). *Cult.* https://dictionary.cambridge.org/dictionary/english/cult

Caper, R. (1996). Play, experimentation and creativity. *International Journal of Psycho-Analysis, 77*(5), 859–869.

Carstensen, L. L., Isaacowitz, D. M., & Charles, S. T. (1999). Taking time seriously: A theory of socioemotional selectivity. *American Psychologist, 54*(3), 165–181.

Chonody, J. M., & Teater, B. (2016). Why do I dread looking old? A test of social identity theory, terror management theory, and the double standard of aging. *Journal of Women and Aging, 28*(2), 112–126.

Cicirelli, V. G. (1999). Personality and demographic factors in older adults' fear of death. *The Gerontologist, 39*(5), 569–579.

Cicirelli, V. G. (2002). Fear of death in older adults: Predictions from terror management theory. *Journals of Gerontology Series B: Psychological Sciences and Social Sciences, 57*(4), P358–P366.

Coyote, P. (2007). *Summer of love: 40 years later.* www.petercoyote.com/sfchron052007.html

Cruikshank, M. (2008). Aging and identity politics. *Journal of Aging Studies, 22*(2), 147–151.

Dass, R. (1971). *Be here now.* Harper Collins.

Davis, F., & Munoz, L. (1968). Heads and freaks: Patterns and meanings of drug use among hippies. *Journal of Health and Social Behavior, 9*(2), 156–164.

Dunn-Froebig, E. P. (2006). All grown up: How the counterculture affected its flower children (Graduate thesis). University of Montana.

Ellis, L., & Wahab, E. A. (2013). Religiosity and fear of death: A theory-oriented review of the empirical literature. *Review of Religious Research, 55*(1), 149–189.

Ellis, L., Wahab, E. A., & Ratnasingan, M. (2013). Religiosity and fear of death: A three-nation comparison. *Mental Health, Religion and Culture, 16*(2), 179–199.

Erikson, E. (1963). *Childhood and society.* Norton.

Erikson, E. (1982). *The life cycle completed.* W. W. Norton & Company.

Evans, C. (2018). *Broad band: The untold story of the women who made the internet.* G. P. Putnam's Sons.

Featherstone, M., & Hepworth, M. (1991). The mask of ageing and the postmodern life course. In M. Featherstone, M. Hepworth, & B. Turner (Eds), *The body: Social process and cultural theory* (pp. 370–389). Sage.

Fisher, J. (2010). Development and application of a spiritual well-being questionnaire called SHALOM. *Religions, 1*(1), 105–121.

Gaskin, S. (May 12, 1999). Rocinante. www.chebucto.ns.ca/Current/AEF/raps/rocinante.html

Gibson, H. J., & Singleton, J. F. (2012). *Leisure and aging: Theory and practice.* Human Kinetics.

Gilleard, C. (1996). Consumption and identity in later life: Toward a cultural gerontology. *Ageing and Society, 16*(4), 489–498.

Gilleard, C., & Higgs, P. (2014). *Cultures of ageing: Self, citizen and the body.* Routledge.

Gilleard, C., Higgs, P., Hyde, M., Wiggins, R., Blane, D. (2005). Class, cohort, and consumption: The British experience of the third age. *Journals of Gerontology Series B: Psychological Sciences and Social Sciences, 60*(6), S305–S310.

Godbey, G. (2008). *Leisure in your life: New perspectives.* Venture.

Gurvis, S. (2009). *Where have all the flower children gone?* University of Mississippi.

Hanegraaff, W. J. (1996). *New age religion and Western culture: Esotericism in the mirror of secular thought.* Brill.

Hanegraaff, W. J. (1999). New age spiritualities as secular religion: A historian's perspective. *Social Compass, 46*(2), 145–160.

Harrison, A. K. (2013). Thick description. In R. J. McGee & R. L. Warms (Eds), *Theory in social and cultural anthropology: An encyclopedia* (pp. 860–861). Sage.

Hill, P. C., & Pargament, K. I. (2008). Advances in the conceptualization and measurement of religion and spirituality: Implications for physical and mental health research. *American Psychologist, 58*(1), 64–74.

Hoffman, J. (2010). The psychedelic 1960s, hippies in their 60s: Substance abuse in the elderly. *The Consultant Pharmacist, 25*(9), 570–576.

Howard, J. R. (1969). The flowering of the hippie movement. *Annals of the American Academy of Political and Social Science, 382*(1), 43–55.

Issitt, M. (2009). *Hippies: A guide to an American subculture.* ABC-CLIO.

Jastrzębski, J., Rogoza, R., & Ślaski, S. (2020). The hierarchical structure of fear of personal death: From the general factor to specific forms. *Psicologia: Reflexão e Crítica, 33.* https://prc.springeropen.com/track/pdf/10.1186/s41155-020-00152-x.pdf

Jung, C. (1934/1967). *Collected works, Vol. 7.* Routledge.

Kawulich, B. B. (2005). Participant observation as a data collection method. *Forum: Qualitative Social Research, 6*(2), article 43. www.qualitative-research .net/index.php/fqs/article/view/466/996

Kelly, J. R. (1996). *Leisure* (3rd Edition). Allyn & Bacon.

Kelly, M. E., Duff, H., Kelly, S., Power, J. E. M., Brennan, S., Lawlor, B. A., & Loughrey, D. G. (2017). The impact of social activities, social networks, social support and social relationships on the cognitive functioning of healthy older adults: A systematic review. *Systematic Reviews, 6*(1), 1–18.

Kerr, S. M. (2009). *Homebirth in the hospital: Integrating natural childbirth with modern medicine.* Sentient.

Keyes, C. L., & Ryff, C. D. (1998). Generativity in adult lives: Social structural contours and quality of life consequences. In D. P. McAdams & E. de St. Aubin (Eds), *Generativity and adult development: How and why we care for the next generation* (pp. 227–257). American Psychological Association.

Kleiber, D. (1999). *Leisure experience and human development.* Basic Books.

Kleiber, D., & Nimrod, G. (2008). Expressions of generativity and civic engagement in a "learning in retirement" group. *Journal of Adult Development, 15*(2), 76–86.

Kleiber, D., McGuire, F. A., Aybar-Damali, B., & Norman, W. (2008). Having more by doing less: The paradox of leisure constraints in later life. *Journal of Leisure Research, 40*(3), 343–359.

Koenig, H. G. (1995). Use of acute services and mortality among religious and non-religious coopers with medical illness. *Journal of Religious Gerontology, 9*(3), 1–22.

Kolsbun, K. & Sweeney, M. (2008). *Peace: The biography of a symbol.* National Geographic.

Kozinets, R. V. (2010). *Netnography: Doing ethnographic research online.* Sage.

Lalich, J., & Tobias, M. L. (2006). *Take back your life: Recovering from cults and abusive relationships.* Bay Tree.

Lattin, D. (March 2, 2003). Twilight of hippiedom/Farm commune's founder envisions return to the fold as ex-dropouts age. *SFGate.* www.sfgate.com/bayarea/article/Twilight-of-hippiedom-Farm-commune-s-founder-2666839.php

Lifshitz, R., Nimrod, G., & Bachner, Y. (2019). Spirituality and wellbeing in later life: A multi-dimensional approach. *Aging and Mental Health, 23*(8), 984–991.

Lowsky, D. J., Olshansky, S. J., Bhattacharya, J., & Goldman, D. P. (2014). Heterogeneity in healthy aging. *Journals of Gerontology Series A: Biomedical Sciences and Medical Sciences, 69*(6), 640–649.

Luong, G., Charles, S. T., & Fingerman, K. L. (2011). Better with age: Social relationships across adulthood. *Journal of Social and Personal Relationships, 28*(1), 9–23.

Malone, J., & Dadswell, A. (2018). The role of religion, spirituality and/or belief in positive ageing for older adults. *Geriatrics, 3*(28), 1–16.

McAdams, D. P. (1993). *The stories we live by.* Morrow.

McAdams, D. P., & de St. Aubin, E. (1992). A theory of generativity and its assessment through self-report, behavioral acts and narrative themes in autobiography. *Journal of Personality and Social Psychology, 62*(3), 1003–1015.

McAdams, D. P., & Logan, R. L. (2004). What is generativity? In E. de St. Aubin, D. P. McAdams, & T-C. Kim (Eds), *The generative society* (pp. 15–31). American Psychological Association.

McMillan, D. W., & Chavis, D. M. (1986). Sense of community: A definition and theory. *Journal of Community Psychology, 14*(1), 6–23.

Meaney, G. J., & Rye, B. J. (2007). Sex, sexuality, and leisure. In R. McCarville & K. MacKay (Eds), *Leisure for Canadians* (pp. 131–138). Venture.

Means, R., & Evans, S. (2012). Communities of place and communities of interest? An exploration of their changing role in later life. *Ageing and Society, 32*(8), 1300–1318.

Meston, C. M., & Buss, D. M. (2007). Why humans have sex? *Archives of Sexual Behavior, 36*(4), 477–507.

Miller, T. (2011). *The hippies and American values (2nd Edition).* University of Tennessee.

Miller, T. (2015). Searching for a commune center: Religious and spiritual communes. In *The 60s communes: Hippies and beyond* (pp. 92–127). Syracuse University.

Moieni, M., Irwin, M. R., Seeman, T. E., Robles, T. F., Lieberman, M. D., Breen, E. C., ... & Cole, S. W. (2020). Feeling needed: Effects of a randomized generativity intervention on wellbeing and inflammation in older women. *Brain, Behavior, and Immunity, 84*, 97–105.

Moran, G. F. (1988). Cares for the rising generation: Generativity in American History, 1607–1900. In D. P. McAdams & E. de St. Aubin (Eds), *Generativity and adult development: How and why we care for the next generation* (pp. 311–334). American Psychological Association.

Moretta, J. A. (2017). Communes and the counterculture. In *The hippies: A 1960s history* (pp. 211–257). McFarland and Company.

Natural Health Movement (2020). *Pioneering producer: Farm Foods popularizes soy foods to America.* www.youtube.com/channel/UCP75iMRX018aRGP8nepttPA

Newton, N. J., Chauhan, P. K., & Pates, J. L. (2020). Facing the future: Generativity, stagnation, intended legacies, and wellbeing in later life. *Journal of Adult Development, 27*(1), 70–80.

Nimrod, G. (2016). Innovation theory revisited: Self-preservation innovation vs. self-reinvention innovation in later life. *Leisure Sciences, 38*(5), 389–401.

Nimrod, G., & Ben-Shem, I. (2015). Successful aging as a lifelong process. *Educational Gerontology, 41*(11), 814–824.

Nimrod, G., & Janke, M. C. (2012). Leisure across the later lifespan. In J. Singelton & H. J. Gibson (Eds), *Leisure and aging: Theory and practice* (pp. 95–109). Human Kinetics.

Nimrod, G., & Kleiber, D. A. (2007). Reconsidering change and continuity in later life: Toward an innovation theory of successful aging. *International Journal of Aging and Human Development, 65*(1), 1–22.

Okun, S., & Nimrod, G. (2020). Online religion communities and wellbeing in later life. *Journal of Religion, Spirituality and Aging, 32*(3), 268–287.

Oswald, A. J., & Wu, S. (2010). Objective confirmation of subjective measures of human wellbeing: Evidence from the USA. *Science, 327*(5965), 576–579.

Pantell, M., Rehkopf, D., Jutte, D., Syme, S. L., Balmes, J., & Adler, N. (2013). Social isolation: A predictor of mortality comparable to traditional clinical risk factors. *American Journal of Public Health, 103*(11), 2056–2062.

Pike, S. M. (2004). *New age and neopagan religions in America.* Columbia University.

Polit, D. F., & Beck, C. T. (2012). *Nursing research: Generating and assessing evidence for nursing practice.* Lippincott Williams and Wilkins.

Prenda, K. M., & Lachman, M. E. (2001). Planning for the future: A life management strategy for increasing control and life satisfaction in adulthood. *Psychology and Aging, 16*(2), 206–216.

Ross, A., Talmage, C. A., & Searle, M. (2019). Toward a flourishing neighborhood: The association of happiness and sense of community. *Applied Research in Quality of Life, 14*(5), 1333–1352.

Roszak, T. (1969). *The making of a counter culture: Reflections on the technocratic society and its youthful opposition.* Doubleday.

Roth, A. R. (2020). Social networks and health in later life: A state of the literature. *Sociology of Health and Illness, 42*(7), 1642–1656.

Rozario, P. A., & Derienzis, D. (2009). "So forget how old I am!" Examining age identities in the face of chronic conditions. *Sociology of Health and Illness, 31*(4), 540–553.

Sarason, S. B. (1974). *The psychological sense of community: Prospects for a community psychology.* Jossey-Bass.

Schick, V., Herbenick, D., Reece, M., Sanders, S. A., Dodge, B., Middlestadt, S. E., & Fortenberry, J. D. (2010). Sexual behaviors, condom use, and sexual health of Americans over 50: Implications for sexual health promotion for older adults. *Journal of Sexual Medicine, 7*(5), 315–329.

Schucman, H. (1975). *A course in miracles.* Course in Miracles Society.

Shaw, R., Gullifer, J., & Wood, K. (2016). Religion and spirituality: A qualitative study of older adults. *Ageing International, 41*(3), 311–330.

Shonk, K. (2020). 3 types of conflict and how to address them. Program on Negotiation, Harvard Law School. www.pon.harvard.edu/daily/conflict-resolution/types-conflict/

Smallfield, S., & Molitor, W. L. (2018). Occupational therapy interventions supporting social participation and leisure engagement for community-dwelling older adults: A systematic review. *American Journal of Occupational Therapy, 72*(4), 7204190020p1–7204190020p8.

Stebbins, R. A. (2020). *The serious leisure perspective: A synthesis.* Springer Nature.

Steptoe, A., Deaton, A., & Stone, A. A. (2015). Psychological wellbeing, health and ageing. *Lancet, 385*(9968), 640–648.

Stevenson, D. (2014a). *Out to change the world: The evolution of The Farm community.* Book Publishing Company.

Stevenson, D. (2014b). *The Farm then and now: A model for sustainable living.* New Society.

Stewart, A. J., & Vandewater, E. (1998). The course of generativity. In D. P. McAdams & E. de St. Aubin (Eds), *Generativity and adult development: How and why we care for the next generation* (pp. 75–100). American Psychological Association.

Stewart, K., & Townley, G. (2020). How far have we come? An integrative review of the current literature on sense of community and wellbeing. *American Journal of Community Psychology, 66*(1–2), 166–189.

Stiriss, M. (2018). *Voluntary peasants: Life inside the ultimate American commune – The Farm.* New Beat Books.

Strauss, A., & Corbin, J. (1998). *Basics of qualitative research: Grounded theory procedures and techniques(2nd Edition).* Sage.

Suarez, S. H. (1993). Midwifery is not the practice of medicine. *Yale Journal of Law and Feminism, 5*, 315–364.

Suzuki, S. (1970). *Zen mind, beginner's mind.* Shambhala.

Thorpe, R. (2018). Ageing and the presentation of self: Women's perspectives on negotiating age, identity and femininity through dress. *Journal of Sociology, 54*(2), 203–213.

Tornstam, L. (1996). Gerotranscendence: A theory about maturing into old age. *Journal of Aging and Identity, 1,* 37–50.

Tosun, D., Siddarth, P., Toga, A. W., & Hermann, B, C. R. (2011). Do adults adjust their socioeconomic status identity in later life? *Ageing and Society, 32*(4), 580–591.

Traugot, M. (2019). *A short history of The Farm.* Unpublished manuscript.

Tucker, R. (2018). Inside the hippie cult. Dirt Magazine. www.dirt-mag.com/ arts/griterati/inside-the-hippie-cult-NRDM20180702180709989

van der Meer, M. J. (2008). Sociospatial diversity in the leisure activities of older people in the Netherlands. *Journal of Aging Studies, 22*(1), 1–12.

Villar, F. (2012). Successful ageing and development: The contribution of generativity in older age. *Ageing and Society, 32*(7), 1087–1105.

Wang, J., Mann, F., Lloyd-Evans, B., Ma, R., & Johnson, S. (2018). Associations between loneliness and perceived social support and outcomes of mental health problems: A systematic review. *BMC Psychiatry, 18*(1), 1–16.

Watson, T. J. (2008). Managing identity: Identity work, personal predicaments and structural circumstances. *Organization, 15*(1), 121–143.

Weathers, E., O'Caoimh, R., Cornally, N., Fitzgerald, C., Kearns, T., Coffey, A., … & Molloy, D. W. (2016). Advance care planning: A systematic review of randomised controlled trials conducted with older adults. *Maturitas, 91,* 101–109.

Weiner, R., & Stillman, D. (1979). *Woodstock census.* Viking.

Weisner, T. S. (2001). The American dependency conflict: Continuities and discontinuities in behavior and values of countercultural parents and their children. *Ethos, 29*(3), 271–295.

Westerhof, G. J., Whitbourne, S. K., & Freeman, G. P. (2012). The aging self in a cultural context: The relation of conceptions of aging to identity processes and self-esteem in the United States and the Netherlands. *Journals of Gerontology Series B: Psychological Sciences and Social Sciences, 67B*(1), 52–60.

Whitbourne, S. K., & Weinstock, C. S. (1986). *Adult development.* Praeger.

Wink, P., & Dillon, M. (2002). Spiritual development across the adult life course: Findings from a longitudinal study. *Journal of Adults Development, 9*(1), 79–94.

Wink, P., & Scott, J. (2005). Does religiousness buffer against the fear of death and dying in late adulthood? Findings from a longitudinal study. *Journals of Gerontology Series B: Psychological Sciences and Social Sciences, 60*(4), P207–P214.

Woodward, K. (1991). *Aging and its discontents: Freud and other fictions.* Indiana University.

York, M. (1995). *The emerging network: A sociology of the new age and neo-pagan movements.* Rowman and Littlefield.

Zwakman, M., Jabbarian, L. J., van Delden, J. J., van der Heide, A., Korfage, I. J., Pollock, K., … & Kars, M. C. (2018). Advance care planning: A systematic review about experiences of patients with a life-threatening or life-limiting illness. *Palliative Medicine, 32*(8), 1305–1321.

# Index

CPSIA information can be obtained
at www.ICGtesting.com
Printed in the USA
BVHW061924141222
654262BV00007B/41